The Promise of Paradise

CREATING THE NORTH AMERICAN LANDSCAPE

Gregory Conniff
Bonnie Loyd
Edward K. Muller
David Schuyler
CONSULTING EDITORS

Published in cooperation with the Center for American Places,
Harrisonburg, Virginia

The Promise of Paradise

Recreational and Retirement Communities
in the United States since 1950

Hubert B. Stroud

Johns Hopkins University Press   Baltimore and London

© 1995 The Johns Hopkins University Press
All rights reserved. Published 1995
Printed in the United States of America on acid-free paper
04 03 02 01 00 99 98 97 96 95   5 4 3 2 1

The Johns Hopkins University Press
2715 North Charles Street
Baltimore, Maryland 21218-4319
The Johns Hopkins Press Ltd., London

ISBN 0-8018-4926-8

Library of Congress Cataloging-in-Publication Data will be found
at the end of this book.

A catalog record for this book is available from the British Library.

Contents

Preface and Acknowledgments

This book is the product of more than two decades of research on various aspects of the retail land sales industry. My interest began in the early 1970s as a graduate student at the University of Tennessee, where I began the study of recreational land development on the Cumberland Plateau. This was the beginning of what was to become a long-term endeavor, with extensive fieldwork in Tennessee, Arkansas, Texas, Colorado, Florida, Oregon, New Mexico, and Arizona.

Geographers and other scholars devoted little attention to the problem of recreational land development in the early 1970s. Although this has changed to a certain extent, there are still relatively few sources of information on the topic. An important purpose of this book is to help fill this void. Consequently, one of my first objectives is to provide, from a geographical perspective (the spatial point of view), information about the location and size of large recreational-retirement communities. Other aims of the book include a consideration of the system of operation, the environmental and economic impacts, and the public policy implications of recreational-retirement communities, beginning with the 1950s. These communities are important elements of landscape change, and they can create many environmental, economic, and consumer problems. An understanding of how these projects work, where they locate, and their magnitude of operation should be useful to government officials and others interested in growth management.

I am indebted to many people for their assistance and support in writing this book. First, I acknowledge the support of Arkansas State University, which included a sabbatical and frequent reassignments for research, which have been indispensable to the completion of this project. I am especially indebted to my mentor, Theodore H. Schmudde, who, two decades ago at the University of Tennessee, introduced me to the topic of amenity land development and interested me in the way such development changes geography. I particularly appreciate his direction, his patience, and his thought-provoking ideas.

I owe a special debt of gratitude to John H. Corbet, colleague and friend, who over the years has provided insightful criticism of my work and who has been a continual source of inspiration and motivation. John's suggestions on how to portray some of my data are especially appreciated. To my wife, Judith, and my son, Brandon, I am grateful for their patience and their support of my research and writing. They have been particularly understanding during our research trips to southern Florida in the middle of summer and have endured many sweltering afternoons in the car driving through subdivision after subdivision trying to help me find the perfect photograph to illustrate my work. At Johns Hopkins University Press and the Center for American Places, George F. Thompson has been a patient and invaluable reader/editor and helped me make substantial improvements in this book.

This volume would not have been possible without the cooperation of many corporate officials, sales personnel, local, regional, and state planners, consultants, engineers, land-use attorneys, property and tax appraisers, U.S. Department of Housing and Urban Development officials, the Florida Department of Environmental Regulations staff, and real estate agents. My deepest appreciation is extended to the following: John McIntosh, Jim Reed, Tom Swafford, Brian Keller, Chris Van Hoy, and Robert Albertson, officials with Fairfield Communities, Incorporated; Richard Anderson, director of operations, Westinghouse Gateway, Incorporated; Dennis Getman, vice president and general counsel, Avatar Holdings, Incorporated; Jim Colegrove, director of public affairs, AMREP Corporation; Frank Schnidman, senior research fellow, FAU/FIU Joint Center for Environmental and Urban Problems; John Outland, Department of Environmental Regulations, Tallahassee, Florida; Richard Morgan, Northwest Florida Water Management District; Roger Henderson and Lynn Herbert with the Office of Interstate Land Sales Registration, HUD; and the following local and regional planners: Charles and Susan Gautier, Alton Roane, Donald Craig, Mark Rosch, William Spikowski, David Burr, Paul O'Connor, Wayne Daltry, Larry Didion, Tyson Symroski, Max Forgey, Mary Gibbs, and Bob Generous.

I owe a special thanks to Ed Reilly, Linda Douthitt, and Susan Rainwater for their assistance in editing, typing, word processing, and countless other tasks that helped put the finishing touches on the manuscript.

I would like to acknowledge the journals that have published some of my research articles, small segments of which appear in this manuscript. Portions of chapters 1, 5, and 11 were published previously under these titles, in the following journals: "Environmental Problems Associated with Large Recreational Subdivisions," *Professional Geographer* 35 (1983): 304–7; "Raw Land to Time-sharing in Arkansas," *Arkansas Business and Economic Review* 16 (1983): 12–16; and "Problems Associated with Recreational Land Development in Arkansas," *Arkansas Journal of Geography* 1 (1985): 18–22.

Two works, *Subdividing Rural America*, by the American Society of Planning Officials and others, and Leslie Allan, Beryl Kuder, and Sarah Oakes, *Promised Lands*, were seminal to this book. Although the information in these publications is now dated, they are two of the few pertinent sources on the subject and were extremely useful to me as I prepared the chapters on economic and consumer issues.

I have made every effort to ensure the accuracy of facts and interpretation, but I apologize for any errors that may have inadvertently occurred. Also, all opinions and conclusions in the book are mine and do not necessarily represent the views of the publisher.

The Promise of Paradise

1 Introduction

The mass merchandising of real estate lots and parcels mushroomed into a multi-billion-dollar industry during the late 1960s. Sales of vacation and retirement homesites in recreational subdivisions totaled more than $5 billion a year in the early 1970s. A large market and high profit margin prompted some of the nation's largest corporations to enter the instalment land sales business. The most successful companies and their stockholders reaped very large profits.

Unfortunately, most of the customers—people from all walks of life—did not share in these benefits. While some buyers were treated fairly, far too many were conned into purchasing property they did not need and really did not want (Morgenson, 1988). Unscrupulous sales tactics by developers primarily interested in generating profits from sales of raw land produced thousands of virtually uninhabited subdivisions across the United States. The industry's image has been tainted by such deception and fraud, and even though legitimate companies are creating viable recreational-retirement communities, all of them have the potential to significantly change the physical environment and the economic and social characteristics of areas where they locate (Paulson, 1972a, 1–5).

This volume assesses the success of these recreational-retirement communities and their problems as they progress through the stages of development. The impact of recreational land development can be both positive and negative. Positive features include putting to use land that might otherwise be only marginally productive, thereby boosting rural economies by generating new tax revenues and consumer sales, stimulating the housing construction industry, and providing recreational opportunities. These benefits must be weighed against the serious problems amenity-seeking populations bring as they move into rural areas, including the reduction of land resources, the environmental devastation of ecologically fragile land, and the overtaxing of local public services (Mosena, 1972, 298–99; Schnidman and Baker, 1985, 508–20).

Although the recreational land sales industry did not begin to take its present form until the 1950s, subdividing land is not new to the American experience. Land fever began to afflict the American people shortly after the federal government was established. In fact, speculative land schemes are as old as the United States and are an American tradition. Land speculation played a major role in opening the West and is a factor in managing contemporary land use (Yearwood, 1971, 113). Land speculation, the subdivision of real estate for profit, and premature subdivision are age-old practices (Cornick, 1938).

By the 1820s, both the federal government and individual speculators had amassed vast profits by selling land parcels to a public hungry for private property. The speculative fever waned by the end of the 1830s, and many newly acquired paper fortunes disappeared in the general economic depression that ensued. Such boom and bust cycles recurred time and again, determined largely by broad swings in the nation's economy. When the general economy improves, retail land sales companies emerge from their periodic hibernation to capitalize on people's desire to buy land.

The possibility of making fortunes by buying and selling real estate has long intrigued speculators; unfortunately, the history of such schemes is marked by land fraud, in which worthless land was sold to unsuspecting buyers. Nonetheless, land speculation is a legitimate business (Vaux, 1974, 1).

Throughout American history, development companies have transferred land long before any development could be absorbed by the local economy. A good example of such premature subdivision occurred in Florida from 1916 through 1925, when speculative activity created enough subdivided lots within a ten-mile radius of Miami to accommodate 2 million people (Vanderblue, 1927, 114–16). Such speculative subdivision, while most significant in Florida, happened throughout the United States (Sussna and Kirchhoff, 1971, 595). In 1825, for instance, when the first boats traveled the Erie Canal between Buffalo and Albany, incentives grew to subdivide land prematurely, and supply of "urban" lots began to exceed demand (Cornick, 1938, 5). In addition to the 1920s boom, notable booms also occurred in New York in 1835 and 1865. Each boom was followed, of course, by a bust. Today, the supply of "urban" lots still exceeds demand (U.S. Dept. of Housing and Urban Development, 1993).

During the 1950s, property in suburban subdivisions became popular. Lots were mass-marketed by a few firms, principally in Florida and in California's remote desert regions. These companies created a nationwide market for property sold on the instalment plan by mail, often sight unseen (Allan, Kuder, and Oakes, 1976, 3–4). This type of land development soon became a national phenomenon; raw or partially developed acreage was "improved," subdivided into small parcels, and offered for sale on liberal terms. Land hustling became almost as much a part of contemporary America as superhighways and rock concerts (Paulson, 1972a). Such developments appeal to a broad segment of the population (W. Martin, 1971, 3). From this boom was born the present-day recreational land development industry (Mosena, 1972, 297).

The success of this industry can be attributed to several factors: the desire of millions of Americans to own land, promotional efforts by land developers, the amenities of a rural environment (pull factor), the desire to escape an urban environment (push factor), the availability of large tracts of relatively inexpensive land located near interstates or major highways, and the absence of government regulations.

As our society became more urbanized, congested, and chaotic, more people began to look for an escape from the pressures of city life. Some turned to rural areas where small parcels of property are offered in large land developments. Advertisements touted such property as having tremendous investment potential, perhaps quoting Andrew Carnegie: "90 percent of all millionaires became so through owning real estate" (Parsons, 1972, 1). Millions of Americans were convinced by such promotions to buy vacation homesites in large subdivisions.

Land sales expanded during the 1950s, and by the late 1960s rural land was being subdivided at an unprecedented rate. Though these subdivisions were concentrated in a few states, there was hardly a state in which subdividers were not converting farms, forests, deserts, swamps, or mountains into lots. Widespread growth continued until 1973, when the industry encountered several problems: an economic recession, increased development costs, more rigorous consumer and environmental regulations, an oversaturated market, negative publicity, and an energy crisis. Demand waned quickly. Recovery was slow, but by 1977 there were some positive indicators. The slump eliminated many marginal developers, and those who remained offered the consumer a better product. While some positive signs remain, it is unlikely that the industry will ever again reach the peaks it attained during the years from 1969 through 1973 (Ragatz, 1976).

In response to these setbacks, developers have changed their operational techniques (Lachman, 1990). Greater buyer sophistication coupled with more stringent regulations in some states has prompted them to, for example, subdivide smaller tracts, provide basic services to lot owners, and implement such plans as time-sharing and undivided interest plans (Chant, 1986). Several land development companies expanded into the creation of resort communities, constructing elaborate infrastructures and building and selling vacation homes. Consequently, home sales became an important source of revenue for many developers.

The second-home market was complicated somewhat by the Tax Reform Act of 1986, which establishes limits on losses and on deductions for interest, depending on how the owner uses the home. For tax purposes, a second home falls into one of three categories: primary residence (rented for less than fifteen days); part residence and part rental; and primarily rental (rented for more than fourteen days, with personal use not exceeding fourteen days). Because of these changes, developers must work harder than ever to sell prospective customers a second home. Families that intend to rent their vacation home for part of the year must do advanced tax planning. Families using their vacation home for most of the season and renting it for fourteen or fewer days are not subject to the limitations of the act (Cavanaugh, 1988). Land developers now prefer to build communities of primary-resident houses, along with the amenities needed to attract an upper-income clientele (Gautier, 1990).

Location and Size

Land sales subdivisions are defined as any land divided into at least a hundred lots for the purpose of sale as part of a common interstate promotional plan. The U.S. Department of Housing and Urban Development's Office of Interstate Land Sales Registration (OILSR) records recreational subdivision filings and produces a voluminous catalogue report in which it tabulates large-scale operations. If all of HUD's 1993 subdivision listings are included, the total exceeds 22,000, of which 6,827 require full disclosure (table 1.1). The emphasis in this volume is on these projects, which are active, offer a hundred lots or more for sale on the interstate market, and submit a statement of record and a property report to OILSR. As classified by OILSR, the remaining subdivisions are inactive, exempt from OILSR regulations, or unregistered (Henderson, 1993; Herbert, 1993; Stroud, 1983b, 304).

Much of the serious impact of recreational subdivisions can be linked to their development methods and their location. Unfortunately, these subdivisions are concentrated in ecologically fragile lo-

Table 1.1 Recreational Subdivisions on File with the Office of Interstate Land Sales Registration, 1993

State	All Types	Full-Disclosure Required — Less than 1,000 Acres	Full-Disclosure Required — More than 1,000 Acres	Lots	Acres
Florida	2,612	768	150	2,117,034	1,627,124
Texas	3,225	755	73	1,280,752	896,909
California	1,748	535	86	976,131	749,857
Arizona	1,632	645	84	590,919	792,613
New Mexico	449	142	39	518,810	573,003
Colorado	932	362	71	319,203	696,981
North Carolina	1,195	265	23	275,318	233,887
Missouri	626	143	17	264,926	148,480
Pennsylvania	519	202	35	222,833	199,784
Arkansas	471	85	14	194,456	154,602
Virginia	491	149	15	157,742	128,362
Michigan	614	107	13	126,579	179,028
Nevada	381	59	12	118,561	187,369
Tennessee	429	78	14	113,501	83,252
Georgia	551	82	13	118,964	118,894
Washington	508	153	8	108,601	73,675
Oklahoma	478	87	4	107,879	63,000
Mississippi	221	67	8	95,335	50,233
Ohio	220	51	8	93,785	45,528
South Carolina	438	83	10	97,156	65,215
Oregon	603	99	11	84,000	96,246
Kentucky	391	101	2	74,407	33,910
Indiana	333	58	6	73,587	199,771
Utah	270	100	12	72,149	91,969
Other States	3,563	857	66	741,866	695,853
Total	22,900	6,033	794	8,944,494	8,185,545

Source: Data compiled from U.S. Dept. of Housing and Urban Development (1993).

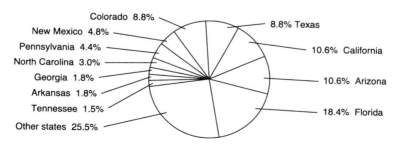

Figure 1.1 Percentage of recreational subdivisions of 1,000 acres or more, by state, 1993.

Source: Data compiled from U.S. Dept. of Housing and Urban Development (1993)

Figure 1.2 Number of large U.S. recreational-retirement subdivisions, by state, 1993

Source: Data compiled and mapped from U.S. Dept. of Housing and Urban Development (1993)

cations, in places with aesthetically pleasing features, or in places that can be promoted for their amenities. These concentrations are evident from comparisons of numbers of subdivisions by state: 57 percent of all recreational subdivisions of 1,000 acres or more are found in five states, 73 percent are in only ten states (U.S. Dept. of Housing and Urban Development, 1993; figures 1.1 and 1.2). Major concentrations occur in Florida, across the desert Southwest, along the Front Range of the Rockies, in the Pocono Mountains of northeastern Pennsylvania, and in several counties near Austin and Houston, Texas. Of the 794 subdivisions depicted in figure 1.2, Florida alone has 150 of them clustered in its central and southern parts. Several of these concentrations are in the Sunbelt, a location many subdividers prefer. Projects range from extremely small subdivisions to gigantic developments, some of which exceed 100,000 acres. One of the largest, Horizon's Rio Communities in central New Mexico, covers approximately 240,000 acres and is subdivided into 172,000 lots, enough to house the entire population of Albuquerque and then some.

The percentage of land in each U.S. county devoted to recreational subdivisions has been mapped to allow comparisons of development activities, regardless of county size (figure 1.3). Counties in central and south Florida, southern Colorado, New Mexico, Arizona, and northeastern Pennsylvania have high concentrations of recreational subdi-

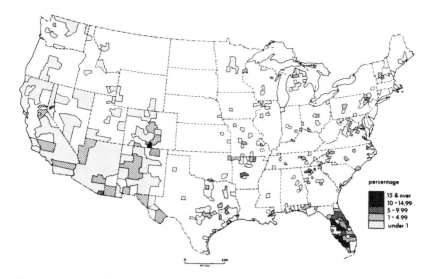

Figure 1.3 Percentage of U.S. land area in recreational-retirement subdivisions, by county, 1993.

Source: Data compiled and mapped from U.S. Dept. of Housing and Urban Development (1993)

visions. Costilla County, Colorado, and Lee County, Florida, have more than 20 percent of their total land area in recreational subdivisions over 1,000 acres in size. Charlotte County, Florida, has more than 18 percent, and another 16 counties have between 5 and 15 percent in such development. An additional 111 counties have between 1 and 5 percent of their land devoted to these large subdivisions, and lower percentages are found in several smaller counties in widely scattered locations (Stroud, 1983b, 307).

In addition to large recreational subdivisions, many states have hundreds or even thousands of relatively small subdivisions that, in aggregate, are a major component in overall land development. Florida, for example, has over 2,000 subdivisions of less than 1,000 acres (figure 1.4). These smaller subdivisions are often located near larger subdivisions. For example, Lee and Collier counties, located along Florida's southern Gulf Coast, have a relatively high percentage of their land area in subdivisions of 1,000 acres or more, but their greatest number of subdivisions are under 100 acres. These smaller-scale operations take advantage of the flow of customers to neighboring large subdivisions. As a result, seven Florida counties have a relatively large number of subdivisions, varying in size; these counties are Citrus, Marion, and Putnam in north-central Florida and Pasco, Polk, Lee, and Collier in central and southern Florida.

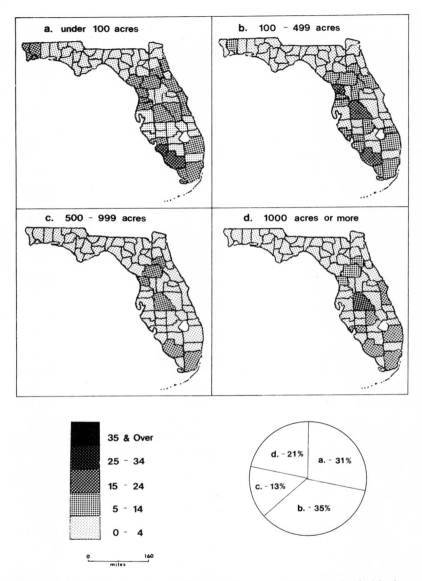

Figure 1.4 Distribution of recreational-retirement subdivisions in Florida, by size, 1993.

Source: Data compiled and mapped from U.S. Dept. of Housing and Urban Development (1993)

Arizona, with nearly 1,500 subdivisions, ranks fourth in the nation in total number of land developments. Although Arizona has large counties and extensive, virtually uninhabited areas where raw land prices have traditionally been low, most of its subdivisions are small. These small subdivisions are concentrated in Maricopa and Yavapai counties in west-central Arizona and in Mohave County, where the greatest number of large subdivisions are also located (figure 1.5). Developers of the small projects in Maricopa and Yavapai counties apparently capitalized on demands for vacation homesites by the urban populations of Phoenix and Prescott (Bloom, Weimer, and Fisher, 1982, 613–14). As with many small subdivisions in Florida, the cluster of small subdivisions in Mohave County is attributable in part to developers' attempts to locate near large subdivisions to take advantage of the customer flow they create. Small subdivisions are strongly concentrated in or near counties with large cities (Phoenix, for example), whereas large subdivisions are located in the more sparsely populated portions of the state, such as Mohave County in western Arizona.

Many factors influence decisions about site selection. The availability of large tracts of relatively inexpensive land is one. For land development to be financially successful, profits must be made above the investments in site improvement and lot promotion. Vast tracts of land are needed to provide the developer with a large inventory of lots, most of which are sold on instalment contracts. The high concentration of large recreational subdivisions in Florida's Lee and Collier counties, for example, is in part attributable to the availability of large landholdings in these two counties after the depression of the 1930s. During the 1950s in this area, one land development company acquired 370,000 acres for less than $100 per acre (L. Carter, 1974, 228–40). And in the 1960s and early 1970s, land on the Cumberland Plateau in Tennessee was sold to recreational subdivision developers for less than $150 per acre (Stroud, 1974, 130). Land in the Ozarks region of northern Arkansas was sold to developers for less than $200 per acre during the 1960s (Stroud, 1977). In the 1950s and early 1960s in the arid and semiarid areas of west Texas, New Mexico, Arizona, and southern California, hundreds of thousands of acres were purchased by land developers for less than $50 per acre (Srader, 1981; Stroud, 1983b, 306).

Another important site selection factor is accessibility, whose significance can be determined by measuring the distance between recreational subdivisions and a major highway. Many of these subdivisions are located adjacent to interstates. There are concentrations of these subdivisions west of I-25 in Colorado, adjacent to I-45 and I-35 near

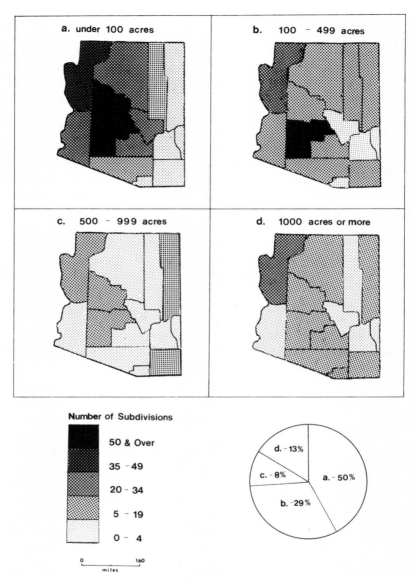

Figure 1.5 Distribution of recreational-retirement subdivisions in Arizona, by size, 1993.

Source: Data compiled and mapped from U.S. Dept. of Housing and Urban Development (1993)

Austin and San Antonio, Texas, along I-40 on the Cumberland Plateau in Tennessee, and along interstates in eastern Pennsylvania, Florida, and California. There are other large subdivisions located within twenty-five miles of interstates, including several near I-40 and I-25 in New Mexico, those west of I-25 in central Colorado, and others in California, Arizona, and Florida. At distances of fifty to a hundred miles from interstates, subdivisions are less numerous but include several projects north of I-40 in northwestern Arizona, east of I-5 in east-central California, and in the Ozarks of Arkansas. Only 2 percent of large recreational subdivisions are located more than a hundred miles— or a two-hour drive—from an interstate; examples include subdivisions in east-central Nevada, central Oregon, and southwestern Colorado (Stroud, 1983b, 306).

Even though recreational or second-home property is often promoted as real estate with a location that provides an owner the opportunity to "get away from it all," several studies indicate that the most desirable location for such property is near a large urban area. A comparison of the location of metropolitan statistical areas (MSAs)* and recreational subdivisions reveals large concentrations of these subdivisions near or within MSAs, with more than 50 percent of them less than fifty miles from an MSA. The clustering of such development near Phoenix, Austin, Houston, and Denver supports these findings (Bloom, Weimer, Fisher, 1982, 613; Stroud, 1983b, 307).

Perhaps the most significant factor in site selection is the absence of government regulations and land-use controls. An absence of regulations makes land development simpler but may make it virtually impossible for government officials to stop land-use practices that will degrade the environment. A survey of local land-use controls reports that 70 percent of communities had been subdivided before the adoption of regulatory controls (American Society of Planning Officials, 1976, 97–98). Another survey discloses that during the early 1970s, a time when recreational land development was at a peak, only about 40 percent of nonmetropolitan counties (fewer than 100,000 people) and less than 60 percent of urban (metropolitan) counties had zoning ordinances (ibid., 97–99). These percentages provide a strong indication, therefore, that much recreational land development occurred without the scrutiny of government officials (Stroud, 1983b, 307).

---

* An MSA is defined by the Bureau of the Census as one or more central cities with at least 50,000 inhabitants in the urban core plus any contiguous counties with more than 75 percent of their population engaged in nonagricultural activities, with county boundaries as the statistical measuring unit.

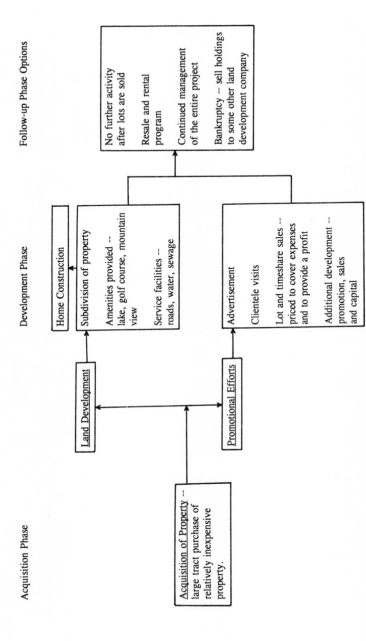

Figure 1.6 Recreational-retirement land development, operational framework

Source: Adapted from Stroud (1978); revised in 1993, using information from Fairfield Communities corporate officials

The System of Operation

Developers of large recreational subdivisions work within an operational framework designed to rapidly convert land into salable "vacation homesites." The framework is essentially the same for all recreational land developments, although each might use variations of the model (figure 1.6).

During the land acquisition phase, developers acquire large tracts of relatively inexpensive land that meets their development requirements. The land must be easily financed, with little or no cash down, and zoned for subdivision. Ideally, it should also have scenic and developable terrain, soil with suitable load-bearing capabilities and adequate drainage, a potable water supply, and adequate utilities. After acquisition, the developer moves into the development phase, which combines the construction of on-site facilities and the implementation of an elaborate promotional campaign. A showcase core area and a road network (usually unpaved) are built, the latter to provide access to lots. The core area has an attractive entrance, paved roads, and large, well-constructed sales and administrative office buildings, which contrast sharply with the remainder of the project.

Much of the success and a major portion of the expense of the operation are from promotional efforts. Because of a limited local demand, developers create a market through regional or even national promotion. Sales personnel often consist of an experienced sales manager and an independent sales staff, who are paid on a commission basis (Lawson, 1988). Some corporations, preferring to teach inexperienced sales personnel newer, more subtle marketing techniques, operate their own sales training schools. Regardless of how the salespeople are trained, the promotional framework is designed to make buying a lot easy for customers. Most companies have an elaborate system for contacting potential buyers: by far the greatest number are contacted by direct mail, but telephone calls and advertisements in newspapers and on radio and television are also utilized, offering free dinners and lodging while the customer visits the development (W. Martin, 1971, 5–6).

Dinner parties are arranged at a restaurant near the customer's home. Here, the merits of the subdivision are discussed and arrangements might be made for the customer to visit the development. On-site inspections are crucial, since the recession rate is much lower for customers who have visited the property (Albertson, 1988; W. Martin, 1971). Private automobiles, buses, airplanes, or limousines transport the prospective buyer to the development site. Cash certificates to cover the cost of gasoline are often issued to families who drive their private automobiles to the property. Flying customers to the development is an extremely effective marketing tool, since air travel quickly transports these customers out of their urban environments, delivers them to a remote subdivision, and isolates them for a highly concentrated sales presentation (W. Martin, 1971, 5–6).

Promotional efforts are designed to sell many lots in a short time. Normally, a lot purchase requires a cash down payment equivalent to 5 percent of the lot's sale price, the balance being due through a conditional sales contract payable over a ten- to fifteen-year period at an annual interest rate of 10 to 12 percent. Interest rates vary depending on the length of the payoff period; substantial discounts in interest rates are given, for example, for shorter time periods. Purchase arrangements are quick and easy and more like purchasing a car than real estate.

Much of the cash generated by lot sales is used for construction and to promote the sale of additional lots. Sales commissions for individual sales representatives range from 12 to 15 percent, with total sales costs running as high as 25 to 30 percent of the purchase price. Additional expenditures are made for advertising and promotion. Thus, the total sales costs for a project can range from 30 to 40 percent of gross sales. General administrative overhead adds another 5 to 10 percent, with construction costs, interest, and carrying charges adding other expensive items to the overall cost of development (ibid., 5–7).

Although some land development companies make sales to as many as 30 percent of the customers who visit their developments, more commonly the percentage of sales is less than 10 percent. Property deeds are usually not transferred to lot owners until the instalment contract is paid in full. As a general rule, the down payment does little more than cover promotional costs, including sales staff, promotional literature, and the housing and transportation of prospective customers. After all the lots are sold, some developers move into other phases of development: home construction, promotion and management of time-share units, lot resales, and management of the development. In some projects the lots are never all sold, the project becomes inactive, and in some instances it fails financially.

Elements of Change

Recreational land development communities have a tremendous potential to create change, both positive and negative. Their impact is intensified because of the aggregates of developments in one location, ill-conceived site selection, and elaborate development and promotional infrastructure. Part of the real estate package sold to lot buyers is the developer's so-called master plan or conceptual model, usually prominently displayed in the sales office to give the prospective customer a view of the "future." Developers try to convince customers that, as homes are built and as human-made amenities (infrastructure) are added, lots will be worth much more in the future. Unfortunately, reality often falls far short of the developer's promises. Many subdivisions fail financially and provide few if any of the promised amenities. Buyers may end up with lots in the middle of nowhere, surrounded by other vacant parcels, and with no services or human-made amenities.

Subdivisions that fail and become inactive are often referred to as platted lands. According to Lorenzo Aghemo (1992), Planning Director for Monroe County, Florida (the Florida Keys), platted lands represent one of the most significant and difficult planning problems for his staff. In the Florida Keys, many subdivided areas are environmentally sensitive, many lots do not meet current standards for development, and lot development is likely to be scattered rather than compact, making it more difficult to provide basic services. Inactive subdivisions create other problems as well, including patchy patterns of land development, complicated land-use arrangements, and the ruining of land for other uses.

Successful subdivisions are not without problems, too, such as environmental disruption and the inability to provide basic services to lots as they are needed. For these and other reasons, it is risky business indeed to rely on a developer's plans or conceptual model of what the development will be like in the future. Proposed lakes, eighteen-hole golf courses, swimming pools, and tennis courts may never materialize, and lot owners may be stuck with property they cannot give away, let alone sell for a profit.

Although the era of large-scale raw land sales has passed, older developments have left behind many problems. This book provides a comprehensive analysis of the environmental, economic, and social impact of large-scale recreational land development; reviews what leading land-use experts say about this important issue; illustrates how some states cope with intense growth and development pressure; and identifies regulatory controls that may help resolve the problems.

PART ONE

The Impact of Recreational Land Development

2 Environmental Problems

One of the worst aspects of recreational land development is the environmental degradation it creates in water and air resources, fish and wildlife habitat, and the aesthetic quality of large tracts of land. In addition it increases erosion and siltation and solid waste disposal problems (Stroud, 1983b, 308–12). Much of the environmental efforts of federal and state governments are directed toward alleviating air and water pollution, but relatively little attention is devoted to the disturbance of scenic landscapes. Because many planners and government officials believe that land-use issues should be resolved locally, public officials and the general public are often caught unawares when a recreational land development boom carves up vast rural and scenic areas rapidly and recklessly (Heritage, 1973, 25). Developers have now subdivided the slopes of the Appalachians and the Rockies, the coastlines of the Atlantic, Pacific, and Gulf of Mexico, and the shores of northern New England lakes. Such massive development was based on a market comprising millions of urban people seeking to escape their cities for a few days a week on interstate highways or by air. Geographer John Borchert labels this era the "auto-air-amenity epoch" (1967, 301–22, 1993). Developers capitalized on the age of convenient travel; their promotions targeted cities a day's drive or less from their development sites. The importance of the automobile is reflected in the aggregations of recreational-retirement subdivisions near interstate highways. Developers also took advantage of the speed and convenience of air travel and offered free flights to customers living in distant cities if they would agree to tour the site and listen to a sales pitch. While the free fly-in technique was used sparingly, some developments—like Cape Coral, Florida—sold thousands of lots this way to a population seeking the amenities of the leisure life.

Various factors determine the environmental impacts from recreational subdivisions, among them the natural characteristics of the site (soil, topography, and wildlife); the development's size, density, design, and improvements; land development techniques and construction practices; and the land-use management system (American Society of Planning Officials, 1976, 45–46; Syme, Seligman, and Macpherson, 1989). Although the environmental impact may be minimal during the early stages, before houses are built and occupied, it increases substantially as home building and occupancy progress. Occupancy may be insignificant at first but can increase dramatically and, whether seasonal or permanent, can dramatically increase the need for water, electricity, and sewers and the strain on natural resources (Syme, Seligman, and Macpherson, 1989). If the development becomes a permanent settlement, the environmental impact from generation of waste and from increased automobile traffic can have negative consequences. Environmental degradation is intensified since many recreational subdivisions are located near water or in areas of great natural beauty (Helweg, 1985, 54–93, 193–238). The future of these subdivisions should thus be given serious consideration.

The building of recreational subdivisions generally hews to lower standards than those followed by traditional suburban subdivisions. Septic systems are widely used, and water supply is often from individual wells, since central water and sewer facilities are not provided outside of the relatively small showcase area. Residents of these subdivisions must also live with monotonous street layouts, insufficient parks, eroding topsoil, clogged drainageways, flood damage, and polluted water. I discussed these problems with the Cape Coral Planning Department staff, which is literally overwhelmed by the problems created by the developers of the massive subdivision. Most of the problems (whose details are discussed in chapter 6) resulted from poor planning and substandard land development practices (Allan, Kuder, and Oakes, 1976, 41–51; Generous, 1991).

Such severe problems stemmed from three basic causes. First, many sites were environmentally sensitive and vulnerable to almost any kind of development. Second, to provide access to lots, developers tore up the land to build networks of dirt roads to all parts of their subdivisions, whether or not there were immediate plans to use the roads or to develop the property. Third, the absence of regulatory guidelines encouraged substandard projects and environmental degradation; developers were free to subdivide their property any way they saw fit, and thus many subdivisions were designed in the easiest, least expensive manner possible. Lots were rigidly superimposed across hilly or mountainous terrain, wetlands, earthquake fault lines, floodplains, and valleys without concern for aesthetics, environment, or hazard (see Beattey, 1994, for the ethics of such development). Whether a subdivision would deface and despoil the landscape or blend with the natural environment was largely determined at corporate headquarters, long before the first infrastructure was built (American Society of Planning Officials, 1976, 7–10). If individual wells and septic systems were used, pollution and depletion of groundwater were likely. If no drainage system was installed, erosion and gullying would likely result. If no land was set aside for solid waste disposal, the new community might find itself within a few years with no place to dispose of its trash (Shultz and Groy, 1986, 592–94). Sadly, far too many subdivisions were built with just such inadequate planning and design. After decades of abuse, the residents of high-growth states such as Florida began to realize that uncontrolled growth and development woulddestroy the very amenities that many Americans were seeking. This awareness led to the passage of regulatory controls mandating planning and development that protects the environment.

An important element of sound environmental planning for large subdivisions is the phasing of development; a subdivision is divided into sections, with lot sales in that section coordinated with the extension of services, so that both proceed together. This process reduces sprawl and saves the developer the extreme financial drain of installing all services at once. Few recreational subdivisions built in the 1960s and 1970s employed phased development (Mandelker and Cunningham, 1979). Developing in controlled phases is becoming much more common, however, particularly in Florida, Oregon, and Vermont. Florida has passed legislation designed to ensure that services to lot owners are provided by the developer as they are needed (Burr, 1992; this legislation and its ramifications are discussed in part 3).

Information concerning the demand for housing and the desire among prospective owners to actually use the development is often unavailable. Few projects have grown substantially, and most have population totals far below the developer's projection. At current rates of growth, therefore, many subdivisions (such as the Forbes Ranch in Colorado) will require hundreds or even thousands of years to become fully built. Environmental research is thus essential if a developer is to plan for sound layout and design and coordinate the needs and impact of the subdivision with the surrounding region. Environmental research also becomes important if a developer is to create a project that conforms to the environmental constraints of a state or region (Allan, Kuder, and Oakes, 1976, 43–44; Joyce, 1991).

Recreational subdivisions located in dry environments are, ironically, in danger of damage from flooding. The torrential cloudbursts that occur in deserts often produce flash floods, and too few subdivisions prohibit residential construction in or near drainageways vulnerable to flooding. Severe flooding has occurred in subdivisions in Arizona and New Mexico, some of them with substantial populations (Didion, 1986). Such problems could have been ameliorated through sound land-use practices at the subdivision's inception (Mandelker and Cunningham, 1979, 31–110).

Very few developers have protected water resources from pollution. They not only failed to use sediment traps and retention ponds to catch dirt, oil, fertilizer, animal excrement, and other runoff pollutants, but they also neglected to replant and reseed areas where vegetation was disturbed by construction work. Such revegetation is crucial, however, in controlling mud and silt at their sources and thus in retaining soil and preventing water pollution. In addition, greenbelt buffer zones on either side of waterways would filter runoff before it reached the water and would also provide attractive recreation areas—but such zones are not common (Allan, Kuder, and Oakes, 1976, 47; Borchers, 1988). Unfortunately, many developers relied on septic systems for sewage disposal and on groundwater wells for water supply. Where lots are small (one-quarter to one-half acre), the potential for groundwater pollution is extremely high. Health codes and environmental regulations are continually being strengthened, but many local governments are reluctant to apply these new regulations to existing subdivisions. Some of these problems could be eliminated by building central sewage plants, but at the same time, effluent from such facilities could also cause pollution problems if the treatment plant is not properly designed (J. Barker, 1989).

The numerous sites selected for subdivision vary tremendously in their suitability for development. Most sites can tolerate at least some development if adequate planning and sound land-use practices are implemented, but in many instances the site's water resources limit the land's ability to sustain a permanent population (Helweg, 1985). If the groundwater's recharging capacities are exceeded, increased mineralization, land subsidence, and water depletion may occur. Limited groundwater supplies could be protected by continuous monitoring of the water's quality and quantity, with an arrangement to switch to another source if there were signs of impairment (Allan, Kuder, and Oakes, 1976, 47–51; Patrick, Ford, and Quarles, 1987, 1–16).

Problems associated with water resources are not limited to semiarid and arid regions. A dropping water table, a need for chlorination, and water shortages are some of the problems that can occur when demand overtaxes supply (Shands and Woodson, 1974; Mackert, 1988). A large recreational subdivision in northern Virginia, for example, gradually became a permanent settlement, increasing the demand for water. Additional wells had to be dug to supplement the two existing wells. Because the subdivision's central water supply system did not meet the state's Health Department regulations (and was finally condemned), the property owners' association had to pay to update the system to meet state standards. Another area, along Florida's Gulf Coast near Tampa, experienced similar water resource problems in the mid- to late 1970s. Rapid growth and development necessitated excessive groundwater withdrawals, which lowered the water level in underlying aquifers, reduced the pressure in several water systems, allowed saltwater intrusion, and forced some communities to declare a building moratorium (American Society of Planning Officials, 1976, 48).

Increased erosion and siltation can also occur if subdivision roads are improperly located and constructed, if construction sites are left unprotected, or if steep slopes are disturbed. Erosion from subdivision roads at Lake Tahoe, California, for example, accounted for a large percentage of the sediment entering the lake (Tahoe Regional Planning Agency, 1971b). Nearly 40 percent of the streams in Nevada County, California, were damaged by siltation, stream bank alteration, and domestic waste from recreational subdivisions (California, 1971). Problems have also occurred in mountainous locations, where slide areas, swelling clays, runoff areas, and other unsuitable surfaces have been used for homesites. During the early 1970s, for example, the Colorado Geological Survey found that 43 percent of the subdivisions reviewed had plans inconsistent with geological conditions (American Society of Planning Officials, 1976, 51). A more recent survey found that 24 percent of the cities and 40 percent of the counties in Colorado reported that subdivisions were platted without regard to topography or geology and that houses built on those sites would be subject to landslide, mud slide, or other geological hazard (Shultz and Groy, 1988).

The construction of a recreational subdivision, particularly if many human-made infrastructural facilities are provided, can dramatically reduce the permeability of the watershed and thereby alter the hydrology of the area. Reduced permeability increases surface runoff and shortens the time between precipitation and peak flows in streams. In the mountain subdivisions around Lake Tahoe, one of every six acres is covered by an impervious surface, such as a paved road or a rooftop, which increases peak runoff, stream bank erosion, and loss of fish habitat in affected streams (Tahoe Regional Planning Agency, 1971a; Machida, 1988).

One of the most severe water resource problems caused by large-scale recreational subdivisions is the massive devastation of wetlands. Dredging and filling causes widespread destruction; although these practices have been outlawed, many coastal areas have already been destroyed. In addition to filling in, polluting, and depopulating estuarine and marsh environments, development along a coast can increase beach erosion and encourage settlement in areas susceptible to flooding and damage from hurricanes and winter storms (Tampa, 1972; Blanchard, 1991).

Generally, if care is not taken to revegetate construction sites and road banks (preferably with indigenous vegetation), disturbance of the natural surface can reduce air quality by creating dust storms, a severe problem in the desert Southwest, where thousands of miles of bladed subdivision roads have contributed millions of tons of dust to the air each year. Some lots in a subdivision in New Mexico were covered by one to two feet of sand ("Horizon Corporation Warned to Curb Sand," 1973). In fact, the Air Quality Control Board of New Mexico has ordered the Horizon Corporation to stop sand and dust from blowing off its subdivision roads.

Higher automobile traffic volumes and increased use of wood-burning fireplaces cause additional air pollution. And as recreational subdivisions multiply, problems with solid waste disposal will increase as well. The jurisdictions in which subdivisions are being developed may be faced with the expense of disposing of a great volume of waste material. Time, equipment, and personnel may also be required to clean up roadsides in areas around these subdivisions (American Society of Planning Officials, 1976, 54; Shultz and Groy, 1988, 593).

In addition, the replacement of the natural environment with the structures of recreational subdivisions may alter the habitat of fish and wildlife. In certain situations, the change can be positive, particularly for those who prefer bass fishing in artificial lakes. All too often, however, subdivision has a negative impact, since many species of wildlife are highly intolerant of human activity. When natural and undisturbed habitats are crucial to a species whose daily patterns or normal migration routes are disturbed, the species may die out. In south Florida, for example, the Florida panther, wading birds, and other species are threatened as their habitats continue to be disturbed by suburban development and urban sprawl (Hammond, 1991).

Recreational subdivision is concentrated in some of the nation's most aesthetically pleasing landscapes. The construction of a dense network of roads and the removal of vegetation for construction can destroy a marsh vista, intrude upon a skyline, scar a mountainside, and totally disrupt the aesthetic quality of a region. Aesthetic disruption can range from the invasion of a wilderness by development to what the Nantucket Islanders call loss of "charm," as small villages are transformed by growth and development (American Society of Planning Officials, 1976, 56; Laitin, 1988).

Vulnerable Locations

Developers of recreational subdivisions make site selection decisions based on several important factors, among them the aesthetic quality of the property. Highly scenic land is an important part of their promotional plan. Scenic land, such as mountains with expansive vistas, is ecologically fragile and susceptible to environmental deterioration if subdivided and developed. Environmental problems created by large-scale recreational subdivisions in several ecologically fragile areas are analyzed below.

MOUNTAINS

One feature of mountain ecology is vertical zonation—distinct vegetation zones that are related to the rainfall and temperature of the zones. It is possible to travel great distances ecologically by climbing a relatively short distance up the slope of a mountain (Costello, 1975, 57–75). Each vegetation zone contains its own distinct wildlife community. Vegetation protects steep slopes from erosion, a naturally occurring problem, which is however exacerbated by human activity. By providing a covering of litter, vegetation protects the surface from pounding rainfall, and by providing openings in the soil, vegetation increases the soil's absorption of water from rain and melting snow. Mountains also contain the headwaters of many major streams, such as the Colorado, Rio Grande, and Arkansas rivers, and thus cannot tolerate land development of any kind. Mountains also contain areas vulnerable to landslides, earthquakes, and flash floods. For many reasons, therefore, mountains are unsuitable for large-scale land development (Ives, 1979, 12–45).

The inhabitation of mountains was, for the most part, limited throughout much of America's history, in both the East and West. For westward-bound settlers, mountains were barriers and wildernesses to be avoided. People went into the mountains only to hunt and trap, to mine, and to explore until the last three or four decades (Costello, 1975, 239–62). However, as the United States changed to an urban, affluent society with more and more leisure time, delicate mountain regions have been subjected to ever-increasing pressures from a host of recreational activities, particularly skiing (Budenkov and Hamilton, 1991, 4–5). Because of the great demand for recreation, the rustic, widely scattered cabins of the hunter or fisherman have been replaced by large-scale recreational subdivisions. The resulting environmental problems are as enumerated above: overtaxed water supplies, disrupted vegetation, and soil erosion. During rainstorms, dislodged soil may dramatically increase the siltation of lakes and streams. Septic systems in thin mountain soil may seep sewage effluent into mountain streams and reservoirs (Allan, Kuder, and Oakes, 1976, 384). Even though recent state regulations restrict the use of septic tanks, many are already in use. And although uncontrolled subdivision development has been restricted in some locations, substandard, environmentally unsound development practices have already been utilized (Shultz and Groy, 1986, 5−6).

Several studies emphasize the environmental impact of subdivisions in mountains, including the Massanutten Mountains−Blue Ridge area in Virginia. Here, recreational subdivisions contributed to soil erosion, hydrological change, water pollution, and scenic blight; rural counties were converted into urban and suburban areas; and officials sold forested mountains and clean streams for short-term revenue gains without considering either the long-term environmental costs or that the land had such development limitations as steep slopes and poor, thin soil. In one Virginia subdivision, well water, once abundant and pure, began to flow slowly and required chlorination (Shands and Woodson, 1974, 1−2; Loyd, 1988).

According to a study of subdivisions in the Colorado Rockies, development significantly alters the natural landscape; the appearance of mountain areas changes when roads, utility lines, and buildings are constructed. Development also modifies watersheds and disrupts wildlife by replacing natural habitats with human-made features, including paved streets, parking lots, and rooftops of homes and other buildings (Howe et al., 1972). A recreational subdivision of nearly 10,000 acres located a few miles southwest of Pueblo, despite the advantages of a beautiful setting in a mountain valley some 6,000 feet above sea level and its location near Interstate 25 and the industrial center of Pueblo, has many problems. The most significant limitation is water, because legal rights to enough water for the development's projected population were not obtained (Allan, Kuder, and Oakes, 1976, 387−90). In addition, the developers failed to provide adequate open space, located lots on steep slopes and flood-prone land, and did not implement an erosion control program. Because roads were bladed across the entire subdivision, many are now either overgrown or contribute to soil erosion. Although lots on steep slopes, some exceeding 25 percent, can be built on with proper engineering and architectural design, a better alternative is to leave steep mountain slopes undeveloped, since they have a high erosion potential and are, at best, extremely expensive to build on (ibid., 410–12).

These problems are significant enough from an environmental standpoint to seriously question the desirability of having a new community built in a location with so many environmental limitations. Robert Twiss (1973, 233–46) discusses the merit of predevelopment planning for such areas, pointing out that the management and preservation of critical areas is an important goal in planning. In other words, good landscape design and planning has beneficial effects that extend beyond the boundaries of the area being protected. Realizing the need for regulation and control, a Montana Department of Commerce manual provides details about the intricacies of Montana's Subdivision and Platting Act (Montana, 1986).

But even given all the problems created during the 1970s and the continued environmental disruption in the 1980s, most state and local governments have failed to establish effective regulatory controls. And even when legislation, such as Montana's Subdivision and Platting Act and Colorado's legislation mandating subdivision notice requirements, has been adopted, it has failed to address many of the problems created by large subdivisions. One significant limitation is associated with how subdivisions are defined and exempted (Shultz and Groy, 1988, 602–3): for instance, developers of large tracts of land may be excluded from regulation. Such loopholes are very popular, indeed, in Montana, where over 70 percent of all divisions of land took advantage of exemptions. The increasingly popular thirty-five-acre and forty-acre miniranch is a strong indication that, in many instances, developers are willing to alter the product they market rather than go through the review process. Other problems in state subdivision control laws are associated with the lack of direction given to local governments, which are required to administer the laws, and with the failure of the laws to take into account regional and statewide impacts of land development (ibid., 604–6).

DESERTS

Deserts occupy a relatively large portion of the southwestern United States. The driest areas are on the eastern side of the Sierra Nevada and Cascade mountains. These rain shadows (dry leeward locations) are shielded from the rain, often producing extremely humid climates on the windward sides of the mountains. Such deserts and semiarid regions may also be far removed from sources of moisture and thereby subject to only occasional rainfall, which often occurs in violent thunderstorms. A single cloudburst may provide several months', or even a year's, rainfall. The desert's plants—cactus, creosote bushes, sage-brush—though common, do not cover the desert floor. The thin soil, bare rock, and sand of these arid areas are exposed to pounding rain, intense sun, and high winds, environmental factors that limit both plant and animal life (Bender, 1982). Deserts are frequently surrounded by semiarid regions, where climatic conditions are not quite as severe. Semiarid regions have denser vegetation, primarily short grasses. Extending across millions of acres in some states, these regions are extremely important to the cattle industry as rangeland but are unsuitable for land development because of their fragile plant and animal life (Humphrey, 1958; Johnson, 1982, 1261–86).

Arid and semiarid regions, with their thin soil, sparse vegetation, and limited rainfall, are particularly vulnerable to changes made by human activity. Their environmental conditions, especially their extreme aridity, make deserts much slower to recover from human-made changes. Despite these limitations, these regions are subjected to pressure from a number of sources (Beaumont, 1989). Although as much as 50–60 percent of the desert Southwest is federally controlled, the private sector owns millions of acres of land, some of which is being urbanized and suburbanized because of rapid population growth in Albuquerque, El Paso, Phoenix, Tucson, and other metropolitan areas. The region is also the location of several gigantic recreational subdivisions, some exceeding 100,000 acres. Large tracts of relatively inexpensive land, coupled with the desire of millions of Americans to own property in the Sun Belt, made recreational subdivision extremely attractive to many land developers during the 1960s and 1970s (Evans and Thames, 1981, 2–3; Stephenson, 1987).

Large land development companies with massive operations in southern California, Arizona, New Mexico, southern Colorado, and western Texas include Horizon Corporation, Forbes Incorporated, and General Acceptance Corporation (GAC). These developers did not, for the most part, adequately prepare for the environmental constraints of building in arid and semiarid locations (Stroud, 1983b, 309–11). As noted, the most severe environmental problems are flooding, soil erosion, and scarce water. Much of the rainfall in arid environments occurs in heavy downpours, with one thunderstorm yielding as much as ten inches of precipitation in an hour. Such downpours easily overtax natural drainage networks, and flash floods are common. These problems are greatly intensified where a dense network of dirt roads is superimposed on the landscape without regard for the natural drainage network or the protection of natural vegetation. Roads also intensify the erosion of soil from an already highly erosive, sunbaked surface of bare ground, loose debris, rock, and sand.

Possibly the most critical environmental limitation is an extremely scarce water supply. Few surface streams run year-round; even if they do, the rights to their water were allocated years ago through a water rights system referred to as *prior appropriation*. Subsequent purchasers of real estate, even of land adjacent to a stream, may not have any legal rights to its water. Subdividers solve this dilemma by suggesting that lot owners use individual wells, but since water tables are deep, drilling costs can be prohibitive. Even if the cost is not exorbitant, a large number of wells can easily overtax aquifers, cause the water table to drop, and allow increases in mineralization from saltwater intrusion. Tucson, for example, relies for its water on an aquifer whose future looks bleak.

Developers also suggest that lot owners with property outside the developed core, usually 90–95 percent of property owners, use septic systems for sewage disposal. Septic tanks on small individual lots may not cause immediate problems as long as occupants remain widely scattered, but the use of wells along with a high concentration of septic systems is not an environmentally sound practice and can cause health problems.

In recent decades, primarily during the 1970s, scholars expressed concern about the environmental impact of recreational subdivisions; these include a comprehensive analysis by James Jezeski et al. (1973) on the impact of subdivision on "semi-primitive" environments in Montana, H. J. Vaux's (1977) study of subdivision in the southern California desert, and Gary Soucie's (1973) study on subdividing the desert. Vaux points out that desert ecosystems, once disturbed, are not easily repaired and a large subdivision may irreversibly destroy fragile desert ecosystems (276). Soucie writes that massive bulldozing of a desert can have severe consequences, as is evident in a subdivision built by McCulloch Properties, Inc. (MPI), developers of Lake Havasu City and other large subdivisions. In fact, in an interview, a Maricopa County supervisor tells Soucie that "McCulloch doesn't need a subdivision permit; they need a mining permit." Soucie emphasizes that the greatest environmental damage occurs from desert land being broken for roads and streets. Fragile plant communities will be uprooted forever, dust storms will blight neighboring areas, and winds and floods will erode the bladed roads into permanent gullies (28–35).

The environmental problems created by the subdivision of a large tract of land in southeastern Arizona illustrates just how inappropriate many sites can be for development. Established in 1969 by GAC, this eighty-six-square-mile subdivision occupies a semiarid valley between two mountain ranges. The site is, of course, inappropriate for large-scale subdivision for several reasons. First, the property is located in a groundwater recharge area; development will cover up much of the permeable surface through which rainfall percolates into the ground and will reduce the amount of water returning to the aquifer. Several cities are dependent upon this aquifer for their water supply. In addition, the terrain includes several sharp ravines and hilly land, where slopes for some lots range from 15 to 35 percent and, as a result, are susceptible to severe erosion. Some property is subject to flooding, because the lots were platted by a preceding company in or along the bed of the Santa Cruz River. The lots were subsequently redrawn, and approximately 3,000 acres along the river have been withheld from lot sales (Getman, 1988). Although project officials took a positive step by leaving an open space along the river, they were not totally committed to leaving it undisturbed, particularly if problems emerge concerning water rights (Allan, Kuder, and Oakes, 1976, 287–89).

WETLANDS

Wetlands—bogs, swamps, marshes, estuaries, salt meadows, and sloughs—are extremely important both environmentally and economically. These fragile ecosystems, if left alone, store water that later recharges aquifers, absorbs dirt, filters pollution, and shelters and feeds plants, fish, and animals. Only recently have these many important functions become widely recognized (Federal Interagency Committee for Wetland Delineation, 1989, 1–7), and there has been, particularly in the past, tremendous pressure from land developers and farmers to drain wetlands for construction and agriculture (Mitsch and Gosselink, 1986, 3–14).

Environmental problems in Florida illustrate the difficulties associated with the development of wetlands. After 1900, Florida's natural environment experienced rapid change as people sought to increase the amount of land available for settlement. Wetlands were drained, mangroves and marshes were filled, seawalls were constructed, and meandering streams were straightened and channeled. Environmental degradation became particularly widespread after World War II because of explosive increases in population and land development (L. Carter, 1974, 4–5). Florida's population increased from 2.7 million in 1950 to more than 12 million in 1990, making it one of the fastest growing states in the nation and the fourth most populous state.

Areas in Florida with a large amount of land in recreational subdivisions were compared with areas of developmental tolerance to illustrate the conflict between land development and environmental preservation (Stroud, 1983b, 309). It was found that areas with slight or no tolerance for development were highly developed, a prime example of recreational subdivisions being built in sensitive and intolerant areas in spite of their being ill suited for development. Luther Carter (1974, 15–17) defines an intolerant area as one in which development, especially if not carefully controlled, will cause the loss or degradation of one or more of the following: a watershed or aquifer recharge area; a natural beach, scenic bay, or freshwater lake; a habitat essential to native plants and animals; and prime agricultural land. Higher elevations, in the panhandle and other parts of northern Florida, are more tolerant of development, but these areas have experienced the smallest amount of recreational subdivision—in part because of the unavailability of large tracts of land and the momentum for growth established years ago in peninsular Florida.

Large recreational subdivisions are concentrated along the Atlantic and Gulf coasts of Florida, with many large projects being completely or partially in the wetlands. Lee County, Florida, for example, with its long coastline and extensive wetlands, has the highest concentration of recreational subdivisions in the United States; its largest subdivision is located entirely within a wetland. In other counties, General Development Corporation, Deltona, and ITT have built subdivisions either totally or partially on coastal wetlands (Allan, Kuder, and Oakes, 1977, 56). The building of many of these subdivisions was made possible by a dredge and fill technique, which has now been virtually eliminated by environmentally sensitive land-use and water resource legislation (Office of Technology Assessment, 1984, 69–84). Unfortunately, these tighter controls came along after hundreds of thousands of acres had already been destroyed.

Wetlands cannot withstand any kind of development, let alone the total alteration of the environment that occurs during dredging and filling. Dredging excavates a channel and filling creates a strip of "dry" land with the earth removed from the channel. The method allows areas under three or four feet of water to be converted into a network of canals and narrow strips of land approximately three or four feet above sea level. Consequently, an environmentally productive and economically significant ecosystem is replaced by poorly drained, flood-prone real estate. Although most widespread in Florida, dredge and fill has destroyed wetlands across the United States.

While canals are important in constructing subdivisions in wetlands, they are not "improvements." These canals may stagnate, especially those in upland areas where tides cannot flush them, and they are vulnerable to pollution from septic tanks and other sources. Many of these ill-conceived drainageways become choked with aquatic plants that thrive on the nutrients in stagnant water. Canals may also degrade aquifers, particularly if the soil is porous. Canals also drastically increase surface runoff and thus contribute to a declining water table and to water shortages (Allan, Kuder, and Oakes, 1977, 62; Morgan, 1988).

A massive 90,000-acre subdivision located near Florida's southern Gulf Coast in Collier County typifies the problems that occur when wetlands are subdivided. The project began in 1960, before the importance of wetlands was fully understood and before specific regulations prohibited dredge and fill. Because extensive drainage was needed to create "dry" ground for homesites, a network of canals was installed to drain the property and lower the water table. The changes created by the multi-million-dollar canal drainage system has had disastrous consequences. Serious fires have occurred in areas of dried-out swamp vegetation, and some hydrologists believe it is only a matter of time until this subdivision becomes an arid environment, with dead trees, dry soil, and smoke from numerous fires (Whiting, 1973; Blanchard, 1991). Unfortunately, the changes made during the building of this development have an impact far beyond its boundaries. For instance, water was diverted from the western portion of the watershed that serves Big Cypress Swamp and the precious Everglades.

In 1972 the federal government took major steps to prevent such disastrous consequences in the future; the Water Pollution Control Act prohibits any dredging and filling that would have a negative impact on city water supplies, fisheries, shellfish beds, wildlife, or recreational areas. The law, enforced by the U.S. Army Corps of Engineers, applies to navigable waters and adjacent wetlands (Allan, Kuder, and Oakes, 1977, 63–64). Such protective legislation is essential but will not resolve mistakes made in previous years. The restoration of existing subdivisions is difficult, since tens of thousands of lots have been sold to disparate buyers. Converting land to its original state may require that local governments "take" the property with just compensation to owners. However, local governments are often broke; also, they are often reluctant to use their police power, although they have the legal authority to do so in certain situations.

The site of a large land development in Lee County, Florida, being built by Westinghouse Gateway Communities, Inc., while it has several limitations, is at least in the interior mainland, away from the coast. There are some wetlands on the site, but much of the land is outside designated wetlands. Unlike developments of the past, this project, which began in 1986, was required to meet many regulatory requirements, including the development of regional impact (DRI) process, as mandated by the Land and Water Management Act of 1972, and the more recent concurrency requirement, specified in the Growth Management Act of 1985 (Craig, 1991). Gateway, as part of its master plan, had to develop a water management system that would incorporate and protect existing wetlands and at the same time allow the proper flow of water across the property (Anderson, 1991). No dredge and fill or canals are allowed within this 5,400-acre project, which is being developed in manageable phases (Burr, 1991). Although this project still has many unresolved problems, many potentially devastating development techniques have been eliminated, and developers are working with local officials to build an environmentally sensitive project. Even though all environmental problems cannot be eliminated, they can be lessened when developers protect wetlands, inventory the site for endangered species, and follow a master plan that has been scrutinized by government officials (Joyce, 1991). Developers can then promote their project as environmentally sensitive to customers—who are becoming more and more environmentally conscious.

PLATEAUS

Recreational subdivisions are also located in plateau areas, which are often not as environmentally sensitive as wetlands, deserts, or mountains. The Cumberland Plateau, particularly along Interstate Highway 40 in Cumberland County, Tennessee, is the location of several relatively large subdivisions. This plateau, rising abruptly from 800 to 2,000 feet above sea level, is a broad, relatively flat, tableland, with bold cliffs, swift-flowing streams, deep canyons, picturesque valleys, and rugged terrain. It was a forbidding barrier to early settlers, and its rugged terrain and poor, thin soil provided few opportunities to its first inhabitants. However, many of the features that discouraged early settlement now attract vacationers, who enjoy rugged terrain and scenic vistas, and developers, who capitalize on the plateau's land development opportunities.

The Cumberland Plateau has served as an upland retreat for years, but recreational land development was limited, and few vacation homes were built in earlier decades. The only vacation homes were widely scattered A-frame cottages on private land. But since the mid-1960s, land subdivision has mushroomed. Projects have multiplied, particularly in Cumberland County near Interstate 40. Recreational subdivisions now claim more than 52,000 acres of what was previously undisturbed timberland.

Much of the Cumberland Plateau is covered by trees, and so it is desirable to people looking for an aesthetically pleasing wilderness or rural environment. The terrain has gentle to moderate slopes; vegetation regrowth is often rapid because the region receives approximately fifty inches of precipitation per year; there are no dust storms even when roads remain unpaved; and flash floods are not a problem, although some erosion and siltation do occur along newly bladed roads and at construction sites. In addition, the soil is suitable for construction, and percolation tests are favorable for septic systems as long as they are not too closely spaced (Stroud, 1983b, 311). With the exception of the arid and semiarid Colorado Plateau, these upland landscapes generally are better suited for recreational subdivision than many sensitive locations. Although plateaus—in this case the Cumberland Plateau in Tennessee—are environmentally more tolerant of development, such extensive and premature subdivision on this terrain remains questionable. Demand for the property is largely created by elaborate promotional schemes; most lots remain vacant, and the chances of buyers reselling their property are minimal (Stroud, 1974, 79–80).

Assessing Impact

There is a need today, as never before, to make ethical and wise land-use decisions. This need is particularly true in places that are experiencing rapid population growth and an increasing demand for sites suitable for land development. As the supply of vacant, undeveloped land diminishes, it is of paramount importance for government officials to develop a strategy for assessing the impact of land development projects, to improve their ability to make quality land-use decisions, and to assess the environmental impact of rapid growth (Barlowe, 1979, 3; Beattey, 1994; Thurow, Toner, and Erley, 1975).

Planners, geographers, landscape architects, ecologists, and other concerned professionals have dealt with the problem of environmental assessment for years, and many methods have been established for assessing the environmental impact from land development. An approach developed in the late 1960s analyzes the land's opportunities and constraints—the elements or components favorable for certain kinds of use and unfavorable for others. This approach stresses allowing the nature of the land to determine what use is best suited to it (McHarg, 1969; Johnson, Berger, and McHarg, 1979, 935–55).

An evaluation method suggested by Donald Davidson (1980, 30–36) is to assess not only environmental characteristics but also the economic viability, social consequences, and environmental impact of a proposed development. Larry Canter (1977, 20–21) suggests that a comprehensive assessment should include a description of the environmental setting, an impact prediction and assessment, and the preparation of an environmental impact statement. A description of the environmental setting provides the baseline information against which impact prediction and assessment can be made. Impact prediction and assessment involves projecting the environmental setting into the future both with and without the proposed action and then performing the necessary calculations to assess the consequences.

Selina Bendix and Herbert Graham (1978, 157–74) outline what they call an eco-plan. They suggest the need to analyze a site and consider a project's goals (what is planned) simultaneously. Planners would then use site analysis data and the development goals of project officials to arrive at an economically sound and environmentally acceptable plan. An excellent and timely work by Walter Westman (1985, 3–26) suggests a seven-phase sequence for impact assessment: defining the study's goals, identifying potential impacts, predicting significant impacts, evaluating the significance of the findings, considering alternatives to the proposed action, making decisions, and doing postimpact monitoring. Frederick Steiner (1991) is also an excellent source for wise land-use planning.

Local government officials must understand what they are dealing with prior to an assessment so they can evaluate the positive and negative aspects of any land subdivision. Such a holistic approach would avoid the mistake of considering environmental impact assessment in isolation and would facilitate its coordination with other aspects of the planning process (Clark, Bisset, and Wathern, 1980, 5–6; Steiner, 1991). Unfortunately, too few local governments bother with environmental impact assessments unless they are mandated by law, and too many are in cahoots with realtors and developers.

UNDERSTANDING DEVELOPERS' SYSTEM OF OPERATION

Later chapters describe the way developers promote their real estate and how they go about transforming raw land into a recreational-retirement community. If local officials understand their system, remind themselves of their public responsibilities to people and land, and realize that most developers are motivated only by profits, they will be better prepared to assess impact and to recommend procedures and policies to regulate these developments. Since many developers subdivide land years or decades before there is a need for homesites, local officials can mandate that subdivision occur only after market studies show a demand for the proposed lots. Florida, Oregon, and Vermont already require development in controlled phases, and Florida has imposed a concurrency requirement for all developments. Concurrency stipulates that developers must provide services as they are needed by property owners (Roane, 1990).

Another important aspect of recreational land development is its elaborate infrastructure: roads to provide access to each lot; administrative buildings; a variety of housing units, including condominiums, villas, garden apartments, duplexes, and single-family detached homes; and such amenities as golf courses, lakes, swimming pools, tennis courts, and hiking and biking trails. These can all significantly degrade the environment unless care is taken to minimize damage through environmentally sensitive design and planning. If local officials are aware of the planned infrastructure prior to development, they can make better decisions about the feasibility of the site for development and the appropriateness of the project for the community. If a county is going to be required to maintain the roads after the developers complete the project, which is often the case, officials must consider the cost of such maintenance. If developers plan canals and waterways to provide better drainage and outlets to the sea, for example, local officials need to take into account the potentially serious environmental problems associated with such wetland degradation and to question the suitability of the site for development.

Recreational land developments must attract a large number of people to the development site. Developers promote the project to a large clientele and sell lots to a certain percentage of customers (around 10 percent of visitors purchase a lot). The influx of a large population, even if it is seasonal, will make a substantial impact on the community. Furthermore, one of the most important features of recreational subdivisions is their potential to become permanent communities with large populations. Fairfield Bay in Arkansas, for example, has a permanent population of approximately 2,200 people, a substantial increase since its beginning in 1966 but small in comparison to its potential population. Developers at Fairfield Bay have sold over 16,000 lots (homesites), which means that the community has a potential population of approximately 50,000 people.

Even more alarming is the population potential of Cape Coral, Florida. The project, begun in 1958, was subdivided into over 138,000 homesites. This vast, vacant subdivision, at the start, had only a few permanent residents. In 1970 it still had only 11,000 permanent residents. In 1993 the population exceeded 80,000, but its potential population, based on number of vacant lots, is well over 400,000 people. Cape Coral's potential for growth is particularly worrisome since developers made no provisions to accommodate such growth. Almost all the basic services needed in this rapidly growing city are inadequate; two of the most significant problems are limited supplies of potable water and streets that are not designed to handle the traffic. Since little predevelopment planning took place and since few regulations were in existence at the time, the result was tremendous environmental devastation and a total disregard for the provision of basic services to lot owners.

Fortunately, the land development atmosphere has changed dramatically in recent years, but the Cape Coral example shows what results when predevelopment planning and environmental assessment are lacking. An awareness that, although these projects may seem relatively insignificant at the outset, they have the potential to become quite large is crucial for local government planners and decisionmakers. The case of Cape Coral illustrates the dire need to plan ahead.

Sound land-use planning and design include using street patterns that conform to the natural terrain rather than a rigid gridiron pattern that ignores the environment; using a cluster design rather than scattered development and sprawl; providing open space (usually 25 percent of the total acreage); excluding lot sales in areas of critical environmental concern, such as prime agricultural land, groundwater recharge areas, and wetlands; restricting lot sales in such hazardous areas as floodplains, steep slopes, and earthquake zones; reducing land alteration by constructing roads only in areas scheduled for immediate development, preserving the topography, and limiting devegetation to building sites and roads (Allan, Kuder, and Oakes, 1976, 101–14; see also Stokes et al., 1989).

Since water is crucial for most recreational subdivisions, both to supply households and as a scenic attraction, vital and sometimes extremely limited water resources should be protected through the following: using natural swales as drainage systems; building sediment traps and buffer zones between lots and waterways; immediately replanting disturbed vegetation, using indigenous, low-maintenance plants; limiting septic systems to one-acre (or larger) lots, with adequate percolation rates and proper distances from bedrock, groundwater recharge areas, and surface waters; requiring central sewage treatment facilities for smaller lots and in places where soils are unfavorable for septic systems; forbidding major stream rechanneling and wetland dredging and filling; and using groundwater only up to its environmentally safe yield to avoid saltwater intrusion, mineralization, land subsidence, and groundwater depletion (ibid., 114–27).

One of the biggest obstacles to putting these guidelines into practice is that state and local government officials are not convinced they are necessary. Until these guidelines become part of state and local land-use statutes, there are few effective means to regulate recreational subdivision or to ameliorate their negative impact on the environment. If the public does not demand effective controls over the environmental menace of these subdivisions, we could soon be saying farewell to our few remaining natural lakes, rugged seacoasts, and beautiful mountain landscapes. Based on the present degradation from such development, future degradation could cause the greatest environmental loss in our history, far more significant than the impact of earlier land booms in Florida and the desert Southwest (Heritage, 1973, 25). Even our everyday landscape is harmed by developers' greed and the ignorance of government officials.

CAPABILITIES OF THE LAND

The key to establishing sound land-use planning is to consider the ecology of the site proposed for development. Consequently, the first step in developing a meaningful ecological plan is site analysis. The necessary data can be obtained from maps and aerial photographs and from studies of geosystems, hydrosystems, biosystems, inland wetlands, coastal wetlands, uplands, open spaces, cultural systems, historic sites, and other components of the physical and cultural landscape (Bendix and Graham, 1978; McHarg, 1969; Steiner, 1991; Stokes et al., 1989). Government officials need to assess the potential environmental impact of proposed land development, an assessment that is comprehensive, systematic, and reproducible (Canter, 1977, 20–22). An interdisciplinary approach is suggested, since the subdivision of land and its subsequent development potentially affect so many parts of the physical and cultural landscape.

In areas being developed, a plan should aim to achieve the best fit between a human activity and its landscape. The landscape should be thought of as consisting of elements, or components, including soil, vegetation, hydrology, geology, wildlife, and climate. Each offers opportunities and constraints for each kind of use (Johnson, Berger, and McHarg, 1979). Development tolerance zones can then be established and mapped prior to land subdivision. Local government planners and officials can then use these zone maps to help them decide whether to approve or disapprove subdivision projects. Zones not suited for development would not be developed. Moreover, zones that will tolerate development can be further subdivided. Ideally, the pattern of land use assigned to the landscape will be determined by the physical properties of the land (ibid., 935–36).

Unfortunately, this approach almost entirely ignores the cultural aspects of land. Various components of the landscape affect and are affected by one another. An understanding of how the whole system works should indicate what events might occur as a result of some proposed land uses. Therefore, existing land use should be inventoried and mapped so that decisionmakers know current uses and how these uses coincide with the development tolerance zones. Before decisions can be made about proposed developments, officials need to know the existing uses of land surrounding these proposed developments. A consideration of the cumulative impact of all developments is essential to a comprehensive assessment of the environmental impact of land development.

Objective professionals, especially landscape architects, should be hired to make a comprehensive site analysis and inventory of the land. Such an inventory might logically begin with an analysis of the geology of the region. The kind of rock under the surface indicates the stability of the land, the presence or absence of void space (openings for water storage) for groundwater, and the suitability of the region for development. Much of this information can be found on geological maps made by the U.S. Geological Survey, Federal Center, Denver, Colorado.

The analysis of the surface configuration will identify areas too steep for development and areas in floodplains or wetlands. This information is available from topographic quadrangles, also from the U.S. Geological Survey. The nature of the soil should be studied to provide information on drainage, water tables, and soil groups. This information can be obtained from general soil surveys published by the Soil Conservation Service in the U.S. Department of Agriculture. Understanding the local hydrology is also significant, since decisionmakers should know the location of recharge areas, direction of groundwater movement, aquifer yields, depth of the water table, location of surface water, flood zones, and drainage basins. Such information is available on maps or in publications and circulars provided by the water resources division of the U.S. Department of the Interior (various years).

Equally important to a comprehensive site analysis is the existing vegetation, which holds the soil in place, protects watersheds, acts as a windbreak, supports wildlife, provides an aesthetically pleasing landscape, and cleans the air. In assessing vegetation, the professional should gather information about the distribution of plant associations, communities, and habitats; about areas important as noise buffers; and about plants as food or as nests for wildlife. While some helpful information is available in published works such as Eugene Odum's *Fundamentals of Ecology* (1959), much of the information must be collected in the field. The wildlife investigation would identify species and their habitats and ranges and movement corridors; these data would also need to be collected by professionals in the field.

The site analysis data should be presented in at least two forms: on maps with overlays to delineate development tolerance zones and in a narrative describing the site. The data should be analyzed using a geographic information system, or GIS, a tool for manipulating geographic information by computer. Once geographic information is in the computer in digital form, the data can be displayed and analyzed with a speed and precision not otherwise possible. GIS can compare many different variables on maps showing relationships among slope, soil, vegetation, and transportation arteries, help analyze sites, and assist in making site selections.

Site analysis should not ignore cultural features, since it is often a combination of human-made and physical features that determines the character of a place. When an area is settled, it is forever changed. While many aspects of culture are difficult to measure, its more concrete properties can be measured—farms, houses, roads, bridges, churches, cemeteries (historically significant burial grounds), and archaeological sites (Indian settlement sites and burial mounds, for example).

UNDERSTANDING DEVELOPERS' OBJECTIVES AND PLANS

While the site analysis is being made, developers should define realistic goals, identify their basic plans, and give the precise location of the proposed project. This initial screening would indicate how the project fits into its development tolerance zone. If a proposed site is suitable for development, government decisionmakers would continue to scrutinize the project to determine the developer's objectives and the specific nature of the proposed subdivision. The master plan would also show basic infrastructural needs, such as road networks, water and sewer lines, administrative buildings, restaurants, golf courses, and tennis courts. This master plan would help government officials understand the magnitude of the development and its impact on the environment. Such information as size (in acres), number of lots proposed, anticipated number of homes, projected population, and associated services (roads, sewers, trash collection, schools, etc.) are essential pieces of information.

One of the most important aspects of land development is the phasing schedule (the time allotted for the development of various segments or units of a project, often done in 500-acre units). Land development and lot subdivision in controlled, manageable phases are crucial to reducing environmental impact. In the past, many subdividers simply subdivided the entire parcel at once, with little regard for when the site would actually be used by the people who purchased the property. Today, however, projects must be more sensitive to the environment, and development in small, manageable segments is a significant part of this protection. Moreover, the subdivision of land only as needed is significant in preventing the overplatting of lots and in avoiding committing lots to potential homesites long before there is a need for building sites. Even this phasing approach will not protect the environment against bad design, however.

Developers of most large subdivisions will have, or at least state that they have, a multipurpose objective, including the provision of quality homes, recreational facilities, and opportunities for real estate investment. Whether these goals come to fruition is highly questionable. Nevertheless, local governments must be prepared for whatever development occurs. Government land planners and decisionmakers need to examine the relationship between the proposed site and the project plans to determine if they coincide. The objective is to blend environmental needs and land use to arrive at an economically sound and environmentally acceptable plan.

Ideally, local decisionmakers would present all pertinent information, including special reports, maps portraying land capabilities and limitations, land-use regulations, and costs to taxpayers in an open forum that includes planners, environmentalists, developers, and other interested parties. In hostile situations, open forums may be difficult to arrange; opposition groups often must become vocal to get a hearing. In either case, the objective is for all interested parties to present their arguments for or against the proposed development before local officials make their final decision on approval or denial. Developers should then be given time to address any shortcomings and to make plans to correct them. The open forum will not work if local officials have already made up their minds and hold forums just to placate the public.

Next, formal meetings should be held with local decisionmaking groups, such as the county commissioners, to discuss a systematic approach to analyzing the site's potential for development. Maps portraying soil characteristics, slope, and any other pertinent environmental and cultural concerns should be available for analysis. Using overlays, these maps can be compared with the developer's site plan depicting roads, utility lines, and other infrastructure. Comparisons among these maps should allow officials to identify environmentally sensitive (and culturally important) areas and to establish areas suitable for buildings and other infrastructure. An environmental impact study is essential to adequately assess all the ramifications of a large development. It lists proposals for development; describes the area's physical and biological features; identifies probable impacts on the natural, cultural, and social environment; assesses unavoidable adverse effects; suggests alternatives; and presents ways to improve the project or to mitigate negative impacts.

The demands on local officials have never been greater. Not only are they required to address environmental concerns, they must also deal with social and economic issues, which necessitates thoroughly examining environmental, social, and economic problems brought about by any development. The data developed in response to environmental laws and local regulations may require interpretation and explanation so that those involved at the local level can understand them. Government officials must present information to developers and the general public clearly and concisely.

The development process can be greatly enhanced if local officials follow through after their assessment process. As a project progresses, frequent inspections should be made by appropriate officials. During the early stages, soil erosion and sediment control are the major environmental concerns. Keeping disturbed areas to a minimum, controlling runoff, and retaining sediment can keep storm water within a controllable range. As long as officials are knowledgeable about the need for environmental protection, they are likely to support careful monitoring. If on the other hand they have little understanding of environmental planning and design, they will need to be educated and their actions monitored by community groups—otherwise, projects could be approved and allowed to develop based on narrow engineering concepts rather than on a holistic approach.

Bonita Bay, a new community south of Fort Myers, Florida, within the coastal zone of southern Lee County, is an example of a project that has observed environmental regulations. Developers, taking advantage of greater environmental awareness among prospective clients, promote the importance of preserving the environment, at the same time providing a high-quality community (Trudnak, 1989). Of course, developments like Bonita Bay still are not without environmental degradation, particularly those located near environmentally sensitive coastal wetlands. Any development has an impact. But, although not all environmental problems are solved, sound planning and design, with a commitment to minimize landscape alteration, can lead to environmentally compatible land use and a more aesthetically pleasing landscape.

Finally, developers should have plans in place to mitigate environmental degradation, including providing buffers along streams and other bodies of water, revegetating disturbed areas with native vegetation, and minimizing tree removal. Government officials might prepare a list of questions to determine what mitigation plans are in place, such as the following:

—Is the development planned to occur in controlled stages?
—Have arrangements been made for the provision of buffer zones along streams and other bodies of water?
—Are plans in place for the revegetation of disturbed soil?
—Have arrangements been made to minimize tree removal?

—Are plans in place for the provision of basic services as they are needed at individual lots?

Answers to such questions can provide local governments with the information they need to make wise land-use decisions (Joyce, 1991).

3 Economic Concerns

One of the dilemmas local governments face is ensuring that new development provides an economic stimulus for the community without degrading the environment, draining current tax revenues, or exceeding local abilities to provide housing, medical care, schools, and sewer and water hookups. But some communities have been so eager to reap the benefits from new developments that they fail to consider their negative impacts. This has been the case with large recreational subdivisions; local officials, unfamiliar with the full implications of such development, welcomed these projects because of the anticipated tax revenues and construction jobs, without consideration for provision of services or other problems associated with uncontrolled growth. Land developers can provide convincing evidence to local officials of the benefits to be provided by their projects (Craig, 1991). They argue that their subdivision will increase revenues in a variety of ways, including taxes paid on vacation property and homes, money spent in the area by vacationers, purchases of construction materials, increased land values, loans made locally for the purchase of lots, and wages paid to local people employed by the project as clerks, secretaries, cooks, maids, sales staff, and administrators.

Several factors determine the economic impact of recreational land development. Sales of unimproved raw land, for example, tend to generate little tax revenues, since property taxes are based on improvements. Unimproved projects also generate little spending by developers and lot owners. Fortunately, these subdivisions cost the local government very little for public services. A major cost may result, however, from the change in land use from agriculture or timberland to residential if residences are never built but alternative economic uses are precluded (American Society of Planning Officials, 1976, 61; Jaffe and Sirmans, 1982, 3–19). Developments with a lot of amenities produce substantial tax revenues but require more public services. The cost-benefit relationship is likely to change as development progresses (Schofield, 1987, 37–99). In the early stages, when homes are being built, revenues from property taxes tend to exceed the cost of public services. As the subdivision becomes fully developed or if it becomes a permanent settlement, service costs may exceed revenues.

Recreational subdivisions can generate large expenditures for engineering, site design, infrastructure, housing, and amenities. Whether this money is spent locally varies, depending upon the diversity of the economy and upon decisions made by the developer. If local labor forces are insufficient or unskilled, developers may bring people in from the outside. Moreover, if materials and supplies cannot be purchased locally, developers must purchase them elsewhere.

Important questions, which often are not asked, are, can the local community meet the increased demands generated by the development? If not, will revenues from the development cover the cost of expanding these services? Can the local community meet these greater demands? Are existing schools, police and fire protection, and basic services adequate? (Roane, 1990; Sampson, 1988). Other economic concerns result if recreational subdivisions stimulate more growth; it is common, for example, for other subdivisions to locate near large recreational subdivisions and add to the strain on local services, particularly if the subsequent developers do not make arrangements to meet the needs of the new property owners.

To determine the fiscal impact of a recreational subdivision, the costs of providing public services to development sites should be compared with the tax revenues generated by the development. Basically, the most important question is whether new tax revenues will cover new costs. Government officials must be apprised of what services the development requires and how costs and revenues will vary over time. The fiscal impacts from development are usually more serious in rural communities, where public services are inadequate or unavailable. These communities may be forced to raise taxes, increase user charges, or create special taxing districts to cover the costs of providing services to vacation homeowners. On the other hand, more developed communities may absorb the impact of recreational land development.

Positive Impact

LAND VALUES AND TAX REVENUES

One of the most important economic benefits of recreational subdivisions is the increased tax revenues as land increases in value. Measuring such changes in land value is difficult, particularly for real estate somewhat distant from the subdivision site (Adams and Mundy, 1991; Jundt, 1980, 39–53). On the Cumberland Plateau in Tennessee, for example, rural land was valued at approximately $100 to $150 per acre during the late 1960s and early 1970s, prior to subdivision. In 1972, after substantial recreational development had occurred, land adjacent to large projects was valued at $500 or more per acre. Speculative and inflationary prices were applied to tracts of land adjoining major subdivisions, and as a result, adjacent tracts were offered to developers at $500 per acre. Moreover, the price continued to inflate, and two years later the asking price was $1,000 per acre (Stroud, 1974, 130–43).

Normally, property in recreational-retirement subdivisions is assessed in the same manner as property in suburban subdivisions. However, many county governments, particularly during the 1970s, gave recreational land developers a tax break on lots they had not sold. In Deschutes County, Oregon, for instance, recreational lots still owned by the developer were taxed at only 45 percent of the normal rate at which vacant, single-family lots owned by individuals were taxed. The tax laws were changed in the late 1980s, however, and developers are no longer given a discount on their unsold lots (D. Reed, 1993). In Wisconsin, a state statute permits lower assessed valuations on developer-owned lots. Although taxes increase when lots are sold, the most significant increases occur when homes are constructed. For example, in several towns in Windham County, Vermont, owners of second homes pay as much as 40 percent of the total property taxes of the town (Turner, 1993). And property tax revenues from the Quechee Lakes subdivision in Vermont now provide approximately 30 percent of the total revenue for the town of Hartford (American Society of Planning Officials, 1976, 68–69; Standon, 1993).

A study by Clyde Richey (1972) compares the assessed valuation and property taxes, before and after subdivision, of property on a lake in Wisconsin. At the time of the comparison, the developer had created a lake, cut roads, staked out the lots, cleared the brush, and cleaned the shoreline, but the project was far from completed. One year before the subdivision was approved, the land was assessed at $3,917, for a property tax of $114. Two years after certification for subdivision, the assessed valuation was $128,000 and the property tax was $3,858.

This thirtyfold increase occurred when the development process was only in its middle stages; many more improvements were to follow. Richard Brown's study (1970) of a vacation-home community at Lake Latonka, Pennsylvania, provides another example of positive economic impact. This development added income to local businesses and increased tax revenues without increasing the demand for government services. Developers of the 1,600-lot subdivision spent $500,000 for land acquisition, $2 million for site preparation, $3 million for home construction, and $1.5 million for management and promotion. These expenditures yielded approximately $14 million in gross business activity from 1965 to 1970.

In another study, Gordon Lewis (1975) found that Snowmass (in the Aspen, Colorado, ski complex) contained 5 percent of the population but 19 percent of the assessed value of Pitkin County. While receiving 18 percent of the county's expenditures, it contributed 22 percent of the county's revenues. These findings indicate that vacation-home developments can increase tax revenues and the overall tax base without substantially increasing the county's expenditures. Local officials are more than willing to authorize such developments because of these anticipated benefits but seldom consider the possibility that these revenue-generating features may change—or never materialize.

The most substantial change in land values occurs within the boundaries of the development. Initial lot prices are largely dependent on the lot's proximity to primary amenities but, in general, range from $6,000 to $30,000. Inflated lot prices may reach $100,000 or more, according to the intensity of land use and the amenities offered. The highest priced lots are those near primary amenities or with panoramic views. Lot prices drop rapidly the farther away they are from such attractions. Remoteness and inaccessibility are, therefore, apparently not desirable even to people who leave suburbia to "get away from it all" (Stroud, 1974, 130–31; Van Hoy, 1993).

Lots can be sold at urban prices as long as the demand for vacation-home property is high; thus, lot prices are based entirely upon a developer's ability to attract a large number of buyers. These prices may become totally unrealistic if the developer's promotional schemes fail, a major concern of developers, especially if direct mail advertising, a popular means of attracting customers, generates fewer and fewer customers.

Changes in land values within the subdivision invariably affect the surrounding community. Prior to land development, for instance, timberland on the Cumberland Plateau was taxed at approximately $0.50 per acre. During the mid-1970s, taxes on lots in recreational subdivisions on the plateau were between $7.00 and $12.00 per year. Taxes on lots with vacation homes on them ranged between $80.00 and $160.00 per year. Tax rates have changed over the years, and by 1992 timberland was being taxed at approximately $1.50 to $3 per acre (depending on the current market value), taxes on unimproved recreational lots ranged from $24 for the least expensive to more than $150 for a choice lot. Tax revenues from improved lots (those with vacation homes) ranged from $289.90 for a house and lot valued at $60,000 to $723.75 for a house and lot valued at $150,000.

These increased revenues have changed the operating capital of Cumberland County. Assessments at Fairfield Glade, for example, generated approximately 25 percent of the county's total 1992 tax revenue. This positive economic impact is partially offset by the added expenses of providing services to a larger population. While the exact cost of county services for Fairfield Glade is difficult to measure, the expenditures on road maintenance, health care, schools, fire and police protection, and other services are expected to escalate as more roads are dedicated to the county and as the population matures and requires more services (Stroud, 1974, 134–35; Barnwell, 1993).

Similar increases in land values occurred in association with Fairfield Bay, a resort in north-central Arkansas. Land in more remote sections of the county—distant from recreational subdivisions—sold for between $50 and $150 per acre in the late 1960s and early 1970s, while lots within the subdivision, usually only one-third of an acre or less, ranged from $6,500 to $30,000. With its championship golf course, nationally known tennis center, and beautiful lake, Fairfield Bay has emerged as one of the prime recreational resorts in the region and has dramatically increased the land's revenue generation. Prior to development, this land was little-disturbed timberland. It now has more than 1,300 housing units, a town center, numerous human-made amenities, and a permanent population of over 2,100 persons, and it pays property, sales, income, and other taxes.

In 1984, improved lots in Fairfield Bay had an average assessment of $343, while raw land in the development was assessed at an average of $7 per acre. Lots with houses had an average assessed value of $3,000, with a time-share per unit assessment of $6,500. Other human-made amenities and community facilities had a cumulative estimated assessment of $545,200 in 1984 (Hammer, Siler, and George Associates, 1984, 18–19). Assessed value is calculated by multiplying the fair market value by 20 percent. Taxes are then determined by multiplying the assessed value by the tax rate (0.0369 in 1992 in Van Buren County, Arkansas). For example, a $100,000 house and lot in Fairfield Bay would yield a tax bill of $738 ($100,000 × 0.20 = $20,000 × 0.0369 = $738; Smiley, 1993). The real estate taxes on

Fairfield Bay property rose from less than $22,000 in 1979 to more than $1 million in 1992. In addition, personal property taxes of more than $100,000 were levied on boats, automobiles, and equipment belonging to Fairfield Bay residents. But all of these taxes have not been paid to the tax collector (Squires, 1993) because of financial difficulties associated with the company's reorganization after bankruptcy (R. Coyle, 1993).

Additional income from the subdivision is generated by taxes on sales, income, gasoline, cigarettes, spirits, and other items. In total, since Fairfield Bay's beginning in 1964, the county has received millions of dollars in revenues that it would not have received had the project not been established. Of the more than $3.2 million in tax revenues generated in Van Buren County in 1992, for example, approximately one-third was attributed to Fairfield Bay. The amount of this revenue actually paid to the county by Fairfield Bay remains to be seen.

EMPLOYMENT

The number of new jobs created by recreational development is largely dependent upon whether the subdivision progresses beyond raw land sales. Raw land sales create a flurry of construction activity when roads, administrative offices, and the showcase core are built, but few long-term jobs are provided. For the most part, administrative and sales personnel are brought in from the outside. A few local residents may be hired as construction labor, secretaries, and security guards, but ultimately the impact of a subdivision on employment is largely dependent upon the developer's intentions and success in progressing beyond a raw land sales operation to the creation of a new community.

Fairfield Bay epitomizes the impact of such complete development on jobs. The subdivision directly employs operating, maintenance, sales, clerical, and construction workers. In 1992, the subdivision employed 225 persons during the winter season and 325 during the spring and summer. In addition, 12 free-lance sales agents earned commissions from the sale of lots and housing units (R. Coyle, 1993). As these employees spend most of their salaries locally, additional jobs are created in trade and service establishments, which then purchase supplies from other businesses. This multiplier effect increases the economic impact of the development on both the county and the state. Economists indicate that, for every job created in a basic industry in a county, 1.02 jobs are created in service industries. The size of the multiplier is lessened by purchases of goods produced outside the region. The multiplier for the state economy is 2.12, significantly higher than for the county (Hammer, Siler, and George, 1984, 6–9). Although its current population may be relatively small, a new community can significantly boost the economy in new jobs alone. Other significant growth indicators are increases in demand for public utilities, goods and services, and other items purchased locally.

OTHER GROWTH INDICATORS

Since most of the households in these new communities are new to the area, their incomes represent new income. In Fairfield Bay, in 1992, for example, its more than 2,000 households earned more than $35.8 million in wages (R. Coyle, 1993). Further, visitors spend an average of $125 per day and time-share unit owners spend approximately $100 per day. In 1992, guests and time-share visitors spent over $2.25 million. Retail sales associated directly with the development increased dramatically, jumping from $11.2 million in 1979 to over $21 million in 1984, representing a significant economic impact on Van Buren County and the state (Hammer, Siler, and George, 1984, 63). In 1992, retail sales were only $10 million, reflecting the problems associated with bankruptcy and reorganization and the sharp cutback in marketing programs (R. Coyle, 1993).

Increases in demand for public services, such as electricity, water, and telephone, are also indicators of growth. The demand for telephone and television cable hookups also escalates. Much of this growth produces a positive economic benefit because of the increased workload for electricity, telephone, and other service-oriented companies.

Evidence of this economic growth is provided by a study of the impact of second-home development on northeastern Pennsylvania, which finds that second-home owners in a single subdivision spent $1,062.20 locally and an additional $1,478.10 regionally. If these data are valid for a seven-county area of northeastern Pennsylvania, estimated expenditures by owners of the estimated 32,021 second homes in the United States reached $82 million a year (Economic Development Council of Northeastern Pennsylvania, 1976). Economic impact is dependent, however, on several variables, many outside the control of local officials (Drake et al., 1968, 33–43). As these developments mature, their economic impact can change dramatically. If developers provide basic services for homeowners and maintain roads and other infrastructural facilities, the economic impact is likely to be positive. When the developer's plans are inadequate or where these plans fail, positive economic impact is much less likely.

Negative Impact

Many hidden costs are associated with recreational subdivisions, but they are often either overlooked or ignored by local governments when they approve development. A study of development in Colorado shows that hidden costs are associated with education, fire protection, and road maintenance. A new development could easily overload schools, particularly in a rural school system. And if the county does not require the new development to provide its own fire protection, then the local government would incur the responsibility and expense of providing it. Usually a subdivision dedicates its roads to the county after one or two dwellings are built on them. Then it is the local government's responsibility to keep these roads open, no matter how few people use them, and the cost could be exorbitant (Howe et al., 1972, 96–98).

A study of recreational subdivisions in Utah shows that the possibility of economic gain to local economies was the justification most frequently given by local officials for their receptive attitude toward recreational subdivisions. They felt that these developments would benefit landowners selling their agricultural land and would therefore increase tax revenues as land values increased and the tax base expanded. As the study discovered, this line of reasoning is not always valid: first, the establishment of a recreational subdivision invariably leads to land speculation and the resultant nonuse of land; second, it entails demands for services that small rural counties can ill afford (Workman et al., 1973, 1–10).

Interestingly, in Utah the countywide tax assessment rates on unimproved lots in these subdivisions were less than half the countywide rates for property outside these recreational subdivisions. These lower rates resulted from the Utah State Tax Commission's (USTC) policy concerning speculation: "value" and "full cash value" of property mean the amount at which the property will be taken in payment of a just debt due from a solvent debtor. Consequently, unimproved lots are not assessed at the sale's price if speculation is obvious to the USTC. These artificially low taxes kept the developer's cost of holding land low. Land speculation continued, but considerable tax revenues were lost each year. According to some county commissioners, counties do not receive enough in taxes from these unimproved lots sold to pay for billing costs ("Land Boom Swells . . . ," 1973). Thus, other county residents were subsidizing the owners of undeveloped rural lots.

In Beaver County, Utah, for instance, the loss was nearly $13,000 in tax revenues in 1972 due to an assessment rate of only 5.67 percent on unimproved lots and a countywide rate of 12.38 percent (Workman et al., 1973, 1–10). The Utah tax code has now been changed, and unimproved lots no longer receive a tax advantage. In fact, it is the permanent resident who now gets the tax break; unimproved lots are taxed at 95 percent of their value, while a house and lot that is occupied for at least six months of the year (i.e., a permanent residence) is taxed at only 66 percent of its value. An unimproved lot with a market value of $5,000 × 0.95 = $4,750 × 0.008781 (tax rate) = $41.70 per year in tax revenues. A permanent residence, on the other hand, valued at $80,000 × 0.66 = $52,800 × 0.008781 = $463.63 in tax revenue (Limb, 1993). In view of the potential tax income needed to sustain a second-home population if and when a subdivision advances beyond the speculative stage, it is certainly logical to design tax laws to generate more revenue and discourage speculative ventures. Otherwise, rather than representing a positive cash flow, recreational subdivisions, particularly those that advance beyond an initial stage, are likely to be an economic drain on local governments.

Despite these negative aspects, many feel that tourism and recreation land development are among the few ways to provide an economic stimulus for rural areas. Economic opportunities are few in rural areas of the desert Southwest, for example. Agriculture does not provide a basis for economic growth, and manufacturing and mining are not appropriate in many locations. As a result, many rural counties welcome recreational subdivisions, often without considering what the economic costs might eventually be.

UTILITIES

Since relatively few recreational subdivisions provide their own central systems, extending water and sewer facilities to a new development is likely to be a major consideration for local governments. Most developers rely on private wells and individual septic systems or on community water systems owned by a property owners' association, but such an approach may not be adequate for the subdivision's needs, particularly if its population escalates dramatically.

The problems associated with the provision of water and waste disposal vary. In the whole state of New Mexico, for example, there is enough water for only 850,000 people without diverting water from farms and industry or buying water rights outside the state. But the state's population exceeds 1.2 million, which has forced New Mexico to purchase water rights from Arizona. Despite this, there are enough subdivided recreational lots in New Mexico to triple its present population. As early as the late 1960s, some local governments began refusing to provide water to new developments and adopted utility extension policies. The city of Albuquerque, for example, will not extend services to adjacent subdivisions unless a formal request has been made for annexation. Developers of Volcano Cliffs, a subdivision west of Albuquerque, requested and received approval for the annexation of portions of its property, and services have now been extended to some of the lots (Cloud, 1993). Service extension policies and other short-run solutions may save local governments money in the beginning, but what will happen when lot owners move into these subdivisions and force a change in policies? The residents of recreational communities often take an active role in local community affairs. Where population totals are small (Cumberland County, Tennessee, for example), a resort community with a population of 2,000 to 3,000 is an important portion of the population and could significantly influence the outcome of local elections or referendums.

Many rural governments have approved high-density recreational developments with septic systems as the only means of human waste disposal. In Pike County, Pennsylvania, almost 90 percent of recreational subdivisions used septic systems in soils not suited for them (Wulhorst, 1988). Several recreational subdivisions in northern Georgia have no public sewage systems and no plans to add them in the future (Peterson, 1988). Similar situations exist throughout the country. Utilities such as electricity, telephone, gas, and television cable may also be difficult to provide, particularly if settlement is widely scattered. Unable to absorb the expense of extending lines to only a few customers, many utility companies pass the cost on to the customer, usually on a cost-per-mile basis. But this cost can be prohibitive to the lot owner.

ROADS

Roads may be one of the largest expenses for local governments. Although developers assume the cost of road construction within their projects, these roads are often substandard dirt roads. Most of them remain unimproved for years. The financial burden of improving and maintaining roads eventually falls to local governments. The law in many states requires that local jurisdictions not accept road dedications unless there is an ordinance detailing construction standards. Under such an ordinance, property owners must bring the road up to these standards before dedication can occur. If the cost of maintenance is beyond the means of local governments, a special maintenance district may have to be established, which assesses lot owners for maintenance costs. In Tennessee, for example, counties have developed minimum standards for roads before they can be dedicated. These standards include a hardtop surface (tar and chip), a minimum width, and the proper ditch line cuts for drainage. Fairfield Glade recently dedicated fifty miles of hard-surface (tar and chip) interior roads to the county. Since these roads are relatively new and meet current standards, the county does not anticipate major maintenance expenses in the near future. Yet within a few years, these roads will need to be repaired; it will cost approximately $3 per foot, or a total of $792,000, to completely refurbish fifty miles of tar and chip road surface (Fields, 1993).

Roads leading to recreational subdivisions may also require maintenance and improvement. Most rural or county roads are not adequate to handle the heavy traffic load created by a recreational subdivision. For example, in the mid-1970s Okanogan County, Washington, spent approximately $5,000 to maintain an access road to a subdivision whose residents provided only $1,637 in taxes to the county road department and an additional $1,309 to the county's general fund (American Society of Planning Officials, 1976, 65). Similarly, Cumberland County, Tennessee, had to completely redesign a seven-mile stretch of access road from Interstate 40 to one of its largest recreational subdivisions. The road, designed for county traffic, could not accommodate the high volume of vehicles traveling to and from the development. Peavine Road (the access road from Interstate 40 to Fairfield Glade) had to be widened and straightened in 1980 to alleviate traffic problems created by the resort community. In addition, a five-mile portion of the road had to be resurfaced in 1985 at a cost of $274,000, again largely because of heavy traffic from Fairfield Glade (Gravely, 1993).

A 1977 study of road expenditures associated with recreational subdivisions used two approaches to determine additional road expenditures (Weber, Youmans, and Harrington, 1977, 40–42). First, Klamath County, Oregon, road files were searched over a five-year period to assess the amount spent on various stretches of the road. Second, estimates of the average annual cost of maintaining county roads were obtained from the public works director. The county's cost of maintaining a 0.2-mile stretch of asphalt road that serves a particular recreational subdivision was estimated to cost an additional $650 per year. This figure was obtained by multiplying 0.2 mile of road by the cost of maintaining an asphalt road ($3,250 per mile).

In a second case, the situation was more complex. The subdivision apparently created pressure for the improvement of a road so that school buses could safely travel it. The county road existed long before the platting of the subdivision. Since the platting of the subdivision, however, the county has regraveled and maintained the road much more frequently. If the road improvements and maintenance would not have been necessary without the subdivision, then the entire costs of the improvements and maintenance should be considered a cost of the subdivision. If, on the other hand, the improvement and maintenance would have been made without the subdivision, then no additional cost should be attributed to the subdivision. An alternative is to apply half of the cost to the subdivision, estimated to cost the county \$2,131 annually (\$1,550 per mile per year $\times$ 0.5 $\times$ 2.75 mile).

SCHOOLS

The pressure that recreational subdivisions placed on local schools came as a surprise to local officials. Permanent subdivision residents may have school-age children, and the subdivision also may generate secondary population growth. School busing costs can be exorbitant, since recreational subdivisions are often in remote locations. During the 1970s, the peak of recreation subdivision activity in many states, a local school district in Okanogan County, Washington, spent over \$2,000 in a single year to bus nine children from one subdivision. And the school budget in a Vermont community more than doubled in a ten-year period as part-time residents became permanent residents (American Society of Planning Officials, 1976, 65–66). While such extreme situations are unusual, educational expenses can increase dramatically as subdivisions establish a permanent population. New classrooms will be needed, and even greater transportation expenses will be incurred.

A good example of a recreational-retirement community impacting a school system is Fairfield Bay in north-central Arkansas. This resort community of approximately 2,200 people has 250 students attending the Shirley Public Schools, a small rural school district that serves a portion of Van Buren County. These 250 students from Fairfield Bay cost the Shirley Public School District more than \$784,000 per year in instructional expenses (based on Arkansas Department of Education figures; Kenzel, 1993). Additionally, the school district spends over \$14,700 per year for three buses that travel more than fifty miles a day to transport these students. These educational expenses accounted for almost 80 percent of the \$1 million in tax revenues due to Van Buren County from the Fairfield Bay community (residents and corporation) for the 1992 tax year. But Fairfield Bay is delinquent on a substantial portion of its taxes.

Most rural police forces cannot handle the additional work produced by recreational subdivisions, particularly during peak seasons. Many police forces remain constant throughout the year, even though the population may more than double during periods when vacationers are using their second homes. In Hall County, Georgia, for example, 224 full-time police officers serve a population of 76,000 and an incredibly large recreational population during the summer. Being situated near metropolitan Atlanta and adjacent to Lake Lanier, Hall County is the destination of approximately 19 million tourists per year, many of whom visit the county on weekends during the summer. Although Hall County's 2.94 police officers per 1,000 permanent residents is above the national average of 2.2, the ratio drops dramatically during peak summer weekends. Since Hall County does not hire part-time or temporary help, the law enforcement staff is often overtaxed during peak periods (Grogan, 1993). Weekend use of Lake Lanier sometimes soars to more than 400,000 people and easily exceeds local law enforcement capabilities (Topper, 1993).

Recreational land developments create other problems for police forces besides heavy seasonal use. Being unoccupied much of the year, second homes are easy targets for burglars, arsonists, and vandals, creating investigative work and a need for police checks of unoccupied homes. In some cases, police departments have to be created where none exist. In other areas, part-time police officers are hired for weekends and summer months. Some developments provide some of these services on site and thereby ease the burden on local governments. For example, Fairfield Glade in Cumberland County, Tennessee, has its own security force, which relieves the county sheriff's department of the need to constantly monitor Fairfield Glade. However, the sheriff's department does assist with burglaries and fatalities. While the impact on county law enforcement is not overwhelming, the potential impact is great, particularly if the on-site security force is eliminated or if the population at Fairfield Glade continues to expand.

The rural counties in which many recreational subdivisions are located have minimal fire protection facilities and rely largely on volunteers. Some counties, however, have no fire protection at all, and as homes are built in recreational subdivisions, the demand for fire protection can easily exceed capabilities. Moreover, homes on steep slopes, in remote locations, in dense forests, or in condominium highrises are particularly difficult to protect. For the first, fire danger is great, and for the second new equipment may be needed.

Small, rural communities in which medical facilities are largely unavailable may be unable to meet the health care needs of the new population. For example, no medical facilities are available within the subdivisions on the Cumberland Plateau (J. Reed, 1984); residents rely on doctors and hospitals in nearby urban areas. An examination of hospital records in Crossville, Tennessee, a city of 6,394 people, reveals a substantial increase in the number of outpatients during June, July, and August, many of whom listed out-of-state addresses as their permanent residences. This seasonal need is indicative of a permanent need in the future as part-time residents become permanent residents (Stroud, 1974, 114). At the same time, local welfare roles can increase as workers are attracted to the area by the prospect of employment. But, many of the jobs created by recreational subdivisions are temporary and seasonal, which tends to aggravate the unemployment problem. Unless these citizens find gainful employment elsewhere, they become negative, rather than positive, forces in the economy. Although unemployment insurance provides some relief, it is only temporary and does not alleviate the unemployment problem.

Recreational subdivisions also increase the cost of running local government, which includes tax administration and collection, record keeping, licensing, inspection, land-use planning, and zoning. The most difficult situation arises when a large recreational land development is planned in a sparsely populated rural county with a minimal government staff and inadequate facilities to handle the operations of government. Grand County, Colorado, had to hire a planning staff and employ several planning consultants to write subdivision and zoning regulations because of a proposed 1,000-acre ski resort. In Pasco County, Florida, the planning and zoning budget rose from $15,000 the first year it was created to more than $320,000 in only a two-year period because of mounting development pressure. Unimproved recreational subdivisions have resulted in a large number of tax defaults by disgruntled lot owners, especially on purchases made sight unseen. In Taos County, New Mexico, where defaults have occurred on 10 percent of the subdivided lots, officials must trace titles back ten years and transfer them to the state. This added administrative burden, coupled with the low tax rates on unimproved property, can cause counties to spend more than they receive.

The costs associated with large-scale land development are not insignificant. If local officials are aware of these and other potential expenses, provisions can be made for covering such expenses before land development is approved. Local governments can stipulate that the land development company contribute to an escrow account to cover these costs. If, after a certain period of time (five to ten years) there are no educational or other costs directly attributable to the new community or if the development is generating enough tax revenue to cover expenses, the money could be returned to the developer. In all likelihood, however, tax revenues will be inadequate to cover expenses, and supplementary (or alternative) sources of revenue will be needed.

Evaluating Economic Consequences

The economic benefits and costs of recreational developments may shift continually, particularly if the number of the community's residents continues to increase. Local governments should prepare, therefore, for the change and not expect a subdivision to remain in an initial stage, during which it generates more revenue than it requires in services. The maturing of these subdivisions produces additional problems, but with proper management and advanced economic and environmental planning, local governments can reap benefits.

Although the regulation and management of land use can occur through zoning ordinances, building codes, subdivision regulations, planning, and other devices, these techniques are not sufficiently comprehensive to measure the effects of new developments. A systematic, comprehensive approach toward identifying relevant criteria is often missing. Philip Schaenman and Thomas Muller in 1974 suggested a comprehensive approach, using forty-eight impact measures. Only a portion of these are expected to apply to any one development. The impact on the local economy can be measured, for instance, by determining the net change in government fiscal flow, the number of new long-term and short-term jobs provided, the changes in the numbers and percentages of those employed, unemployed, and underemployed, and the changes in land values. Other items in the model include an assessment of the natural environment, aesthetic and cultural values, public and private services, and housing and social conditions.

Obviously, recreational developments can have both positive and negative economic effects on local communities. They may produce property tax surpluses, increase retail trade, and create new jobs at the same time that they increase the cost of public services. Under certain conditions, the result can be a fiscal deficit. The most important consideration is neither the revenue generated nor the added costs but the net income produced by the new development, which is largely dependent upon the stage of development of a subdivision, local tax distribution policies, and the location of the subdivision with respect to political boundaries. During the early stages, there may be a tax surplus. After the development has become a permanent settlement, there may be a tax deficit.

For subdivisions located in two or more political jurisdictions, one jurisdiction may reap tax revenues while the other may pay high costs. This is likely where the developed core is located in one county but with only a network of roads and little development in the other county. A good example is Hot Springs Village, a large recreational community in Garland and Saline counties in Arkansas. Most of the homes and other infrastructures are in Garland County, but a substantial portion of the land area (including roads) extends into Saline County. Because of this particular layout, a majority of the tax revenues goes to Garland County, yet both counties will have the responsibility of providing basic services as the subdivision becomes inhabited. While service from Saline County is insignificant at the present time, this may change dramatically as the community expands outward from the developed core.

Some studies indicate that recreational land development produces tax surpluses rather than deficits (LeJune, 1972; Tillson et al., 1972; Ziner, 1974). But most of these studies were made during the early stage of development. There was no assurance that positive cash flows would continue as these subdivisions progressed into more advanced stages of development. In addition, many rural governments do not always initially provide all the services a recreational subdivision might need. A property owners' association with membership fees might provide services and maintain infrastructure. If the property owners' association becomes inoperative or if its ability to provide services is overtaxed, local government expenditures could escalate dramatically.

Such expenditures would most likely occur if a subdivision becomes the permanent residence of families with school-age children. For example, suppose that 500 lots in a subdivision of 1,000 lots have dwellings averaging $20,000 in appraised value and that these dwellings are permanently occupied by families with two school-age children. Tax revenues to the county would be approximately $86,000 from all 1,000 lots, but the cost to the county would be $200,000 per year, and that does not include services to part-time residents or any expansion of services (Shands and Woodson, 1974). The fiscal balance tips to the negative side, of course, when more permanent residents with school-age children move in. Recreational land development, therefore, has a delayed tax impact, which has prompted some critics to label these developments a "taxpayer's time bomb" ("Subdivision 'Benefits' Mixed Bag," 1972; Schnidman, 1987, 31).

A case study of the local tax impact of recreational subdivisions in

Oregon illustrates how dramatically cost-benefit relationships can change. In the early stages of a subdivision in Klamath County, Oregon, more revenue was generated by the development than it cost to provide services to it. In addition, residents of the development purchased food, entertainment, and other items locally, and local landowners were able to sell land that would otherwise not have been sold. On the other hand, lots purchased by out-of-state people may never be improved and thus stand idle, limiting the potential increase in property values and diminishing the aesthetic appeal of the area. Further, absentee owners are sometimes delinquent in their tax payments, which lowers local government land income. Increased development may eventually cause problems in the provision of services, but forming districts for sewer, water, roads, and schools may be difficult because of absentee ownership. Coupled with police protection, these services can severely strain local government finances (Tillson et al., 1972, 9–10).

But the impact of recreational subdivisions on local communities, whether harmful or beneficial, can be managed. Subdivision design can be modified through land-use planning codes, through changes in the system of taxation, through public expenditure decisions, and other methods. With the proper controls, economic contributions may outweigh economic costs. However, local governments and citizens must evaluate the role of these developments in their communities and take steps to ensure that benefits do exceed costs; otherwise, taxpayers may be paying for the mistakes of ill-conceived recreational land developments for years to come.

In Florida, counties charge developers impact fees, but several counties are experiencing tremendous shortfalls in these fees and are being forced to consider other sources of revenue, including an ad valorem property tax, an income tax, and an increase in the sales tax (Manning, 1991). These problems are partly the result of growth that was allowed to take place without provision for adequate roads, water supply, waste disposal, and the like. According to a recent study of Florida's growth and economic well-being, citizens have been shielded from the truth concerning the cost of public facilities. For example, new wastewater treatment facilities were financed with EPA sewer grants, so the long-term fiscal ramifications of increased sewer demand by any particular development were often ignored. As grant funds for such facilities disappear, the local government must find other ways to pay for the ever-increasing demand created by uncontrolled growth (Siemon, 1988). Much of the growth in Lee County, Florida, for example is occurring in Cape Coral, a lot sales subdivision that emerged in the 1950s as one of the fastest growing communities in the state.

Since no service provisions were made by the original developer, the local government is now scrambling to provide the infrastructure necessary to sustain a Cape Coral population that now exceeds 80,000. There is a paradox in progress (Tuan, 1989).

4 Consumer Issues

Environmental and economic impacts from recreational subdivision have been substantial, but problems associated with the consumer have been the most widely publicized. Hundreds of thousands of buyers have been victims of high-pressure sales tactics, deceptive and fraudulent advertising schemes, and broken promises. Such problems have been most acute in unimproved recreational-retirement subdivisions, where thousands of lots remain unused, for sale, or abandoned and tax delinquent. The dilemma is how to deal with such an unproductive use of land.

Consumer victimization became a serious national issue as early as the mid-1960s. The major consumer abuses fell into three general categories: problems related to sales, problems related to obtaining title to the land, and problems related to the provision of services (Allan, Kuder, and Oakes, 1976, 60–61). To determine the severity of these abuses, Senate hearings, conducted by the Subcommittee on Frauds and Misrepresentations Affecting the Elderly, were held on interstate land sales. The hearings produced lengthy documentation of recreational real estate industry practices, and the evidence prompted federal legislators to pass the Interstate Land Sales Full Disclosure Act of 1968. In addition, the Office of Interstate Land Sales Registration (OILSR) was established as the federal agency that would enforce the act and thereby regulate the recreational land sales industry. Owners of lots in interstate land sales projects were given an opportunity to air their complaints in public hearings sponsored by OILSR, and surveys and studies were designed to obtain information about consumer dissatisfaction. By the mid to late 1970s, literally thousands of property owners' responses were obtained. Complaints ranged from problems associated with deceptive sales practices to problems with financing irregularities.

During and shortly after interstate land sales peaked in the early 1970s, several books and articles specifically addressed problems associated with consumer abuse. Some of the more significant works include Vince Conboy's *Florida's Billion Dollar Land Fraud* (1972), Morton Paulson's *The Great Land Hustle* (1972a), Dorothy Tymon's *America Is for Sale* (1973), and Anthony Wolff's *Unreal Estate* (1973). Newspaper and journal articles also appeared with titles such as "AMREP Accused of $200-Million Swindle of 45,000 Land Buyers" (1975); "Warning: Land Frauds are Flourishing" (1967); "Million Recovered by State for People Bilked Buying Land" (1969); and "The Land of Enchantment Is also the Land of Ripoffs" (Page, 1977), indicating the many problems caused by what some refer to as "fast-buck land subdividers." Although land developers vary tremendously in their commitment to producing legitimate new communities, few are without consumer-related problems. The following discussion assesses the general nature of consumer abuse, examines existing consumer protection regulations, and suggests ways to alleviate many of the problems.

The Problem

Dorothy Tymon, in her introductory chapter entitled "The Land Exploited," points out that the most outrageous swindles were perpetrated by some of the nation's most dignified blue-chip corporations, including General Development, McCulloch Oil, AMREP, Horizon Corporation, Forbes Magazine, and International Paper Company. These companies and many others convinced millions of Americans to buy a piece of America before it was all gone, or as Tymon notes:

> What the eager buyers do not seem to realize is that in most instances they are not buying land at all. Underneath the advertisement of mountain views, river views and desert views; of lake fronts, canal fronts and ocean fronts; of pink sandy beaches and cozy snug harbors is a cleverly merchandised scheme whereby the purchaser of most subdivisions is not buying or investing in land. He is not even lending money to the so-called "land developer," but often is simply giving his savings and earnings to a company such as International Telephone and Telegraph and paying the company interest on top of it (Tymon, 1973, 11–12).

Vince Conboy's book has a similar tone. He asks, "Why do frugal, hard-working people with above average intelligence buy 'wilderness acreage or useless lots' in Florida from high-pressure, phony strangers when they have excellent real estate investments in their own home states or foreign countries?" Conboy says that buyers have paid millions of dollars for so-called free dinners, gas, trading stamps, and discounted vacations and suggests that "get rich" land literature should be thrown in the nearest wastebasket. Despite attempts by government agencies to alert the public, Florida's "land-a-rama" still appeals to many people, who lose their common sense when exposed to the "sun and sand hucksters" (Conboy, 1972, 8–9).

Wolff's *Unreal Estate* underscores this insatiable appetite for land. "Tens, even hundreds of thousands of Americans are paying some $6 billion a year for homesites in far-off land subdivisions." Lots are sold as "potential vacation homesites" or for investment to unsophisticated buyers based on slippery or false promises. In many cases, the land being sold is inappropriate for either purpose. Such real estate is successfully promoted in part because of the customer's naive belief in easy money or easy living (Wolff, 1973, 2–4).

In a survey conducted by the *Christian Science Monitor* in the early 1970s, more than 40 percent of lot buyers responded that they were generally dissatisfied with their lot purchase (Cahn, 1973, 11). Similarly, more than 50 percent of the respondents to a survey in Siskiyou County, California, stated that their recently purchased lot in a recreational subdivision had not fully met their expectations. Complaints centered on the developer's failure to deliver promised improvements, deceptive sales practices, the poor investment potential of the property, the failure of the developer to provide adequate utility services, financing irregularities, property use restrictions, and excessive real property taxes (American Society of Planning Officials, 1976, 90).

Misrepresentation and outright fraud have been the source of the most serious problems. In the late 1960s, Gulf American Corporation (now General Acceptance Corporation) pleaded guilty before the Florida Land Sales Board to charges of fraudulent sales practices. Sales activities were suspended for thirty days, and the company was fined $5,000. It also had to refund money to anyone affected by the more than 1,200 cases of land switching in Collier County and another 600 cases in Lee County (Conboy, 1972, 80). Late in 1971, the state of California won a temporary restraining order against the land sales subsidiaries of Boise-Cascade on the grounds that the firm's salesmen had used fraudulent sales tactics at several subdivisions (Rodgers, 1972, 50). Boise agreed to a $58.5 million settlement, out of which a $24 million fund was established to cover refunds to buyers who wanted their money back. The remaining funds were used for administrative and maintenance costs and for providing promised improvements ("Boise Cascade," 1973). Such costs and other problems caused the demise of many large land sales corporations. Boise-Cascade ended its involvement in land sales during the mid-1970s, and many other major corporations are not nearly as active as they once were.

Other tactics, although not fraudulent, resulted in many dissatisfied customers. The most significant of these was the hard-sell approach in which "free" dinners and "free" gifts attracted prospective customers. Clients who accepted free dinner invitations expected a sales presentation, but they were not prepared for the intensity and skill of the sales pitch. High pressure tactics were the key to many land sales that probably would not have occurred otherwise.

Problems were also created by the naivete of customers about the real estate business in general and interstate land sales in particular. These buyers did not have the information necessary to make intelligent investment decisions, since it was difficult to obtain information about natural hazards, the cost of basic services, and other limitations. Many lot owners found they were unable to build on their property because of the exorbitant cost of providing even the most basic services (American Society of Planning Officials, 1976, 89–91).

While consumer abuses declined somewhat during the 1980s, problems continue. A recent example is General Development Corporation (GDC), one of the largest land development companies in Florida. GDC filed for bankruptcy in April 1990. Prior to the bankruptcy filing, the former president and chairman of the company pleaded guilty to defrauding nearly 10,000 customers by increasing the price (sometimes more than three times the actual value) of homes they were selling by using misleading (fraudulent) appraisals. Problems with fraud and inadequate cash flow created a financial situation that necessitated the bankruptcy proceedings. Even established land development companies can be ruined financially either through their own deception and fraud or by lack of financial support, bank credit lines, and loan guarantees (Fins, 1990, pp. 106–7; Henderson, 1991).

Consumer Protection
EXISTING REGULATIONS

Consumer abuses begin with the sales tactics used by many land developers. Most lots are sold by persuasive salesmen (or women) who offer a quick and easy way to purchase real estate and who convince customers to purchase a lot by making a small down payment, signing a long-term instalment contract, and making small monthly payments. Because the emphasis is on selling property as quickly as possible, developers have shown little concern for whether the customer receives a fair value for his "investment" or whether the land is ever used (Paulson, 1972b). After a time, many buyers realize they cannot afford the payments and default on their contract, thus losing not only the land but also their down payment and equity. But even a customer who makes all the payments and receives a deed to the property may discover that the lot has little or no resale value, that utilities are limited to a small "developed" core, and that the community has few residents.

Even though consumer protection was initiated by consumer interest groups during the late 1960s, abuse has continued to plague the industry. Some of the most objectionable tactics include urging purchasers to sign blank contracts to be completed by the company at a later date, offering free vacations that turn out to be sales promotion gimmicks, refusing to make refunds when lot purchasers change their minds, and failing to provide information about how much lots will appreciate over a given period of time. Problems are concentrated among the elderly, and classic examples include sales made sight unseen either by mail or by phone. During an inspection of the land in subsequent years, lot owners often discover that their lot is under water or unusable because of a lack of services. Many couples are stuck with a parcel they cannot use and with no definite way to get their money back.

Such land sales tactics prompted many states to pass consumer protection legislation. Federal legislation was passed for the first time in 1968 and became effective on April 28, 1969. The Office of Interstate Land Sales Registration (OILSR), with the appointment of a new administration in March 1972, began an aggressive consumer protection program against unscrupulous developers. The new OILSR administrator was upset that no one had regulated the industry for years and eagerly initiated a new offensive against abuses (Gardner, 1973). However, the present law is limited primarily to disclosure of information.

Other agencies providing indirect scrutiny of the land sales industry include the Federal Trade Commission and U.S. Postal Service. The Postal Service becomes actively involved in land sales only after a consumer has filed a complaint of mail fraud with the postal inspector. The Federal Trade Commission, which has broad powers to protect the public from unfair business practices, has investigated the land sales industry in depth and is particularly concerned with the state-

READ THIS PROPERTY REPORT BEFORE SIGNING ANYTHING

This Report is prepared and issued by the Developer of this subdivision. It is NOT prepared or issued by the Federal Government.

Federal law requires that you receive this Report prior to your signing a contract or agreement to buy or lease a lot in this subdivision. However, NO FEDERAL AGENCY HAS JUDGED THE MERITS OR VALUE, IF ANY, OF THIS PROPERTY.

If you received this Report prior to signing a contract or agreement, you may cancel your contract or agreement by giving notice to the seller any time before midnight of the seventh day following the signing of the contract or agreement.

If you did not receive this Report before you signed a contract or agreement, you may cancel the contract or agreement any time within two years from the date of signing.

NAME OF SUBDIVISION   FAIRFIELD BAY

NAME OF DEVELOPER   FAIRFIELD COMMUNITIES, INC.

DATE OF THIS REPORT   NOVEMBER 15, 1990

Figure 4.1   Cover page of a property report prepared by a developer
Source: Fairfield Communities (1990)

ments or claims made in land development advertisement. While only an indirect protection, these agencies have succeeded in curbing some of the most abusive companies (Herbert, 1993). Land-use legislation at the state level, while not specifically directed at land sales, does help control it.

The Interstate Land Sales Full Disclosure Act requires land sellers to disclose certain information to buyers through a property report presented to the buyer by the developer (figure 4.1). This report contains information in a question and answer form and includes the firm's

**DEPARTMENT OF HOUSING
AND URBAN DEVELOPMENT**

Land Registration, Purchaser's
Revocation Rights, Sales Practices and
Standards, and Formal Procedures and
Rules of Practice

Guidelines for Exemptions Available
Under the Interstate Land Sales Full
Disclosure Act

OFFICE OF
INTERSTATE
LAND SALES
REGISTRATION

**Including Amendments Through April 1, 1990
and Subsequent Technical Corrections**

Figure 4.2 Cover page of the document outlining a developer's registration requirements with the Office of Interstate Land Sales Registration.
Source: U.S. Dept. of Housing and Urban Development (1990)

financial condition, estimated date of completion of improvements to be installed by the developer, and much more. The disclosure act applies to persons who sell property in interstate commerce developments of 100 or more unimproved lots of twenty acres or less in size (U.S. Department of Housing and Urban Development, 1984a). Developers must also file a statement with OILSR detailing the information summarized in the property report (figure 4.2).

The property report must include accurate information about encumbrances, mortgages, and liens on the property; roads, utilities, and other local services; topography and climate; water supply; flooding and soil erosion; hazards and nuisances; taxes and such other facts and figures that will be useful in evaluating the merits of a development. Since the law requires disclosure, rather than regulation, there are many shortcomings. For instance, developers can sell any type of lot they wish so long as they disclose specific facts in the statement of record to HUD and in the property report to buyers. Lots can be located in places so isolated that services will never be provided, or they might be underwater. Such practices could be significantly reduced or even eliminated if the OILSR law were strengthened beyond the current disclosure mandate. If OILSR is to become more regulatory, Congress must pass a law that provides for more vigorous management of the land sales industry. Since such legislation is unlikely—primarily because of intense lobbying from the real estate industry—OILSR will be forced to work under the present relatively weak law.

Additional indirect protection is provided by the Truth in Lending Act, which provides three days for a buyer to cancel a contract if he or she uses the land as collateral for a loan. This three-day grace period applies only if the buyer intends to use the land as a principal residence. The clever developer circumvents this requirement by including in the sales agreement the statement that the purchaser does not intend to use the property at the present time as a principal residence.

As it stands now, OILSR has the authority to suspend a company's right to engage in interstate land sales and can ask the Justice Department to bring criminal charges against violators. Of the more than 3,400 active subdivision filings with OILSR for fiscal year 1991, approximately 170 were issued suspension orders. Developers have twenty days to respond to the order. Most developers request a hearing, which provides additional time for the developer to amend abusive behavior. Since most developers are anxious to avoid suspension, they correct their mistakes; only about ten subdivisions are actually suspended each year. The OILSR Full Disclosure Act provides for fines of up to $5,000 and jail sentences of up to five years. Accordingly, each prospective buyer must be given a detailed, written property report, but if the seller fails to furnish such a report, the buyer can cancel the deal at any time and have his or her money refunded. If a seller fails to comply with any provision of the act, or has committed fraud, the buyer may sue for damages up to the purchase price of the lot plus any improvements and reasonable court costs (Henderson, 1991).

Along with the boom in land sales during the early 1970s came numerous consumer complaints about companies engaged in land sales ("Land Sales Boom," 1972). OILSR received 5,000 complaints covering a wide range of abuses in only a two-year period during the early 1970s; despite scant public knowledge of the newly formed agency, the flow of complaints swelled to 50 per week in 1972. Some twelve years later, well after the peak in land sales, OILSR received 2,952 complaints from October 1, 1984, through September 30, 1985 (Henderson, 1986). Consumer complaints declined during the 1980s, and by 1990 the annual total was 1,547 (Henderson, 1991). OILSR officials indicate that the types of abuses that were so problematic during the 1960s and 1970s are continuing today. The decline in abuses is more the result of a reduction in land sales than in improvements in developer behavior. The $25 million in refunds in 1990 and $19 million in 1991 to dissatisfied lot owners is an indication that many abuses are continuing (ibid.). As is apparent from these statistics, it takes more than a good law to solve the problem; it requires strong enforcement.

During its first few years, OILSR was buried under layers of officialdom and hampered by a small staff and an authority based on disclosure rather than regulations. Problems also result when enterprising sales staffs use the registration requirement for their own ends, telling consumers that the government has approved their subdivision, which is never the case. And although it is good advice never to buy land without seeing it, just looking at a chunk of undeveloped desert, swamp, or woodland does not tell buyers whether the site has been used as a toxic landfill, or whether there are legal encumbrances on the title, or whether there are easements or rights of way; it doesn't tell them the resale value of the property. Second mortgages or tax liens, for example, may take precedence over the lot owner's claim to the land if the developer runs into financial problems. In short, there are many compelling reasons why consumers should pass up the "free" dinner and vacation offers from land development companies. A more rational approach to buying recreational or retirement property is to visit the area, talk with a number of real estate brokers, and sign nothing until one is fully convinced that the property will be a sound investment. Caveat emptor, or let the buyer beware, originated in early Roman marketplaces to warn citizens of fraudulent sales. This is good advice, particularly for those interested in buying property on the interstate land sales market. While regulations have been strengthened, the consumer is responsible for determining the value of a lot and the legitimacy of a land development operation. Moreover, before purchasing a lot offered by a promotional land sales subdivision, prospective buyers should know their rights, know the facts about the development and the lot they plan to buy, and understand the tactics of high-pressure sales campaigns.

Any land sales company offering 100 or more unimproved lots for sale or lease by mail or other means of interstate commerce must register with the Department of Housing and Urban Development. Failure to comply with the law is punishable by up to five years in prison, a $10,000 fine, or both. Developers must provide OILSR with a copy of the corporate charter and a financial statement; the title policy and copies of deeds and mortgages; information on local ordinances, health regulations, schools, hospitals, and utilities; plans for roads, streets, and recreational facilities; and such supporting documents as maps, plats, and letters from utility companies. Many states have also enacted consumer protection laws supplementing federal legislation (L. Platt, 1987, 181–88). OILSR requires a rather comprehensive report from the developer, but the information is usually compiled without the scrutiny of a disinterested party or agency. The buyer should also remember that, although the federal law requires the issuance of a property report prior to the sale, the federal government in no way has judged the merits or value of the property.

Most lots are purchased through a sales contract. For those subdivisions under OILSR jurisdiction, buyers are provided specific rights depending on the date the contract is signed. Contracts signed before June 21, 1980, should indicate that the buyer has a "cooling-off" period of three business days, during which the buyer may cancel the contract, simply by notifying the seller, and receive a full refund. Contracts signed after June 21, 1980, provide for a seven-day cooling-off period following the day the contract is signed, and the contract must state that the seller will give the buyer a warranty deed within 180 days after the contract is signed. If the contract does not contain the clear property description necessary for filing with the proper authority, the customer may cancel his or her agreement within a two-year period. The contract should also clearly state the right of the buyer to a notice of any default and indicate what the limitation is on the amount of money the seller may keep as liquidated damages (D. Martin, 1980).

In addition, the prospective buyer should be aware that there are several exemptions from the law and that some promotional land sales operations are not covered by the law and do not issue property reports. The following situations allow exemption from the law: tracts with fewer than 100 lots; lots in a subdivision where every lot is twenty acres or more; lots upon which a residential, commercial, or industrial building has been erected or where a sales contract obligates the seller to build one within two years; certain lots sold only to residents of the state or metropolitan area in which the subdivision is located; low-volume sales operations, in which no more than twelve lots a year are sold; lots that meet certain local codes and standards and that are zoned for single-family residences by enforceable codes and restrictions; and subdivisions comprising multiple sites of fewer than 100 lots each, even though the lots are offered under a common promotional plan (U.S. Dept. of Housing and Urban Development, 1984a).

UNSCRUPULOUS PRACTICES

Unsophisticated buyers may still get caught by a high-pressure sales pitch and sign a sales contract before they realize they are making a commitment. The subdivider and lot salesperson may conceal or misrepresent facts about current and resale value, and buyers may be encouraged to believe that their lots represent an investment that will increase in value as regional development occurs. Between one-third and one-half of the buyers of recreational lots are primarily seeking speculative investments (American Society of Planning Officials, 1976, 92). The most significant cause of the premature subdivision of land is buyers who speculate for financial gain (Shultz and Gray, 1986, 2). People investing in recreational lots are wagering their purchase price against the odds of further improvements being made to the property, without which appreciation is not likely to occur. The sales agent may, for example, tell buyers that the developer will resell their lots if the need arises. But as much as 40 percent of the initial sales price was used for promotion and commissions for sales agents, so it is unlikely that someone else will give a lot owner more than the original price, or even the same price. Furthermore, the developer most likely has hundreds or even thousands of unsold lots in the same subdivision (U.S. Dept. of Housing and Urban Development, 1989a). In several major recreational subdivisions in southern Arizona, resale prices for lots averaged from a low of 61 percent to a high of 88 percent of their original sales price (Stephenson, 1987). And a random sampling of resale records of a recreational subdivision near Washington, D.C., shows that most lots were resold for less than half the original purchase price (Paulson, 1974).

Property owners may have difficulty finding a buyer at any price. If they live hundreds of miles from their lot, they have little choice but to attempt to sell their lot through a local realtor. Unfortunately for the lot owner, a local market either may not exist or has reached the saturation point (U.S. Dept. of Housing and Urban Development, 1989b). Some developers refuse to honor refund promises made during the promotion and sale of the lot. Refund requests are often countered with arguments about the terms of the refund agreement, and the developer may even accuse its own agent of making a money-back guarantee without the consent or knowledge of the developer.

Misrepresentation of the facts about the subdivision is a particular problem. Incomplete or false information is often given about the legal title, claims against the subdivision, dangers such as cliffs and swamps, poor drainage, restrictions on use, or lack of necessary facilities and utilities. The property report, if required, does provide some protection, and if the company advertises sales on credit terms, the Truth in Lending Act requires that the sales contract stipulate all terms of financing.

Another problem occurs when buyers rely on the subdivider's contractual agreement or oral promise to develop the subdivision, and then the promised golf course, tennis court, or swimming pool never materializes. Another common problem is the developer's failure to deliver deeds and title insurance policies. Since most sales are made by a contract that a deed will be delivered when all payments have been made, the potential for abuse is quite high, and a dishonest developer may not provide the deed even after the last payment has been made. In addition, abusive treatment of customers and high-pressure sales tactics are common ploys. Clients are often rushed into buying a lot; for more resistant buyers, abusive language may embarrass them into a decision to buy. In some cases, hesitant buyers have been isolated in remote sections of a subdivision, with transportation being controlled by the sales agent.

Prospective clients are often lured to subdivisions by offers of "free gifts." The promised gifts may not be provided, or special conditions may be attached to them. At times, customers receive their gifts only after they purchase property. "Free vacations" are another means of attracting prospective buyers to the subdivision for an intense, high-pressure sales pitch. In some instances, lots may be advertised at an extremely low price, but when prospective buyers arrive, they are told that all the low-priced lots have been sold. They are then pressured to buy a more expensive one. Even if a low-priced lot is available, it may be poorly located, too small to build on, or under a rattlesnake-infested cliff or on an unstable slope. Another technique is to lure buyers to the property with a $500 to $1,000 gift certificate. But the money can only be applied to the price of a lot—and of course, the price of the lot is inflated to cover the cost of the certificate.

Finally, the developer may withhold the property report until the purchaser has signed a sales contract, or the report may be included in a mass of promotional materials and legal documents. Unaware that the report is in their possession, buyers fail to read and understand it before signing a sales contract (U.S. Dept. of Housing and Urban Development, 1989a).

SUGGESTED IMPROVEMENTS

Developers and buyers can take several steps to prevent consumer abuses. Developers should adhere to all regulatory guidelines (particularly those designed to eliminate false advertisement), sell only unencumbered land, sell only lots that have been properly recorded at the courthouse, insist on an on-site visit by the customer, abandon all off-site sales operations, and use caution before allowing clients to sign instalment contracts. In addition, they should deposit funds received from instalment contract payments into an escrow account until the titles are deeded to the buyers, issue a full refund if services are not provided as promised, require substantial down payments as part of the requirement for contract sale approval, legally transfer unencumbered titles to sold lots, and set aside funds to cover the cost of basic services. It is the customer's responsibility to become informed about how the land sales industry works, including the various investment opportunities that developers will be promoting (ranging from unimproved lots to time-sharing) and the various approaches they may use to sell these options. Such an awareness can prevent the prospective buyer from being caught off guard and overwhelmed by a fast-talking salesperson. Moreover, customers should hire legal counsel for advice before considering the purchase of land.

Customers should insist on nothing less than an on-site visit. Buying lots sight unseen causes more problems than any other buyer behavior. Without an on-site visit, the buyer is totally uninformed about the setting of the property, the availability of services, and many other factors discernible only by looking at the development. However, even though on-site inspection may reduce abuses, it does not eliminate them. An on-site visit can give unscrupulous sales people another opportunity to take advantage of unsuspecting customers by showing them the wrong lot. Or they drive customers around the development in vehicles equipped with two-way radios broadcasting false sales, a technique designed to make the customers think that lots are going fast. They are usually told that lots are being sold so rapidly that it is essential to make a commitment on a lot immediately, before all the choice parcels are taken.

The developer should be required to run credit checks on prospective buyers before instalment contracts are signed. A credit check protects customers from overcommitment and from the loss of their "investments" by default. But few companies bother with credit checks. In fact, many developers do not plan to improve the property so have little reason to find out if buyers can make the payments. If they default, the developers keep all the money they have been paid so far and then can resell the lot. Fortunately, those companies with plans to create viable new communities have more to lose from defaults and more to gain by making credit checks. Since a credit check is a routine procedure among banks and other agents granting credit, the land sales industry should be no exception. An escrow account provides additional consumer protection in the event the developer fails to complete the project. Many factors, including economic recessions, changes in environmental requirements, and lawsuits, can slow down or halt development. An escrow account or surety bond provides at least partial protection if developers fail financially.

Providing basic services to lots is a major problem with some companies. A provision allowing a full refund to the buyer if services are not provided will give the developer an incentive to extend services as needed. And the requirement of a down payment of, say, 20–30 percent should discourage impulsive buying, which frequently ends in default and financial loss for the lot owner.

Buying real estate is supposed to be accompanied by the transfer of a deed that gives the purchaser title to the land. Since land is often bought through a mortgage arrangement, developers may not own or have clear title to the land they are selling. Because of variations in degree of ownership and because certain rights to the land may be owned by someone else, buying real estate is much more risky than buying goods and services. The potential for abuse is great, and the advice of an attorney is necessary before final decisions are made. Some subdividers, for example, sell the same lot to several different customers. Or they sell real estate they do not yet own. In situations where the development company is paying off a mortgage on the land, it may not be able to guarantee that a clear title can be issued to individual lot owners. All too often the company defaults on its loan, leaving lot buyers without a way to obtain titles to their lots. Lots should be offered for sale only after they have been legally recorded (platted) at the appropriate county office and only from land to which the subdivider has title, either unencumbered by a mortgage or other financial obligation or encumbered only by a mortgage that includes a release clause guaranteeing that lot purchasers will receive full title upon payment of all instalments. When lot buyers sign a purchase contract, they should receive deeds—or the titles should be placed in trust or escrow under terms that protect the buyers' property interests. Since the financial position of many land sales companies is tenuous, such precautions will protect the lot owner.

If the lot is to be of use to the buyer, basic services are essential.

Obviously, central water and sewer, roads, drainage, and electricity are necessary if the lot owner plans to build a home—so there should be a provision for, or guarantee of, potable water, a waste disposal system, a drainage system sufficient to prevent flooding from a 100-year-frequency storm, a solid-waste collection system, paved streets and roads built to county standards, and electricity and telephone service at standard cost. Since many projects are advertised as new communities and sell property at highly inflated suburban prices, it is only logical that basic services be provided as needed. Again, an escrow account or surety bond can guarantee that adequate funds are available for provision of these services (Allan, Kuder, and Oakes, 1976, 60–93).

PART TWO

The Development
of "New Communities"

In the 1950s, land developers took advantage of the widespread interest in owning real estate in so-called new towns, or new communities, an interest that peaked during the 1970s as developers capitalized on people's desires to make speculative investments. Some large recreational subdivisions were repackaged as new towns to increase sales, qualify for financial aid, and win local zoning approval. All too often, however, these new towns ended up as bland, primarily middle-class, predominantly Caucasian communities with single-family detached homes and rows of townhouses, condominiums, and other multifamily units. Improvements included curved streets, more open space, human-made amenities, convenient shopping, and an industrial park to pay part of the tax burden, but despite these improvements, many problems remained unresolved, including wasteful and environmentally unsound land-use practices, lot sales based on high-pressure sales tactics, inefficient and unequal distribution of basic services, scattered development, economic and racial segregation, inadequate supplies of reasonably priced housing, and unimaginative landscape and housing design. The worst projects are nothing more than land exploitation schemes, while the best have resolved few of the problems of urban and suburban living.

Why do these attempts to create new communities have so many shortcomings? The answer is that, unlike the European new town model or the successful American greenbelt communities of the New Deal era, these projects were not social, economic, architectural, and environmental experiments but instead were speculative ventures for profit. The new community concept was used to enhance lot sales by promoting the idea that a special place was being created that would provide all the modern conveniences and amenities of city life without its congestion, crime, and pollution. Land development schemes based on speculation and a desire to quickly generate a positive cash flow cannot be expected to produce an innovative new community. Yet thousands of people have bought lots and built homes in these developments, thinking they have found their dream community—only to find as many or more problems as they left behind.

While all land developments have shortcomings, some are much worse than others. Projects that began in the 1950s and 1960s contrast sharply with the subdivisions of the 1970s and 1980s. Although all six recreational-retirement communities discussed in this part have created environmental and consumer problems, none is as severe as those developed in wetlands and deserts when there were few growth guidelines. Built before the value of wetlands was fully understood and before the era of environmental regulation, Cape Coral, Florida, caused major environmental devastation. This city is also marred by a monotonous grid pattern of streets and canals, scattered development outside the developed core, inadequate open space within the core, an insufficient water supply to meet a rising demand, and many other problems attributable to a poor environmental and ecological planning design. Similar unsound practices have occurred across the United States, from Florida to Colorado to California. The problems at Lake Havasu City, Arizona, illustrate the difficulties that arise when desert environments are the sites for new communities.

Fortunately, the era of such poorly designed and ill-conceived subdivisions has now largely passed, and improvements in land-use practices began to emerge during the early 1970s largely in response to innovative regulations adopted by many local governments. Communities such as Fairfield Glade, Tennessee, and Port LaBelle, Florida, with their much improved layout and design, are vast improvements over giants such as Cape Coral. Although many projects have been caught up in lengthy regulatory processes in some states, the end result is a subdivision design that is sensitive to fragile environments. A negative result of the permitting process, of course, is the increase in real estate prices attributable to long delays in development.

It is clear from the following examination of six communities, with dates of origin extending over nearly two decades, that problems are extensive and that we need growth management mechanisms specifically designed to deal with these problems.

5 Fairfield Glade

The Evolution of a Successful Operation in Tennessee

The recreational land development industry experienced many changes in recent years, in response to a slower economy, a more sophisticated clientele, and more stringent regulatory controls (Rodin, 1991). All too often recreational subdivisions were built in isolated locations that lacked either human-made or natural amenities, and their bare lots sold at highly inflated prices through questionable sales tactics (Hansen and Dickinson, 1975, 124–25). During the 1970s there was considerable public outcry against these developers because of both environmental disruption and consumer abuse, and the declining sales resulted in financial ruin for many operations. The companies that did succeed did so through adequate financial backing and flexible and innovative developmental plans that adjusted to the changing market.

A large portion of the thousands of recreational homesites sold each year are in resorts that offer such amenities as golf courses, tennis courts, water sports, shopping malls, restaurants, and a variety of housing, such as villas, townhouses, single-family detached homes, condominiums, and time-share units. Indeed, fewer and fewer customers are content to buy a lot in a subdivision with little more than a network of dirt roads and a developer's promise to provide amenities in the future.

Fairfield Communities, Inc., is one of several recreational-retirement land development corporations that has changed with the times; it has created several "successful" projects, which are rapidly emerging as high-amenity resort communities. One of the most successful projects is Fairfield Glade, an 11,700-acre development on the Cumberland Plateau in Cumberland County, Tennessee. A detailed examination of this project illustrates how a successful operation unfolds and how it adjusts to take advantage of a changing market.

Figure 5.1 Aerial view of Fairfield Glade prior to development. Scale
1 : 10,000 ft.

Source: U.S. Dept. of Agriculture (1964)

The almost instant success of this recreational-retirement community can be attributed not as much to the natural beauty of the property as to the promotional and organizational system of this well-organized corporation. Besides having a sound financial base, this project conducted its promotional effort on a large scale, provided a variety of housing, and built numerous recreational facilities, following the land development plan that it first used in 1966 at a development in north-central Arkansas. The success of its promotional operation can be attributed in part to the organization and experience the company acquired from its earlier operations.

Fairfield Glade is a good example of a successful recreational subdivision that has evolved into a thriving high-amenity resort in a relatively short period of time. Its tract of land is located along Peavine Road in eastern Cumberland County. Before it was purchased for development in 1969, only a small portion of the original 9,600-acre tract had been cleared, and timber covered at least 80 percent of the area. Cleared areas were used primarily as pasture, with little or no land under cultivation. Roads and houses were few (figure 5.1). But

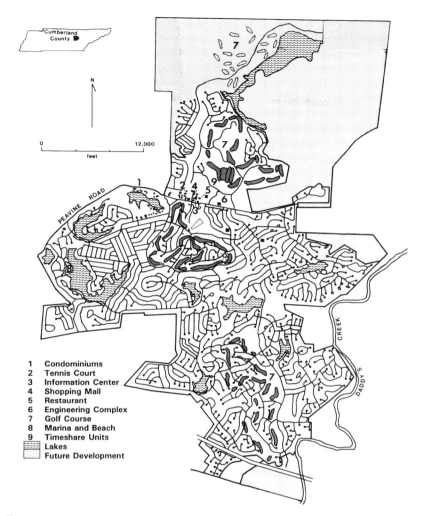

Figure 5.2 Map of Fairfield Glade

Source: Adapted from Stroud (1978), revised in 1993 using information from Fairfield Communities corporate officials

the tranquil setting was soon replaced by a large land development. In 1970 the developers built an extensive network of roads, a sales office, a golf course, a restaurant, tennis courts, and such other infrastructure necessary to give prospective buyers the impression that a high-amenity resort was in progress. In only three years, more than half of the original 9,600 acres was covered by a network of roads (figure 5.2), a sales office, lakes (figure 5.3), and houses.

Figure 5.3 Artificial lake, Fairfield Glade
Source: Photograph by author

By 1973, 244 condominiums and 181 single-family homes had been built, and the permanent population was approximately 500. Over 100 miles of roads extended across 5,000 acres of the development, but the built-up areas were concentrated near the town center (figure 5.4) and covered only about 1,000 acres. By 1980, the project had expanded to 11,700 acres and had 368 single-family dwellings, 256 condominiums (figure 5.5), 53 townhouses, 20 villas, and a 100-unit motel. Its permanent population had increased to 1,100, with a seasonal population reaching 60,000. Visits by prospective buyers increased dramatically, from 5,000 families in 1970 to more than 20,000 families in 1981 and 1982 (Swafford, 1984). By March 1993, the development's permanent population was approximately 3,000, and more than 15,000 lots had been sold. The subdivision had 1,529 single-family detached homes, 171 mobile homes, 256 condominiums, 147 townhouses, 66 villas, 345 time-share units (figure 5.6), the motel, and a shopping mall (figure 5.7). The road network exceeded 182 miles (figure 5.8). There is a concentration of infrastructure along Peavine Road and a large amount of land devoted to human-made amenities, particularly lakes and golf courses (figure 5.9).

Financing

Adequate financing is one of the most significant components of a successful recreational land development operation. Developers of Fairfield Glade, with financial backing from Fairfield Communities, Inc., constructed many permanent facilities and promoted their property extensively. These investments produced a negative cash flow during the first few years of operation. While these expenses are eventually offset by a substantial profit, the developer must have the financial resources to continue deficit spending for three or four years. The inability of many less solvent developments to withstand such delays in profit generation has led to their demise (Stroud, 1974, 84).

EXPENDITURES

An analysis of expenditures during the initial stage of development at Fairfield Glade provides an indication of the sequencing of spending, the cost of each development phase, and the importance of adequate financial backing during the early stages of development.

Land for Fairfield Glade was purchased for less than $200 per acre, with the original 9,600 acres being purchased for $150 per acre. Based on this price per acre, the developers invested approximately $1.8 million to acquire over 11,600 acres of land. Ironically, this cost becomes relatively minor when compared with the capital that was required to promote and develop the property (Stroud, 1974, 88).*

Development costs are the expenditures for improvements made after the purchase of land. These expenditures vary tremendously each year depending on the development phase. In 1969, development costs were slightly more than $58,000, but in both 1971 and 1972 they were around $1 million (table 5.1). The major expense was providing roads to the lot sites and exceeded all other development costs by a four to one margin. Additional money was required to pay the management staff, secretaries, engineers, construction and maintenance workers, maids, and security guards. Although the average annual wages per employee was low since many of them work only three or four months, during the summer, the total cost was still approximately $600,000 per year (ibid., 89–90).

A large portion of maintenance costs are covered by dues paid

---

* Much of the information needed to analyze the financial structure of a land development corporation is confidential and difficult to obtain. Information about total expenditures for structural improvements and annual development expenses was released after many conversations with officials at corporate headquarters. An analysis of these costs provides insight into the capital outlay needed to operate such a project and indicates the capital gains that can be realized.

Figure 5.4 Sales office and other administrative buildings, Fairfield Glade
Source: Photograph by author

Figure 5.5 Condominiums at Fairfield Glade
Source: Photograph by author

Figure 5.6 A time-share housing unit, Fairfield Glade
Source: Photograph by author

Figure 5.7 Shopping mall, Fairfield Glade
Source: Photograph by author

by property owners as members of the property owners' association. Membership is required of each lot owner. By 1973, more than 6,500 lots were sold, but after cancellations the number of property owners who were active dues-paying members of the association was 5,500. Revenues exceeded $600,000 annually, enough capital to cover maintenance expenses, security guards, and other service employees (ibid., 90).

Although a large capital investment is required to instal the necessary infrastructure, an even larger investment is made to promote the property. Developers estimate that it costs approximately $130 in promotional expenses to attract a family to the project site. During the mid-1970s, approximately 15,000 families visited the development, at a cost of $1.9 million per year. An additional expenditure of $1.5 million was used to house the 15,000 guests who visited the subdivision on the three nights and four days of their "free" vacation. In total, promotional efforts alone required an annual expenditure of $3.4 million (table 5.2). Promotional expenses are expected to escalate even more as response rates decline and the cost of providing free lodging increases (ibid., 90–91).

From 1969 through early 1974, over $1.2 million was spent on infrastructural facilities, $2.5 million on road construction, and $1.5 million on wages. The golf course was the most expensive recreational

Figure 5.8 Paved road in an undeveloped portion of Fairfield Glade
Source: Photograph by author

facility. But as costly as all these facilities are, they are relatively minor in comparison to the nearly $11 million spent on promotion (ibid., 91). As one would expect, development expenditures increased sharply after the first year, with the largest occurring in 1971, when many facilities were provided. Promotional costs and employment expenditures also increased as the development became better established and started to expand.

INCOME

Fortunately for the developer, increases in expenses were paralleled by increases in income generated by lot sales. Most lots were purchased through an instalment plan financed by the land development company, with buyers usually making a small down payment and agreeing to pay the balance in monthly instalments. Cash flows during the first few years of operation were relatively small, but as the number of lot owners increased, income increased as well. In 1970 the project received only $258,800 in cash from its $910,000 worth of lot sales, but by 1973, cash income jumped to more than $7 million, from its $16.2 million in lot sales (table 5.3). A comparison of annual expenditures and income received (table 5.1, 5.2, and 5.3) shows that income from lot sales was insufficient to cover costs during the first three years. But

Figure 5.9   A golf green and cart path, Fairfield Glade
Source: Photograph by author

during 1973, with basic investment in facilities past, the rapid rise in income from monthly payments provided a positive cash flow. As is shown in table 5.3, cash received from lot sales exceeded $7.1 million* in 1973 alone. Additional income was derived from home construction. In 1974, revenue from the sale of homes and lots and from property owner association dues totaled approximately $10 million. Expenses for promotion, employment, maintenance, and continued subdivision development, on the other hand, did not exceed $5 million, leaving approximately $5 million in revenue to cover earlier debts and to provide a profit for the corporation (ibid., 92).

As the preceding comparisons show, there is a need for adequate financial resources, particularly during the early years of development. Although lot owners usually do not buy their lots outright, their down payments and interest payments eventually provide a substantial income for the developer. Yet developers who rely on these sales to finance their projects are likely to go bankrupt long before the income is large enough to meet expenses (ibid., 93–94).

---

*This figure is obtained by adding income from cash deposits, cash purchases, monthly payments, and dues.

Table 5.1 Development Expenditures, Fairfield Glade, 1969–1973 (dollars)

	1969	1970	1971	1972	1973	Total
Acquisition of property	1,440,000			285,000		1,725,000
Lot development						
Roads	10,458	253,301	410,850	399,245	307,000	1,380,854
Water	4,760	42,225	140,317	23,596	49,000	259,898
Sewage				290,000	281,000	571,000
Other	43,225	80,226	66,934	96,623		287,008
Infrastructure		355,000	70,000	238,300	83,000	746,300
Sales office		210,000				210,000
Country club				205,000		205,000
Restaurant		108,000				108,000
Civic center					83,000	83,000
Grocery		37,000				37,000
Warehouse			29,000			29,000
Pro-shop			41,000			41,000
Engineering offices				27,000		27,000
Stables				6,300		6,300
Created amenities						
Golf course			175,000	168,000		343,000
Lakes			95,000			95,000
Miniature golf course			9,600			9,600
Golf driving range			17,000			17,000
Tennis courts				17,000		17,000
Swimming pool				68,000		68,000
Total	1,498,443	730,752	984,701	1,585,764	720,000	5,519,660

Source: Stroud (1974).

Table 5.2 Promotional and Employee Costs, Fairfield Glade, 1970–1973 (dollars)

Year	Family Visits	Contact Costs[a]	Housing Costs[b]	Total Promotional Cost	Employee Cost
1970	5,000	625,000	500,000	1,125,000	90,000
1971	12,500	1,562,500	1,250,000	2,812,500	300,000
1972	15,000	1,875,000	1,500,000	3,375,000	500,000
1973	15,000	1,875,000	1,500,000	3,375,000	600,000
1970–73				10,687,500	1,490,000

Source: Stroud (1974).

[a] $125 per family.
[b] $100 per family.

Table 5.3 Income from Lot and Home Sales, Fairfield Glade, 1970–1973 (dollars)

	1970	1971	1972	1973
Cash income				
Deposits	91,000	369,000	806,000	1,625,000
Cash purchases	50,000	180,000	400,000	810,000
Monthly payments	85,800	432,120	1,322,220	3,692,940
Property owner's association dues	32,000	154,375	436,230	1,029,355
Lot sales[a]	910,000	3,510,000	8,060,000	16,250,000
Home sales		380,000	1,310,000	1,450,000

Source: Stroud (1974).

[a] The average price of a lot rose from $3,500 in 1970 to $5,000 in 1973. Lot sales increased from 260 in 1970 to 3,250 in 1973.

Marketing Techniques

LOT SALES

In the early stages, developers depended upon the sale of a large number of lots. Since the property is in a rural area without a large population or a demand for vacation homes, promotional efforts had to encompass nearby metropolitan areas (Chattanooga, Knoxville, and Nashville, among them) as well as other states. Since initial contacts had to convince prospective customers to visit the development, promotional advertisements linked the development with prospective customers in target areas.

Direct mail advertisement was the primary means of reaching customers. These advertisements offered a free vacation and emphasized the scenic and natural beauty of the Cumberland Plateau and the high quality of the resort. A mailing list of potential buyers can be purchased from a listing firm or established by mailing experts employed by the company. A list can cost as much as $50,000 from a listing firm. Postage alone can be high; even at a bulk mailing rate, the postage cost for 3 million mailings would exceed $390,000. The resort has drastically cut back on direct mail, in response to its reorganization following its Chapter 11 bankruptcy in 1991.

Response rates were low even when the promotional mail was received and read. Each year approximately 4 million pieces of mail, plus other advertisement, brought only 15,000 families to the development site during the early 1970s. Fewer than 3,800 families purchased property. Although this response rate is low, it is higher than the response rates for two other land developments on the Cumberland Plateau (table 5.4). Fairfield Glade (Project A) produced only 1.5 property owners from 1,000 mailings. While this response is quite low, it is substantially higher than the response rates at Projects B and C (smaller developments with less money to spend on promotion and infrastructure).

In addition to promotional mailings, salespeople operated out of offices in Knoxville, Nashville, and Birmingham, making telephone calls to middle-income families offering them free vacations. If a family was interested, a salesperson visited the family to explain the terms of the vacation and to collect a $25 confirmation fee, which was refunded when the family arrived at the development site. These offices were more successful in attracting clients to the development than the direct mail system was. In 1972, for instance, 30,000 telephone calls were made in Knoxville, resulting in 3,000 visits to the development site, a response rate of 10 percent. This type of promotion is more expensive than direct mail, but its targeted visitors were more likely to buy a lot (Thompson, 1973; Stroud, 1974, 45–46).

Several factors determined what areas received promotional literature, some of the most significant of which were high family incomes, few local prohibitions on direct mail advertisement, and large populations, especially within a day's drive of the development site. States in the Midwest and states on the periphery of Tennessee were targeted. Families in Ohio and Indiana received mailings in 1970; by 1973, fifteen states—including Michigan, North Carolina, South Carolina, Georgia, Pennsylvania, Virginia, and West Virginia—received the bulk of the 6 million pieces of promotional literature mailed each year (McIntosh, 1973). The success of promotional advertisement can be as-

Table 5.4 Response from Direct Mail Promotional Program, Three Developments on the Cumberland Plateau

Project	Number of Direct Mailings	Percentage of No Responses	Number of Families Accepting the Free Offer	Percentage Failing to Follow Through	Number of Families that Visited the Project	No Sales		Sale of at Least One Lot	
						Families	Percentage	Families	Percentage
A	1,000	99.25	7.5	30	5.2	3.6	70	1.5	30
B	1,000	99.50	5.0	50	2.5	2.1	83	0.4	17
C	1,000	99.50	5.0	50	2.5	2.2	91	0.3	9

Source: Stroud (1974).

Figure 5.10   Home states of lot owners in Fairfield Glade, 1973
Source: Stroud (1974)

sessed by analyzing the number of lot owners from the various states that receive promotional mail (figure 5.10).

TIME-SHARING

Lot sales were emphasized during the first decade of operation, but in 1980, a time-share program was initiated. This was done to partially offset the decline in lot sales in the late 1970s and to introduce an innovative concept in vacation housing. In a relatively short period of time, revenue from time-share sales exceeded income from lot sales (table 5.5). Time-share revenue continued to increase through 1988, when it exceeded income from lot sales by over $10 million. The popularity of time-sharing during the 1980s is reflected in the following statistic: more than 750,000 time-shares had been sold nationwide by hundreds of resorts and land sales companies by 1988 (Crawford, 1983; Englander, 1988). This increase was not to continue, however—in large part because of the bankruptcy and subsequent reor-

Table 5.5 Lot and Time-Share Unit Sales, Fairfield Glade, 1973–1993

	1973	1980	1988	1993
Number of lots sold	1,035	814	467	292
Average lot price (dollars)	5,000	7,873	17,589	22,500
Revenue generated from lot sales (dollars)	5,175,000	6,408,622	8,214,063	6,570,000
Number of time-share weeks sold		1,428	2,313	400
Average price per time-share week (dollars)		4,320	8,137	7,400
Revenue generated from time-share sales (dollars)		6,048,000	18,820,881	2,960,000

Source: Fairfield Communities (1993).

ganization of the company. The change in marketing strategy, which included a dramatic reduction in promotional activity and a declining interest in time-sharing nationwide, resulted in a drop in both lot and time-share sales (J. Reed, 1993; Keller, 1993).

Apparently, despite declining interest in time-shares in many parts of the United States, time-sharing is the wave of the future. Following a period of decline, in part because of image problems, the time-sharing industry has experienced an upsurge in growth since 1991. Working diligently to shed its dubious reputation of fast-talking salespersons pressuring people to buy a lifetime of crummy vacations, the industry was given a boost as Disney and other high-profile companies invested billions of dollars in lavish resorts and more flexible scheduling options. Disney Vacation Development, Incorporated, does not even use the word *time-sharing* in their advertisement and points out how ownership in the Disney Vacation Club is superior to traditional vacation ownership or time-sharing. Although the Disney offering is more flexible in terms of scheduling vacation time and the Disney name does add credibility to the offering, it is time-sharing pure and simple, packaged in a slightly different way. According to representatives from the American Resorts Development Association, time-sharing growth has been tremendous, with nearly 1.2 million households in the United States owning time-share intervals, up from 155,000 households in 1980 and 750,000 in 1988 (Crawford, 1983; Englander, 1988; "Time-Share Industry," 1993). Time-sharing appeals to the developers of Fairfield Glade because it gains the project nationwide attention, provides immediate use of on-site facilities, and gives greater sales flexibility. Moreover, the revenue generated by this new program is crucial, particularly in view of the decline in lot sales (McIntosh, 1983; J. Reed, 1984, 1993).

Resort time-sharing is a purchase that guarantees customers the use of a resort housing unit for a certain period of time each year. Two types of time-sharing are available—one allows the purchaser to buy an ownership interest in the unit; the other allows the purchaser to buy a right to use the living space for a specific number of years but without ownership. Time-share ownership offers both advantages and disadvantages. Owners of a time-share unit at Fairfield Glade can rent, sell, or transfer their shares; they may realize some tax advantages; and they receive a warranty deed from the developer after 50 percent of the payments have been made.

Further, inflation has substantially increased the average price of the resort's rental property, so the purchase of a time-share may be a hedge against this inflationary spiral. A time-share may also be a good value if the savings on vacation rents, meals, and other expenses in ten years equal the amount paid for the time-share. In the early 1980s, for example, an average one-week time-share purchased for $7,000 with an annual maintenance fee of $120 would have cost the owner $8,200 in ten years. A resort living unit renting for $850 per week would have cost $8,500 in ten years, for a savings of $300. In future years, the savings will be greater if rental prices continue to escalate. This comparison is based, of course, on the assumption that the time-share owner does not have other expenditures, such as exchange program fees, and that maintenance fees will remain the same year after year (National Time-sharing Council, 1981; Stroud, 1983a, 14–15).

Today, however, the case for cost savings associated with a time-share purchase is more difficult to make. The average price of a one-week time-share at Fairfield Glade in 1992 was $7,800, and the average maintenance fee had increased to $260 (J. Reed, 1993). In ten years, the total cost of the time-share would be $10,400. Rent for a comparable unit must exceed $1,040 per week if savings are to be realized. As the time-share market becomes saturated, it will be extremely difficult to resell time-shares, and the investment potential and savings possibilities will be much more limited.

A time-share unit is certainly less expensive than the purchase of a vacation home on an individual lot; but the two are not comparable.

Time-sharing is not an investment in real estate, and even if the building in which a time-share has been purchased appreciates substantially over time, an individual owner's interest is only one-fiftieth or one-fifty-second of the condominium unit. This can hardly be considered a money-making investment (Stroud, 1983a).

There are several other disadvantages to time-share ownership, one of the most significant being that one time-share is good for only one week. The time-share investment would increase substantially if it allowed for longer vacation times. But if a customer desired five weeks rather than one, the time-share investment would jump from $7,800 to $39,000 (based on average cost). So the argument that time-sharing is an inexpensive way to have a vacation is questionable. An investment of $7,000 to $12,000 for a single week, even if it is for life, is substantial, especially since the price covers neither the annual maintenance fee, nor an exchange fee, nor the Resort Condominium International fee. In 1992, time-share ownership maintenance fees at Fairfield Glade ranged from $170 to $340 per week, with an average of $260 per week (Welch, 1993). This fee was for only one week of use. The most expensive items are the management fee, the housekeeping and maid service, electricity, and the restricted capital reserve fee (table 5.6). These rates are by no means fixed and can escalate dramatically as a building deteriorates from age and heavy use (remember that forty-nine other families use each unit in a single year). Two weeks are set aside for maintenance.

Another drawback is that time-share owners are committed to a specific week for life, and decisions concerning the desired week must be made at the date of purchase. A week during peak tourist season is much more expensive than a week during the off-season. Fairfield Glade's peak season is May 22 through October 5 and was priced at $12,900 per week in 1993. But a week during the off-season was only $6,400. One's vacation needs may not be the same in subsequent years, yet a particular week has already been selected. There is an exchange program, but exchange requests must be made forty-five days in advance and there is a $39 fee for making the exchange (Van Hoy, 1993). Disney's flextime offering is designed to alleviate the disadvantage of selecting a particular week for life by implementing a point system that allows vacation time to be changed from year to year or as the need arises. Fairfield Glade is in the process of converting to a point system, as well. Similarly, the time-share owner is committed to a single vacation location for life. To add flexibility in location, Fairfield Glade became a member of Resort Condominiums International (RCI), and thus a time-share owner can exchange vacation time in this development for vacation time at any resort that belongs to

Table 5.6 Breakdown of a Time-share Owner Maintenance Fee, Fairfield Glade, 1993 (dollars)

Item	Weekly Expenditure
Operations	
Legal fees	0.98
Audit and tax preparation	0.27
Accounting, data processing, administration	5.47
Board of director's expense	1.01
Fairshare service	8.45
Management fee	24.80
Fire and extended coverage	3.80
General liability	0.83
Directors' and officers' liability	0.36
Postage	1.65
Miscellaneous forms and supplies	2.06
Real estate taxes	6.96
Basic equipment charge (telephone)	6.25
General supplies	0.74
Fax dues	3.00
Master association dues (community club)	8.64
Principle payments (energy management system)	3.03
Interest payments (energy management system)	0.64
Repairs and maintenance (equipment)	5.82
Glass and silver replacement	2.49
Linen and laundry replacement	1.90
Building repair and maintenance, exterior	2.92
Housekeeping and maid service	18.98
Laundry and linen service	6.34
Housekeeping supplies	6.83
Housekeeping (carpet and upholstery cleaning)	13.33
Water	6.45
Electricity	22.34
Sewer	4.50
Building repair and maintenance, interior	19.32
Cable TV	6.24
Pest control	1.81
Other	2.42
Building rental (Store-N-Lock)	0.73
Grounds maintenance	8.78
Garbage pickup and trash removal	1.50
Restricted capital reserve fee	36.36
Total	248.00

Source: Fairfield Communities (1993).

RCI. This program is operated on a first-come, first-served basis, and there is an annual membership fee of $89 for each owner who wishes to participate, with no guarantee that desired exchanges will be made.

Time-share owners are entitled to use the facilities in the development free of charge (tennis court fees are waived for property owners, for example), but these privileges are limited to the particular vacation week they have purchased. This limitation has encouraged several time-share owners to purchase a lot in addition to their time-share week, since individual lot owners have ownership privileges year-round (Albertson, 1988). This is an expensive answer to the problem, since the average price for a lot now exceeds $15,000. Clients often purchase what are referred to as membership lots for this purpose—lots that are unbuildable and sold at a reduced price.

A time-share resort may provide a resale program for clients who decide to sell their week, but the week may compete with the developer's unsold week, reducing the likelihood the owner's week will be resold. Even if the week is sold, it probably will not sell at a price sufficiently high to cover both the developer's commission fee (sometimes as high as 20 percent) and the price paid by the owner. One of the most potentially troublesome problems associated with time-share ownership may occur if a co-owner sues for partition of real estate; this means that one owner could sue to have the building sold. Moreover, the entire building may be sold to satisfy a lien on one owner. While the chances of this happening are slim and the government cannot take more of the proceeds than the pro rata share from the forced sale, the sales price could be far less than the total amount paid by time-share owners (National Time-sharing Council, 1981). Finally, decisions concerning maintenance needs and maintenance fee assessments are out of the hands of the owners. A property owners' association or a board of directors makes these decisions based on a majority vote, and an individual owner may or may not be satisfied with association or board decisions (Stroud, 1983a).

Time-sharing obviously offers developers a vital source of revenue at a time when lot sales are on the decline. At the same time, it provides the customer an alternative means of owning vacation housing. But the viability of such ownership remains questionable, and prospective buyers should use extreme caution before purchasing a time-share unit.

What the Customer Actually Buys

There are often many differences between what the developer "sells" and what the customer "buys." At Fairfield Glade, developers and sales representatives emphasize the rural setting—that ownership of a homesite will enable the owners to escape the pollution, congestion, and pace of an urban environment. At the time lot purchases are made, much of the development is in woodland, and with the exception of a network of roads, the property is natural and has the serenity urbanites may be seeking (figure 5.11). In March 1993, more than 15,200 lots had been sold, but only 1,529 owners had constructed homes on their lots. Although there is an impressive town center, only approximately 2,000 of the project's 11,700 acres are developed. For the most part, a tour of the development reveals only a few homes, the cluster of amenities around the town center, hundreds of acres of open space, and thousands of acres of woodland (figure 5.12). To complement the appeal of a rural setting, the developer emphasizes the variety of service and recreational facilities available to the property owner. In other words, all of the services and amenities that one expects in a city are part of the plan, yet supposedly the result will not have the disadvantages of urban living.

Many lots are sold simply because the sales promotion implies that lot values will appreciate substantially. Despite regulations from the U.S. Department of Housing and Urban Development that prohibit the use of unsubstantiated promises concerning investment potential in land development promotional schemes, developers are apparently successful in conveying this message. According to a property owner's survey conducted by project officials, 24.6 percent of all owners purchased lots solely for investment purposes (Rawn, 1973).

The price the customer pays for a vacation homesite supposedly buys a wooded quarter-acre lot, roads (usually paved), water and sewer hookups, membership in a property owners' association (current fee, $216 per year), a totally planned community, numerous amenities, and an expectation of leaving the problems of urban living behind. However, property owners often find that their lots are serviced by gravel or even dirt roads and that water and sewer lines reach only a small percentage of the lots. Furthermore, much of the lot price includes the cost of promotional advertisement and another large portion covers the developer's expenses, which enables him to continue the process of attracting thousands of additional prospective property owners, all of whom are to enjoy a quiet, peaceful setting. So, ironically, buyers pay for the visits of others, who will eventually destroy some of the amenities they paid for.

Buyers are also supposedly purchasing property that is in great demand. It is difficult to resell vacation-home property, however, unless lot owners are willing to take a sometimes considerable loss. Although developers provide a resale office, it does not seem logical for devel-

Figure 5.11   Lot in an undeveloped portion of Fairfield Glade
Source: Photograph by author

Figure 5.12 Partially disturbed woodland, Fairfield Glade
Source: Photograph by author

opers to resell others' property for a small commission when they could sell one of their thousands of unsold lots for a considerably larger profit. Local realtors list vacation-home property and local newspapers carry advertisements by individual owners, a clear indication that developers' resale programs are not successful.

As a member of the property owners' association, the property owner is responsible for maintaining all the service and recreational facilities that the developer built. The ultimate cost of this maintenance can be exorbitant.

Evidently, many people are seeking an alternative to urban life or to their present residence. But if everyone builds a vacation home, in a development with thousands of lots, the rural, natural, and undisturbed bucolic landscape will disappear, and the area will become similar to a suburban subdivision. If on the other hand, home building and continued growth and development do not occur, property owners may be burdened with lots either that cannot be built on because they don't have the basic services needed for human habitation or that have no resale value. In either case, recreational subdivisions fall short of customer expectations (Stroud, 1974, 79–80).

Adjusting to Financial Difficulty

Fairfield Glade has been more successful than many recreational land developments. It had substantial financial backing from its corporate headquarters. Its development plan was based on knowledge gained at other locations. And it utilized innovative marketing techniques centered on the provision of high-quality amenities. During a time when many developments were beginning to experience economic difficulties, this project implemented a time-sharing program; income from lot sales and sale of time-share units produced over $26 million in revenue. The company has built an amenity resort with an impressive infrastructure and thus has avoided consumer problems by shifting its emphasis from the sale of raw land to the development of a resort community, including a town center with a shopping mall, paved streets, central water and sewer hookups for lots in the developed core, and excellent recreational facilities.

The innovations have not alleviated every problem; the number of lots for sale exceeds demand. Property owners who purchased lots as an investment and wish to sell find that resale is difficult, if not impossible. In addition, most remote lots have few of the basic services needed for human habitation. Although the sale of time-share units has been profitable for the developer, customers experience many shortcomings. These and other problems indicate that, even when a developer makes a conscious effort to create a high-amenity resort community, the interests of the consumer remain secondary to the profit motive. And its elaborate infrastructure and finely tuned promotional framework were not enough to keep this company out of financial difficulties (J. Barker, 1991). The company, incorporated in 1966 and operating twenty-three resorts in ten different states, avoided many of the pitfalls and financial problems of other land development companies for almost twenty-five years. Eventually, however, the company began to feel the effects of a troubled economy and the problems associated with obtaining adequate financial backing. Its financial problems resulted from problems in the savings and loan industry, the collapse of the high-yield bond market, and reduced real estate lending by commercial banks (Howeth, 1990). The following sequence of events highlights what led up to the company's filing of Chapter 11 bankruptcy.

On August 20, 1990, the First National Bank of Boston terminated the company's right to draw additional loans under its $45 million revolving credit facility and demanded that the outstanding revolving loan of $23.2 million be repaid in forty-seven equal monthly instalments, beginning September 15, 1990. The company was forced to significantly reduce lot and time-share sales promotion, further exacerbating its financial problems. On October 2, the company announced that it had not made its scheduled October 1 sinking fund and interest payment of approximately $3.8 million. On October 3, the corporation filed a petition under Chapter 11 of the bankruptcy laws seeking to reorganize and restructure its debts (ibid.). On May 8, 1991, the company and twelve of its subsidiaries filed reorganization plans under the U.S. bankruptcy code. Early indications were that the most significant changes would include a reduction in staff and cutbacks in sales activity. A new board of directors has been selected and operations have been streamlined (McConnell, 1991). The casual observer, however, will notice few changes at Fairfield Glade (Ferguson, 1991).

The final reorganization is now complete. The most dramatic change is in marketing; all but a small percentage of direct mail promotion has been eliminated, and the company relies more heavily on referrals and in-house marketing techniques, whereby it attempts to sell additional lots or time-shares to current owners and their guests. The result of these changes has been a dramatic decline in the cost of promotion, in contract sales (from approximately $26 million per year to approximately $9 million per year), and in sales, engineering, and construction personnel (J. Reed, 1993). The problems that this company is experiencing indicate the volatile nature of the recreational real estate industry—and how quickly a positive financial situation can sour.

6 Cape Coral

South Florida's Largest Gulf Coast City

Land development companies, taking advantage of rapid population growth and the desire among millions of people to invest in Florida real estate, have subdivided more than 1.6-million acres into more than 2.1 million lots in the state. While subdivision activity is also significant in the desert Southwest and the mountains of Colorado, it does not compare with recreational land development in Florida. Sadly enough, this development is concentrated in natural areas with a low tolerance for disruption. This creates a significant growth dilemma: the subtropical and seacoast amenities that attract people to Florida are threatened by the developmental pressures that such growth creates. Since the destruction of these environmental amenities has many negative implications, it is essential that a means be found to ensure the environmental integrity of peninsular Florida.

In 1958, Gulf Guaranty Land and Title Company began to develop Cape Coral, one of the largest recreational subdivisions in Florida. This company eventually became the Gulf American Corporation before merging with General Acceptance Corporation (GAC) in 1969. As a result of the merger, GAC acquired more than 500,000 acres in eleven different subdivisions. After many unfavorable state and federal court rulings on class-action suits, suspension orders from the Office of Interstate Land Sales Registration in 1975, and other problems, GAC went bankrupt and in 1980 sold its remaining holdings at Cape Coral to Avatar Holdings, Inc. Currently at Cape Coral, Avatar has approximately 4,000 single-family homesites for sale, 400 acres zoned for commercial or industrial use, 2,250 acres zoned for multifamily dwellings, and 600 acres of undeveloped land (T. Weiss, 1986; Getman, 1993).

Located along Florida's southern Gulf Coast, Cape Coral extends

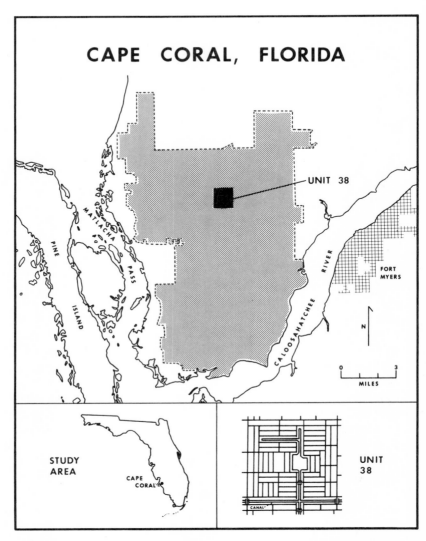

Figure 6.1 Map of Cape Coral. Unit 38 is one of approximately 100 units in the city; the map shows how streets and canals are arranged in the units.
Source: Stroud (1991)

across 65,000 acres, or approximately one-eighth the total land area of Lee County, one of the fastest growing counties in Florida. The county's fifty-two miles of beautiful coastline and a prodevelopment attitude among local officials stimulated its growth. It was not until the early 1970s that minimal subdivision regulations were passed, and even then developers had only to record the plats and adhere to certain street and drainage specifications. By 1970, there were more than 250,000 lots in excess of demand, by far the majority of them in Cape Coral and Lehigh Acres, Lee County's two largest recreational subdivisions (Stroud, 1984).

Cape Coral's peninsula location, between the Caloosahatchee River and the Gulf of Mexico (figure 6.1), is one of the worst possible choices for development from an environmental standpoint. Palmetto (small palm trees) and pine forest and sizable stretches of mangrove estuaries and tidal marshes covered an important freshwater recharge area prior to development (figures 6.2 and 6.3). This ecologically fragile zone stored and purified water draining from upland regions. Although much of Cape Coral is undeveloped, all the property has been platted. Thousands of people in widely scattered locations across the United States and other countries own these lots. Such a complicated ownership pattern exacerbates efforts to change land use or to redesign the subdivision (Tossier, 1983; Generous, 1991).

Developers installed a gridiron of roads and canals (figure 6.4) by dredging and filling. Today, much of the property is dehydrated, devegetated, and sterile (Knight, 1990). Phasing was not used, and only minimal acreage (less than 1 percent of the total area) was provided for open space and parks. Homes were built in a 100-year floodplain, and less than 15 percent of the subdivision is covered by trees. The reconfiguration of the topography through massive excavation for roads and canals destroyed a shallow freshwater aquifer. Eroded soil, urban runoff, sewage from septic tanks, and stagnating and weed-choked canals (figure 6.5) have polluted the groundwater, the Caloosahatchee River, and the Matlacha Pass. Water pollution is intensified by a lack of retention basins for storm water, a lack of buffer zones along streams, a lack of vegetation along disturbed land, and a lack of seawalls to halt erosion along canal banks. In addition, potable water from shallow aquifers is minimal, recharge is slow, and there are problems from saltwater contamination (Morgan, 1988).

Four separate water-bearing layers of rock (aquifers) are located under Cape Coral. The deepest layers are highly mineralized, and the uppermost layer (the water table aquifer) was severely degraded years ago by the construction of canals and roads and from the use of septic systems on small lots. The next most readily available aquifer is the Mid-Hawthorne, a water-bearing layer found in a series of limestone rock ranging from less than 100 feet to as much as 150 feet in depth (Barraclough and Marsh, 1962; Boggess, 1968). Its large quantities of relatively shallow fresh water made the Mid-Hawthorne the primary source of water for the cities of Cape Coral and Fort Myers and for individual homeowners outside these cities. The aquifer soon became

Figure 6.2 Wetlands along the western margin of Cape Coral. Plastic sheeting (only recently installed) is to help protect this fragile mangrove from sediment and other pollutants.

Source: Photograph by author

Figure 6.3 Pine and palmetto forest in an undeveloped portion of northern Cape Coral.

Source: Photograph by author

overtaxed, and the result was a water-level decline of more than fifty feet in some locations. Concern over this precipitous decline prompted Cape Coral officials to dig deeper wells to tap the Lower Hawthorne, an aquifer with a relatively large volume of water and fewer competing interests. But water from the Lower Hawthorne has a high mineral content, making it unpotable. Cape Coral officials then invested in a reverse osmosis (R/O) water treatment plant to remove some of these minerals. (R/O plants also desalinate brackish water.) Booming Fort Myers was also forced to find alternatives to the Mid-Hawthorne aquifer and now uses surface water from the Caloosahatchee River (McCoy, 1993). The region has a large potential water supply from both surface and subsurface sources; the problem is to provide water at reasonable cost to customers. Currently, at least, the limiting factor is cost of treatment rather than shortage of water (ibid.).

In addition to environmental problems, property owners at Cape Coral were subjected to unscrupulous sales practices. The company has been sued for phony claims by the Florida Real Estate Commission and dissatisfied customers (Tymon, 1973). Despite its modifications in sales practices, prompted primarily by Federal Trade Commission rulings in 1974, the developer's overall consumer protection record is poor. GAC neither conducted credit checks on prospective customers nor required on-site visits before lot purchases were made. Although it promised a refund to purchasers who bought sight unseen and who requested it within two days after a visit to the lot, the vast majority of the lots sold at Cape Coral were on the instalment plan and involved costs that were not refundable: interest payments on the sales contract, county taxes for the ten-year payment period, survey fees, charges for drilling a well and installing a septic system, and fees for a county percolation test. Furthermore, the exchange and resale program left much to be desired; exchanges had to be made prior to the receipt of the deed, exchange lots had to be of equal or higher value, and only the principal paid, not the interest, was applied to the cost of another lot. Exchanges were further restricted by the requirement that additional lots had to be available before the swap could occur, because the number of lots available for exchange dwindled rapidly during the mid-1970s. GAC sold hundreds of thousands of lots, but resale is virtually impossible (especially if the property owner expects a profit) unless the lots are in the southern section—the waterfront and yacht club area, where development began (Cobb, 1993).

The problems created by these sales practices have caused many legal battles, with settlements being reached in some of the class-action and Federal Trade Commission suits. Further, poor land use, complex ownership arrangements, the GAC bankruptcy of the mid-1970s, and

Figure 6.4 Aerial view of Cape Coral. The Caloosahatchee River and Fort Myers are located in the southeast corner of the photograph. Scale 1 : 60,000 ft.

Source: U.S. Dept. of Agriculture (1984a)

Figure 6.5 A weed-choked canal in Cape Coral

Source: Photograph by author

Table 6.1 Population Growth, Cape Coral, 1970–1993

Year	Total Population	Percentage Increase	Percentage of County Population
1970	11,470		10.9
1974	19,180	17.2	13.0
1978	24,787	17.2	13.5
1980	32,103	29.5	15.6
1984	43,902	36.8	19.5
1988	63,742	45.2	21.2
1990	74,991	17.6	22.4
1993	81,444	8.6	23.6

Source: Cape Coral (1988); Cobb (1993).

the conflicting demands of consumers, creditors, and regulatory agencies will take years or even decades to resolve, assuming there is a solution.

The Fort Myers–Cape Coral metropolitan statistical area has grown faster than almost any other MSA. Cape Coral alone had 74,991 permanent residents in 1990, an increase of more than 42,000 new residents since 1980, or a 133 percent increase. From 1980 to 1990, it increased in population more than any other city in the six-county southwest region of Florida and is now the largest city in Lee County (table 6.1). In addition, the median age of the population has declined since 1970. Although the percentage of fifty-five-to-seventy-four-year-olds has declined, a large portion of Cape Coral's population is still of retirement age, and over 22 percent of the city's permanent population was sixty-five years or older in 1990 (Cape Coral, 1988, 16; Cobb, 1993).

But the current population and high growth rates are not impressive when one considers the city's acreage and its potential population. Cape Coral covers 103 square miles of land and has more than 138,000 platted residential lots. More than 1,200 miles of roads and 400 miles of saltwater and freshwater canals lace the subdivision (figure 6.6). Assuming three residents per lot, Cape Coral's 138,000 lots could house over 400,000 people; approximately 26,000 lots have been built on since subdivision began in 1958. An average of 400 lots are built on each year. The figure is much higher than for most recreational subdivisions, yet if the present rate continues, it will require more than 280 years for all of the 138,000 lots to be built on. This is assuming water and other services will be available. In view of the current availability of potable water and the problems associated with

Figure 6.6 Large canal and condominiums in the developed portion of Cape Coral

Source: Photograph by author

septic systems on quarter-acre lots, it is extremely unlikely all the lots will ever be occupied (Stroud, 1991).

Growth is most likely in and around the developed core, where basic services are available. The vast majority of the property will remain much as it is today, a barren landscape crisscrossed by deteriorating roads and weed-choked canals. Although the developed core is large in comparison to those of most recreational subdivisions, it is small in comparison to the total area. So development covers only about 15,000 acres, leaving approximately 50,000 acres of platted land with no city services. Consequently, the contrast in landscapes at Cape Coral is dramatic. While a portion of the property resembles a city, with schools, businesses, a city hall, and other features, this urban core is surrounded by a vast wasteland of streets and canals but no inhabitants. Such an operation indicates that the primary objective of the developers was to generate income through lot sales. The developed core appears almost as an afterthought and is dwarfed by the surrounding ghost subdivision.

It is not surprising that Cape Coral has a relatively large planning department in view of all the problems created by its developer. City officials must find an adequate supply of potable water, solve high-volume traffic flows on poorly designed streets, provide services to the urban core as well as to the widely scattered population outside the core, restore the tree canopy destroyed by the developer, provide open spaces and parks in the high-density core area, protect endangered species, such as the burrowing owl, and provide adequate drainage and flood control. These and other problems highlight the need for predevelopment planning and indicate what can happen when developers ignore the natural constraints of a site (Knight, 1990).

7 Rio Rancho

New Mexico's Fastest Growing Community

Rio Rancho began in 1961 on 54,000 acres of land situated 11.5 miles northwest of Albuquerque on the West Mesa of the Rio Grande River (figure 7.1). An additional 31,000 acres were purchased in 1971; subsequent acquisitions brought the total acreage to more than 91,000 acres. AMREP (American Realty and Petroleum Company) purchased the original 54,000 acres for less than $200 per acre. The first lots sold for approximately $1,500 per acre, but by the mid-1970s this price rose to more than $7,000 per acre. These increases occurred without any improvements to the land. Ironically, AMREP paid less than $200 per acre for an additional 31,000 acres ten years after its original purchase (Allan, Kuder, and Oakes, 1976, 141–53).

Rio Rancho is located in a semiarid, low-yield environment. It is cattle rangeland, approximately one mile above sea level and crisscrossed with deep gullies (arroyos) carved out by flash floods during cloudbursts. Without careful design and planning and the implementation of sound land-use practices, Rio Rancho is an unsuitable location for a massive subdivision (figure 7.2). A potential water shortage, erosion, and runoff in association with more than 1,000 miles of bladed dirt roads (figure 7.3) are three of the most obvious environmental problems (Miller, 1987).

Another drawback is that AMREP's environmental planning has been inadequate. Despite its pledges to preserve the natural beauty of the site, the physical layout of the development failed to consider environmental limitations and constraints. Roads were superimposed in a predetermined grid over rolling hills and branching arroyos in what appears a callous disregard for the natural terrain (Sears, 1972, 3–5). Open space was provided not where it was needed but where the land was too rough to be used as homesites, and phased development was not utilized except in the small developed core. No services were planned for the remaining 93 percent of the project except for bladed roads, which have caused dust and sandstorms and severe erosion and gullying. AMREP's failure to provide an adequate drainage system has caused additional problems, the most significant being arroyo wash-outs, flooding, and siltation both on the site and downslope in the town of Corrales (Allan, Kuder, and Oakes, 1976, 155–57). The slope of the terrain at Rio Rancho averages 10 percent, and because devel-opers installed roads without regard to drainage patterns, many lots are susceptible to flooding by water runoff enroute to the Rio Grande River. Therefore, these lots have been severely eroded or covered with sediment—in part because there are no sediment traps or siltation ba-sins (Cinelli, 1975; Sears, 1972).

Rio Rancho does have a small, highly acclaimed, sewage treatment facility; according to the state Environmental Improvement Agency, it is one of the best in New Mexico; spray irrigation and a holding pond prevent sewage from being discharged into any water body. But this facility serves only the developed core (figure 7.4), or no more than 7 percent of the lots sold. Homesites are generally suitable for septic systems, since water tables are deep and soils are relatively pervious (Colegrove, 1986). However, the effect of so many septic systems over such a large area remains to be seen.

The land sales tactics used by AMREP to promote property at Rio Rancho stress selling half-acre desert lots sight unseen to distant buy-ers (Wolff, 1972, 54). Prospective customers are told they can "live like a king," with low taxes and a good job market.* Undoubtedly, consumer protection was poor at Rio Rancho. The credit standing of prospective customers was not investigated, many lots were sold as investments, all payments were retained by the company if the lot owner defaulted, and customer rights to titles were not fully protected. Although AMREP is no longer selling lots at Rio Rancho, its past sales practices created many current problems. Lot owners wishing to build homes on "remote" lots will experience totally unexpected additional costs, including $10.50 per foot for a four-inch-pipe well (well depths

---

* In Barbara Kerr Page, "The Land of Enchantment Is also the Land of Ripoffs" (1977), a photograph caption reads, "With a five-dollar down payment, a buyer can secure a half-acre 'ranchette' near Deming, in southeastern New Mexico." Although the arid rangeland offers few amenities, sales of the scattered lots continue to grow. Deming and surrounding Luna County contain 80,000 half-acre subdivided lots, which would, if built on, house eight times the county's current population (Page, 1977, 8). New Mex-ico, the fifth largest state in land area, has a relatively low cost of living, a warm, dry climate, a poor state economy, apathetic political officials, and other prodevelopment factors that have resulted in fraudulent land sales in excess of $1 billion (ibid., 49).

Figure 7.1 Map of Rio Rancho
Source: Adapted from AMREP Southwest (1990)

range from 200 to more than 800 feet); $1,000 to $1,200 for a septic system; and $10 per foot for electric lines (the cost for extending a line only one mile is more than $50,000; see Herrera, 1993). Lot owners must also pay for telephone lines.

These expenses will be financially prohibitive to most lot owners, who are then left with few options other than selling their property or trading it for a lot closer to the developed core through AMREP's equal exchange program. Lot resale has been very slow throughout the history of the Rio Rancho development, and the few lots that have been resold brought much less than the purchase price. Reselling lots in a recreational subdivision is never easy and is particularly difficult at Rio Rancho, since there is no organized lot resale program. Consequently, many lot owners have few alternatives for recouping their investment.

In spite of these problems, the town of Rio Rancho, on the high mesa northwest of Albuquerque, has come into being. From a mere 1,164 people in 1970, Rio Rancho increased in population by 415.5 percent between 1970 and 1975, and by 1980 its population stood at 10,131 (table 7.1). Substantial growth also occurred during the 1980s, and by 1990 its population was 32,505. Since 1990, rapid population growth continued, with approximately 250 new residents per month, or 3,000 per year, being added (Tucker, 1993), making Rio Rancho the fastest growing community in New Mexico. Half of Sandoval

Figure 7.2 Aerial view of Rio Rancho, with road pattern superimposed. Scale 1 : 60,000 ft.

Source: U.S. Dept. of Agriculture (1982)

Figure 7.3 Dirt road in a remote portion of Rio Rancho. Notice cattle grazing in the background.

Source: Photograph by author

Figure 7.4 Housing units in the developed core of Rio Rancho
Source: Photograph by author

County's population now resides in this thriving town. Incorporated in 1981, it is governed by a mayor and city council, and its revenues totaled more than $20 million for the 1991–92 fiscal year (ibid.).

Rio Rancho's business establishments (figure 7.5) have shown growth just as impressive as the growth in population. In the early 1980s, the community had approximately 30 business establishments; by 1991 there were over 140 retail establishments and 56 industries. Growth will undoubtedly continue in view of the recent decision by Intel Corporation to expand its computer chip manufacturing plant at Rio Rancho (Intel Corporation, 1993). Intel, a world leader in computer chip manufacturing, is moving ahead with a $1 billion expansion, the largest capital project in the history of the computer chip industry for a domestic site and the most expensive single project in Intel history. Its Rio Rancho plant will create up to 1,000 new electronics jobs and approximately 3,000 construction jobs. The expansion will add 140,000 square feet of "clean room" (to keep particles to a minimum) as part of a total Intel expansion of 1 million square feet.

The Intel expansion is expected to have major consequences for Rio Rancho and the surrounding West Mesa. These include not only job growth and other economic stimuli but also several significant negative impacts. Growth can exacerbate housing shortages, overtax water

Figure 7.5 One of several shopping centers in Rio Rancho
Source: Photograph by author

supplies, and intensify drainage problems for communities down-stream of Rio Rancho, as more rooftops, parking lots, and other im-pervious surfaces are created. Of particular concern is the historic town of Corrales, a community that has already experienced flood-ing as a direct result of the building of Rio Rancho (Mather, 1993). Corrales's residents have also complained about the odor from the Intel plant at Rio Rancho (Sanchez, 1993).

Corrales's residents and others living near Rio Rancho are con-cerned about expansion plans not only because of problems created in the past but also because of the magnitude of the expansion. The ad-dition of 1 million square feet is a massive building project, which could drastically alter drainage patterns and exacerbate flooding prob-lems. Moreover, the expansion will require large volumes of additional water. Water taken from aquifers could lower water levels and even-tually deplete water supplies for nearby communities (Davis, 1993). Another concern is access over the Rio Grande River to Albuquerque. Growth and development and the corresponding increase in traffic be-tween Albuquerque and Rio Rancho can compound congestion, par-ticularly during rush hour, on the few bridges across the river.

In spite of rapid population growth and industrial development, Rio Rancho continues to have a relatively low building rate. More than 93,000 lots, potentially homes to an additional 280,000 to

Table 7.1 Population Growth, Rio Rancho, 1970–1993

Year	Total Population	Percentage Increase	Percentage of County Population
1970	1,164		6.6
1975	6,000	415.5	26.3
1980	10,131	68.9	29.4
1984	20,000	97.4	46.5
1988	31,000	55.0	55.4
1990	32,505	4.9	51.3
1993	40,000	23.1	56.3

Source: AMREP Southwest (1988, 1993); population estimate for 1993, Leonard (1993).

300,000 people, remain unoccupied. Thus, much of the environmental and transportation impact at Rio Rancho is yet to occur. If present growth rates continue, it will require an additional 750 years for Rio Rancho to reach its population potential, even if water supplies can be obtained.

A 1981 study found that a high percentage of Rio Rancho residents had a positive perception of AMREP's role in the development of Rio Rancho (J. Weiss, 1981). When asked to rate their expectations of Rio Rancho on the basis of the AMREP promotion, 73 percent were satisfied, 13 percent were neutral, and only 14 percent were dissatisfied. Respondents were also asked to compare the livability of Rio Rancho with their former communities. Fifteen of twenty-two community attributes were rated as better in Rio Rancho than in their former residences. These attributes included climate, scenery, outdoor recreation, and cost of housing. Dissatisfaction included inadequate shopping, recreational facilities, police protection, road repair, and employment opportunities. The list of negative features is surprisingly small in view of the many problems that have plagued the company throughout much of its history.

Rio Rancho has indeed had a rather stormy history, with federal legal actions charging fraud and misrepresentation, customer complaints, and its defaults on sales contracts. The community has survived these problems, however, and now seems to be moving toward becoming a sizable city, based on New Mexico standards. The ability of project officials to overcome many problems, including limited water resources, will be crucial in determining the future growth and development of this community.

8 Lake Havasu City

A Rapidly Emerging Community in the Arizona Desert

Lake Havasu City occupies a 16,700-acre site along the western boundary of Arizona (figure 8.1). It began in 1963 as the first of eight land development projects built by McCulloch Properties, Inc. (MPI). The twenty-five-square-mile development is separated from Lake Havasu, a federal Bureau of Reclamation dam project, by a narrow strip of state parkland. Unlike many recreational subdivisions, developers of this project have built on its lots at a rapid rate.

Robert McCulloch, millionaire chain-saw executive, devised one of the most outlandish and expensive promotional stunts ever used by a land developer to promote a project. He purchased the 140-year-old London Bridge for $2.5 million from the British in 1968 and spent an additional $8 million to have it disassembled into more than 10,000 pieces of granite, shipped to Arizona, and reassembled under the direction of a British engineer (figure 8.2). All of this and more were done to promote the development of what was to be a "model city" in a hot, dry, remote area of western Arizona (Downie, 1974, 153–55).

Lake Havasu City occupies an inhospitable stretch of desert, where rainfall is minimal and temperatures are extremely hot during summer months (figure 8.3). In fact, rainfall averages approximately five inches per year, and summer temperatures reach 115° or higher. This harsh desert climate sustains only sparse, widely spaced, small shrubs and cacti. The site is situated along alluvial fans extending down from the Mohave Mountains, and its sandy soil is deeply eroded by gullies and littered with boulders washed down during storms. The sparse vegetation and intense cloudbursts that characterize desert environments can create serious erosion problems, especially if the surface has been disturbed by development. Residents of Lake Havasu City, therefore,

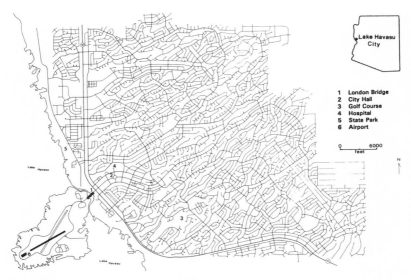

Figure 8.1 Map of Lake Havasu City
Source: Adapted from Lake Havasu City (1991)

must contend with hot temperatures, erosion from rapid overland flow during storms, high winds, and dust storms from the disturbance of topsoil from road construction.

Most of Lake Havasu City's environmental problems are directly attributable to McCulloch's choice of site. Sitting on an alluvial fan, Lake Havasu City is particularly vulnerable to flash floods, which are difficult to alleviate. In fact, flooding problems are magnified, since the developer did not follow the natural limitations of the land. Although improvements have been made in recent years, many homes are too close to washes and drainageways.

The development site was once a wilderness area and wildlife refuge for herds of desert bighorn sheep, desert mule deer, and pronghorn antelope. The antelope is now extinct in this part of the state because of human encroachment. The creation of Lake Havasu and the building of a subdivision near its shore have destroyed the habitat of several bird species, including the heron, crane, and egret. While a few herons and cranes still nest at the south end of the lake, they have difficulty adjusting to the lake and the adjacent urban development and prefer the undisturbed cottonwood gallery forest that grew along the Colorado River before the lake was built (Werner, 1993). Severe water limitations and the widespread use of septic systems on small lots are other potential problems. Commercial and industrial lots and a few single-family lots are served by a central sewer system, but more than 28,000

Figure 8.2   London Bridge, Lake Havasu City
Source: Photograph by author

Figure 8.3   Desert and mountains on the outskirts of Lake Havasu City
Source: Photograph by author

quarter-acre lots were designed for septic systems, which is certainly not sound environmental planning.

Buyers had to contend with many uncertainties once lots were purchased. No provisions were made for refunds, beyond those required by state and federal laws, and if buyers defaulted on sales contracts they forfeited all their land payments plus any payments for taxes, assessments, and improvements. Lot owners must pay fees to special assessment districts established by the developer to finance the cost of installing basic services, including a per acre tax to the Irrigation and Drainage District (assessments vary depending on the size of the lot). The Sanitation District provides central sewer facilities for lots within its boundaries (about 25 percent of the city), and Improvement Districts pay for security lights at selected locations. In 1978, voters decided to dissolve these special districts when their bonds expired. Later, in 1993, realizing that these districts provide an important source of revenue for the city, voters decided to extend the bonds for the Sanitation District until the year 2010 and for the Irrigation and Drainage District until the year 2022 (Massara, 1993).

Lot resales at Lake Havasu City have gone through several changes. During the 1970s and much of the 1980s, lot resale was by no means certain. Many lots were listed by local realtors, but resale was slow. In 1986, for example, approximately 5,000 lots were listed for resale, with no more than 80 selling in a given month (Lee, 1986). By the end of the decade, however, the rate of lot resale and the value of individual lots began to change. Lake Havasu City, with its location along the Arizona-California border, became one of the destinations for families leaving California to escape crime, air pollution, and other urban problems. It also became the choice of families from many northern states. This boom has resulted in a dramatic increase in the average price of a lot, from $5,500 in 1986 to $18,000 in 1993, and has greatly reduced the inventory of vacant lots. Since 30–40 percent of current lot owners have no intention of selling their property, the number of lots available for resale is small (Baumkirchner, 1993).

Improvements in consumer protection were made by virtue of an Arizona sales law, which protects a lot owner's right to title during the contract period and requires that all lots be platted with Mohave County. Although a purchaser does not receive the title until all loan payments are made, the title is held in trust until then (Allan, Kuder, and Oakes, 1976, 328).

Lake Havasu City's 16,700 acres were subdivided into 33,514 lots, most of which were sold within a few years. The city also has multi-family units, motels, mobile homes, and commercial and industrial lots. The population potential created by more than 28,000 single-

Table 8.1 Population Growth, Lake Havasu City, 1970–1992

Year	Total Population	Percentage Increase	Percentage of County Population
1970	5,185		20.1
1974	10,024	93.0	27.0
1980	15,909	59.0	28.0
1985	17,747	12.0	28.0
1988	20,500	15.5	29.1
1990	27,030	52.3	29.4
1992	32,710	21.0	34.3

Source: Arizona (1984, 1985, 1991, 1993).

family lots is approximately 85,000 (based on three people per lot). Although a relatively large number of lots are fully paid for and deeded to their owners, population growth has not met the developer's projections. MPI forecast a population of 20,000 by the mid-1970s, but actual population was only about 10,000 in 1975; in 1990 it stood at 27,030 (table 8.1). In spite of this shortfall, the growth rate at Lake Havasu City is much greater than that at many other recreational subdivisions. Growth rates were dramatic between 1970 and 1980. Growth was not as rapid in the early 1980s but increased substantially by the end of the decade. By 1990, 29 percent of the population in Mohave County lived at Lake Havasu City (Arizona, 1984; Arnon, 1993). If current rates continue, it will require more than 100 years for the project to become fully occupied. This rate, though slow, is much faster than in many subdivisions, which require thousands of years for full occupation to occur if current trends continue.

Although Lake Havasu City has a relatively large number of retirees, the median age of its residents is only 37.1 years. School enrollment figures attest to the fact that the community has a relatively large younger population. During the 1990–91 school year, for example, school enrollment for grades K–12 totaled more than 4,500, higher than one might expect from a subdivision designed as a recreational-retirement community (Arizona, 1991).

From the beginning, developers of Lake Havasu City intended that the project be more than a lot sales subdivision. To raise some of the money needed for large initial investments, McCulloch transferred much of the development costs to property owners, using a loophole in a vaguely worded Arizona statute that allowed him to create special taxing districts. The statute was intended to help farmers finance irrigation systems by providing for the legal establishment of special "irrigation and drainage districts." The Irrigation and Drainage District at Lake Havasu has the power to acquire or lease real estate, to establish charges for services delivered, and to issue tax-exempt bonds. It is responsible for the construction and maintenance of major roads and the community drainage system. Thus, the Lake Havasu Irrigation and Drainage District carries a major developmental responsibility for the community, although the statute that allowed its creation was never intended for use by "new community" developers (Didion, 1986). The district provided a good system of basic services, except for a central sewage system to most lots and a way to deal with flash floods and drainage problems. All in all, the subdivision has progressed more rapidly than most in becoming a new community, even in a most inhospitable desert environment. Lake Havasu City is now the largest city in Mohave County; it also provides employment and recreational opportunities and most basic services. These features prove that a city can be created even in a harsh environment if it has a well-financed development plan and stable management.

Unfortunately, the community also has many of the problems characteristic of land development projects promoted under the guise of new community development. Except for its isolated location, Lake Havasu City is really nothing new and certainly not a model community. The desert landscape is scarred by dirt roads, a confusion of stores and factories, mobile homes, and single-family detached homes. Motels, expensive homes, and an irrigated golf course occupy the choicest locations. The master plan was totally inadequate; much of the city was allowed to just happen in whatever way was most profitable for McCulloch. Although roads extend across the entire project to provide access to distant homesites, many remain unused; but by spreading the community out, the cost of providing basic services increased dramatically. Lake Havasu City provides few positive innovations in the provision of basic services, shopping facilities, pollution prevention, social welfare, or landscape design. Ironically, if the city does grow to its projected population of more than 80,000, it will have practically all the urban problems that many of its citizens left behind (Downie, 1974, 156–64).

9 Fairfield Bay

An Arkansas Ozark Mountain Resort Community

Fairfield Bay is one of twenty-three planned recreational communities in the United States owned by Fairfield Communities, Inc., a company with landholdings in ten states (Albertson, 1988). Fairfield Bay, the corporation's first project, began in 1966 along the north shore of Greers Ferry Lake in Arkansas on a 4,300-acre tract of land (figure 9.1). Initially, the developers provided little in the way of services; a sales office and a network of roads were the first changes made to this little-disturbed portion of rural Van Buren County (Stroud, 1985b, 254).

Fairfield Bay is situated in a steeply sloping portion of the Ozark Mountains, in one of the most beautiful locations in the entire Ozarks region (figure 9.2). The most significant environmental limitations are the steep terrain and the thin mountain soil. With these two exceptions, the site is not nearly as environmentally sensitive as the wetlands at Cape Coral or the desert at Lake Havasu. Yet, any new community, with its elaborate infrastructure and large population, causes problems. One significant environmental problem is caused by the 200 miles of unpaved roads gouged out of the steep terrain (figure 9.3). Many of the roads, constructed years or even decades before they will be needed by lot owners, are used to show prospective customers the small lots for sale. Even though some of the roads follow the natural contour, some have slopes exceeding 15 percent and may always remain unpaved. (Only about 70 miles were paved by November 1993 [Littell, 1993.]) The heavy rainfall common to the area easily washes out these roads and dumps sediment into Greers Ferry Lake and nearby streams. In addition, the roads could destroy the scenic terrain, particularly if cut and fill is used.

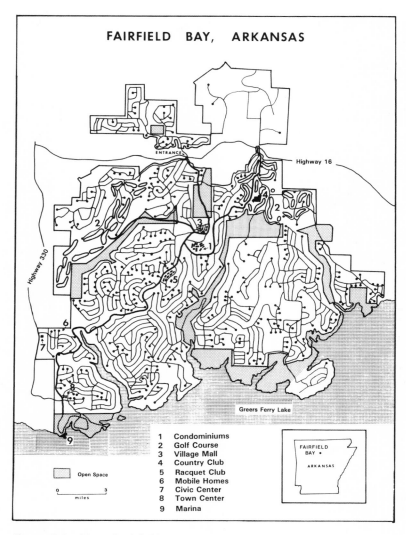

Figure 9.1 Map of Fairfield Bay

Source: Adapted from Fairfield Communities (1993)

Fairfield Bay is, in many respects, similar to a suburban subdivision, except its standards are not as high. For example, septic systems are widely accepted among recreational developers (American Society of Planning Officials, 1976, 49), even though, on small lots, particularly where aquifers are near the surface, such systems can have a devastating impact on the groundwater. At Fairfield Bay, only twenty-six miles of sewer line had been installed by 1993, all within its developed core;

Figure 9.2   Densely wooded mountainous terrain in an undeveloped portion of Fairfield Bay. Greers Ferry Lake is in the background.
Source: Photograph by author

all the remaining lots are to be served by septic systems, even though the thin, rocky soil is not suitable for them. If the number of septic systems is allowed to continue to increase, serious health problems could arise.

More than 16,000 lots have been sold at Fairfield Bay, extending over 9,000 acres. Developers are in the process of extending services outward from the core of the project, but water lines are available along only some fifty miles of road and sewer lines along about twenty-six miles. Property owners wishing to build a home on their lot before services are provided must drill a well, install a septic system, and make arrangements to have electric lines extended to the property. Some homes are as much as three or four miles from areas where basic service facilities are available. Property owners could be stuck with inadequate services for years, especially those with lots several miles from the core area.

Water resources in mountain and plateau regions are limited, because most streams are small and groundwater wells tap only a small amount of water. Water treatment is required for water taken from lakes or streams. Water supplies at Fairfield Bay seem sufficient to meet current demand, but meeting future needs may be problematic even if only half of the lots sold are built on. If homes are built on the ap-

Figure 9.3 Aerial view of the western portion of Fairfield Bay. Greers Ferry Lake is shown lower right. Scale 1 : 20,000 ft.

Source: Arkansas (1980)

proximately 8,000 lots sold, the potential population is 24,000, or ten times the current population.

Although Fairfield Bay developers used high-pressure sales tactics to promote their lots and time-share units, for the most part, its operations have been legal, and lawsuits have been rare. Its most significant consumer problems are common throughout the industry: unauthorized promises made by lot sales personnel during high-pressure promotional tours, instalment contract terms that are unfair to the buyer, inadequate basic services, and poor resale performance. However, Fairfield Bay has done better than most in carrying through on its promises. And although complete services are unavailable outside the developed core, this core is impressive, with its shopping mall, town-

Table 9.1   Population Growth, Fairfield Bay, 1970–1990

Year	Total Population	Percentage Increase	Percentage of County Population
1970	188		2.3
1980	2,081	1,006.9	15.6
1984	2,500	20.1	17.7
1988	2,200	− 12.0	15.9
1990	2,154	− 2.1	15.4

Source: Hammer, Siler, and George (1984); Fairfield Communities (1993).

houses and condominiums, clubhouse, racquet club, marina, fire station, churches, two golf courses, and other facilities. In addition, lot owners receive a warranty deed to their property after the lot is paid for in full. The greatest consumer-related problem is the promise of profits from the resale of lots, because it is unlikely that lots purchased at highly inflated prices will resell at a substantial profit. Resale may be especially difficult if the developer still has unsold lots on hand (Stroud, 1985b, 255–56).

One of the striking features of Fairfield Bay is its dramatic increase in population (table 9.1). In 1993, it was one of the largest single communities in the entire county. Nearly one-half of the county's population growth between 1970 and 1984 occurred at Fairfield Bay. Population peaked at approximately 2,500, in 1984; since then, poor economic conditions and problems with bankruptcy have hampered its growth. While exact figures are difficult to obtain, estimates are that the population declined to 2,154 in 1990 (A. Martin, 1993).

Moreover, the resident population at Fairfield Bay is older and has higher disposable incomes than the indigenous population. A greater spending capability plus other economic benefits associated with the growth of a community provide many positive benefits for the county and state. Some of these positive features include employment opportunities for local residents, a stimulus to wholesale and retail trade, and a boost to property, sales, and income taxes and to the construction industry. In 1973 alone, 106 single-family homes were built. The total now exceeds 1,000 permanent residential housing units. In addition, more than 217 time-share units and 166 mobile homes are available (Littell, 1993).

Fairfield Bay cannot be considered a ghost subdivision, yet the characteristic pattern of concentrated development and vast tracts of undeveloped woodland does exist. Many lots are served by only an unpaved road, and owners who decide to build on their remote lots must drill a well and instal a septic system. There are over 14,400 vacant lots, many of which are unsuitable as building sites because of steep terrain or inadequate services. An average of only fifty-eight lots per year were built on from 1966 to 1984, and fewer than fifteen per year since 1990. At that rate, it will require 250–300 years for the development to become fully built and to reach its population potential of 50,000. If it ever materialized, such a large population would exceed the resources and service capacities of this rural environment. While much could be done to prepare for a substantially larger population in 250 years, certain problems such as limited water resources would be difficult to overcome.

The developers have made the necessary investments to create a highly acclaimed resort with impressive amenities in the core which have convinced many people to invest in the project. The amenities lend a feeling of permanence to the community, an ingredient lacking in many other lot sales subdivisions. However, these amenities do not eliminate the problems of lots too remote for home construction, poor to nonexistent lot resales, environmental degradation, and other problems created by suburban growth in a backwoods location. The bankruptcy and reorganization of Fairfield Communities in 1990–91 illustrates how an economic downturn can trigger a slump in lot sales and a decline in second-home and retirement home construction, which developers often cannot withstand for long. Fairfield Communities and its first land development venture, Fairfield Bay, managed to recover from bankruptcy and are continuing land development, albeit on a reduced scale. Although many of the positive economic benefits, such as the generation of tax revenue, all but disappeared during bankruptcy proceedings, they are expected to rebound now that bankruptcy and reorganization have been completed.

10 Port LaBelle

A "Well-Planned" Florida Community

Port LaBelle was created by General Development Corporation (GDC), one of the largest land development companies in the United States before its bankruptcy in 1990. General Development controlled more than 235,000 acres in Florida alone, including holdings at Port Charlotte/North Port, Port LaBelle, Port Malabar, and Port St. Lucie (General Development Corp., 1982). In 1991, Atlantic Gulf Communities (AGC) acquired most of General Development's property, including all of the acreage at Port LaBelle (Dady, 1993; figure 10.1).

Port LaBelle, located along the Caloosahatchee River in Hendry and Glades counties, is only thirty-three miles east of Fort Myers (figure 10.2). It began during the early 1970s on 31,000 acres of real estate, a site platted into more than 51,000 lots designed to accommodate a population of 129,000 (Gates, 1983; Stroud, 1985c). The new owner, having second thoughts about developing such a large project in a rural setting, amended the original plan and requested a change in the development of regional impact (DRI) agreement approved in 1974 by the local government and the Southwest Florida Regional Planning Council. The new master plan, if it is approved by government officials, will deplat all but fifteen of the original thirty-eight platted units, thereby removing 30,000 lots and 23,000 acres from the original development. AGC also requested that commitments they made concerning the development of commercial and industrial sites and the donation of land for schools and parks be removed from the original plan. The new developers hope to sell the 23,000 acres of deplatted land for approximately $2,000 per acre, to an agricultural enterprise for citrus production. One prospective buyer thinks the land is worth only $1,000 per acre, but no offer can be accepted until

Figure 10.1 Entrance sign at Port LaBelle
Source: Photograph by author

a decision has been made concerning the DRI abandonment request (Trescott, 1993).

General Development Corporation's approach to land development at Port LaBelle was strikingly different from the gridiron pattern of roads and canals and the extensive drainage of wetlands the company used at Port Charlotte. In fact, the performance of General Development in protecting environmentally sensitive land exceeds that of most of Florida subdividers of the late 1960s and early 1970s. The site was laid out in a curvilinear pattern, and lots were concentrated on environmentally suitable land. Much of the development took place on what was already cleared pastureland or on relatively dry, pine and palmetto flatlands. Approximately 4,000 acres of cypress sloughs, wooded or open wetlands, and other areas of valuable vegetation were not developed (figure 10.3). Roads wind around individual trees and oak stands, and vegetation between villages was preserved. From a land development standpoint, it is also important that Port LaBelle's

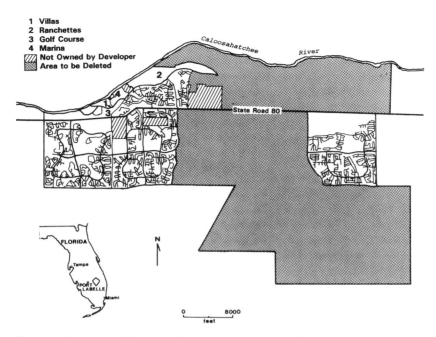

1 Villas
2 Ranchettes
3 Golf Course
4 Marina
▨ Not Owned by Developer
▧ Area to be Deleted

Caloosahatchee River

State Road 80

FLORIDA
Tampa
PORT
LABELLE
Miami

N

0 ———— 8000
feet

Figure 10.2   Map of Port LaBelle. "Area to be Deleted" refers to Atlantic Gulf Community's proposal to abandon plans to develop this portion of the project.

Source: Adapted from Southwest Florida Regional Planning Council files.

31,000-plus acres were from the beginning better suited for subdivision than the land of many other Florida communities. The terrain is higher, between seven and twenty-seven feet above sea level, and not so wet and swampy.

In addition, the company made a commitment to provide lot owners with more than roads and drainage, such as a central water supply, a sewage system, and a paved road to each lot. More important, the project is being developed in small phases rather than all at once. Development is restricted to 60 percent of the property, on a curvilinear street pattern, using a cluster design* that conforms to environmental

---

* Cluster design is a technique that allows the clustering of residential units on a smaller land parcel for each unit than zoning would allow for an individual unit. If, for example, zoning permits three units per acre but requires a minimum lot of 12,000 square feet, a developer's plan could be approved in which the units are "clustered" on individual parcels of only 6,000 square feet provided the density of three units per acre is maintained. This technique encourages innovative design and planning, saves development costs, and provides green areas and open space in common ownership for residents (H. Smith, 1979, 162).

Figure 10.3 Environmentally sensitive land left undeveloped at Port LaBelle
Source: Photograph by author

constraints (figure 10.4). As a result of these practices, Port LaBelle stands in stark contrast to older subdivisions that were platted on wetlands and that followed unsound land development practices (Daltry, 1988; Stroud, 1985c, 193–95).

With its inland location, Port LaBelle is far from Florida's widely publicized coastal growth centers. Hendry County, where approximately 75 percent of the project is located, has been one of the slowest growing counties in southern Florida, and its cattle population outnumbers the human population. Farming is by far the most important land use and provides the bulk of income for Hendry County residents. Although the site of Port LaBelle is more environmentally suitable for subdivision, many problems associated with population growth in such a sparsely populated section of the state remain unresolved. Some of the more obvious are limited job opportunities, inadequate medical care, and the absence of cultural and entertainment opportunities. Moreover, development has occurred in habitats of endangered species and in places that may be susceptible to flooding. Environmentalists are also concerned about the potential degradation of the quality of the water in the Caloosahatchee River. The company has taken steps to purify the site's runoff, but unless extreme care is taken, the subdivision could still have a negative effect on surface water quality (Trescott, 1993).

Figure 10.4 Houses in a cluster design, Port LaBelle. Notice the tree left growing in the middle of the road.

Source: Photograph by author

Port LaBelle developers used elaborate initial planning and followed development practices sensitive to environmental constraints but have not eliminated all potential environmental problems. The environmental impact of suburban-type development is so widespread that it is difficult to avoid certain environmental dilemmas, regardless of how much care is taken by the developer. Even so, sound land-use planning and careful site selection can avoid the subdivision disasters of the past.

Port LaBelle's consumer practices have not been nearly as good as its environmental protection efforts. As is the case with many other land development companies, General Development allowed a minimal rescission period (only three days) during which a refund can be obtained, and it stipulated that all monies paid prior to a default on a sales contract are automatically forfeited to the company. Moreover, there are many hidden costs associated with a lot purchase; fees for extending central water and sewer lines average $3,000 per lot, and there are property owners' association fees, property taxes, and charges for a lot survey and for a hookup to the water system (Dady, 1993).

General Development indicated to local officials that Port LaBelle would bring millions of dollars in increased tax revenues to the state

Table 10.1 Population Growth, Port LaBelle, 1975–1990

Year	Total Population	Percentage Increase	Percentage of County Population
1975	125		1.05
1980	786	528.8	4.23
1985	947	20.0	4.50
1988	1,250	32.0	5.30
1990	1,558	24.6	6.05

Source: General Development Corporation (1988); Gulf Atlantic (1993).

and local governments and that the company was committed to maintaining environmental quality. Because of these promises and because local officials were largely unaware of the widespread changes that would be introduced, General Development encountered little opposition to its plans. At the time Port LaBelle was begun, the Florida Environmental Land and Water Management Act had not been implemented and no other regulatory devices were in place to retard development (Williams, 1988).

Port LaBelle's master plan calls for the development of individual, self-contained neighborhoods, with each neighborhood providing land for schools, shops, and community services. More than 50,000 lots were to accommodate an ultimate population of over 125,000, with a portion living in townhouses, duplexes, and garden apartments. General Development sold nearly 4,000 lots during the first three and one-half years of operation, and by 1976 the project had approximately 130 residents living in homes built by General Development. Seven years later, more than 500 homes served a permanent population of nearly 1,000, and by 1990 the population exceeded 1,500 (table 10.1). Although the original master plan is being drastically altered, the sale of lots and the construction of homes continue, albeit on a smaller scale. As of November 1993, 716 single-family homes, 28 villas, and 32 condominiums had been constructed. These units could accommodate a population of 1,940. The time required for the project to reach its potential population is difficult to determine until a decision has been made concerning the DRI abandonment process. If the abandonment is approved, the developer will be selling only 21,000 lots rather than 51,000. Based on growth rates of the past, it will take an additional 400–500 years for 21,000 lots to be occupied and 900–1,000 years for 51,000 lots to be occupied (Williams, 1988; Trescott, 1993; Dady, 1993; Cottington, 1993).

The planning review of Port LaBelle, conducted primarily by regional planners, was mixed. Positive features include phased development, the suitability of the site for development, and the potential for the development of many middle-income houses. Negative findings include the limited water supply, disturbance of wildlife habitats, inadequate open space, potentially overtaxed schools and solid-waste disposal facilities, and the county's inability to provide health care, police and fire protection, and other community and social services. Even though the developer agreed to set aside land for schools, hospitals, police substations, and the like, obviously, a site alone does not provide public services. The two sparsely populated rural counties (Hendry and Glades) would be hard-pressed to provide them to Port La-Belle. Lot owners from urban locations could be unaware that even the most basic services—medical care, fire and police protection—might be unavailable (Allan, Kuder, and Oakes, 1977, 354–76; Trescott, 1993).

Although Port LaBelle is environmentally sounder than many other subdivisions, problems remain. One of the basic questions is whether there is a need for a new, populous community in a rural area with few jobs, small schools, limited police and fire protection, and a possibly inadequate water supply (Stroud, 1985c, 195; Williams, 1988). Atlantic Gulf Communities' request to drastically reduce the scale of operation at Port LaBelle is an indication that they are well aware of the many limitations posed by a remote location.

PART THREE

Land-Use Regulation of Recreational and Retirement Communities since 1970

The negative impacts of recreational land development are directly attributable to the lack of, or inadequate, land development regulations. The land development boom surprised many rural governments, which had no controls over land-use or development standards (M. Smith, 1987). In a survey of local regulations during the time period when a great deal of subdivision was taking place, over one-third of the respondents reported that their regulations were either "less than adequate" or "very ineffective" (American Society of Planning Officials, 1976, 99). Most regulations were not designed to manage large projects. And what some local governments call subdivision regulations are nothing more than simple platting laws, which require developers only to survey lot lines and roads and file a plat at the county courthouse (M. Smith, 1987, 5).

Another problem is inconsistency among land-use regulations. Some progressive counties have effective land-use management programs, while others have failed to move beyond the most rudimentary land planning. Many unincorporated areas have no planning or zoning at all. These inconsistencies indicate the need for mandatory environmental planning at the local level so that a balance can be established between the needs of the public and the desires of landowners (Schnidman, Silverman, and Young, 1978, 25; and Chinity, 1990).

In a county in Washington State, the subdivision regulations in place during the 1970s applied only to projects with lots smaller than twenty acres, so developers subdividing property into lots larger than twenty acres could avoid even filling subdivision plats. In one Colorado county, unsophisticated zoning techniques allowed recreational land developers to ignore environmental constraints. In one Oregon county, a subdivision ordinance, supposedly written to suit realtors, the county planning commission, and the state Board of Health, did not require developers to provide community water or sewer systems for lots larger than one acre (American Society of Planning Officials, 1976, 100).

Recreational subdivisions often bypass the metropolitan fringe and leapfrog into the hinterlands, surprising rural communities unprepared for rapid growth (Healy and Short, 1983, 112–20). Local officials, unaware of the full implications of recreational land development, have not taken it seriously. They have assumed that lots were being sold to distant buyers, none of whom would really consider moving to the "middle of nowhere." But while it is true that many of these subdivisions may never be fully developed, others may become real communities. Furthermore, although many believe that these projects will be only seasonally occupied and therefore have little impact on local services, and although developers often claim variances from local regulations on the grounds that seasonal occupancy creates less impact and less necessity for services and improvements, this may not be the case. And even though a subdivision is heavily occupied during only one season of the year, water and sewer systems and roads must accommodate users during peak periods of occupancy (American Society of Planning Officials, 1976, 100–102; Craig, 1991).

Changing attitudes toward unbridled growth combined with rising fiscal pressure and a desire by communities to exert more influence over new construction promoted changes in the ways communities regulate newly proposed development. Some communities now apply the same regulations to recreational subdivisions as they do to primary home subdivisions, including zoning, subdivision regulations, and structural and health codes. In addition to conventional methods, new techniques for analyzing and regulating development are evolving continuously and include environmental and fiscal impact analysis and flexible zoning controls (DeGrove, 1984, 1–7; Levin, Rose, and Slavet, 1974; Shultz and Groy, 1988, 597–602). But no matter what the regulations, some problems remain, due to a lack of staff at the local level. Even zoning, the most widely used local management technique, has been inadequate to deal with problems created by these communities (Fischel, 1990). First, local governments are often without clear-cut jurisdictions and may have a very limited understanding of the importance of ecological design and planning. Second, zoning at the local level is woefully inadequate to combat problems of statewide significance (Bosselman and Callies, 1971, 1–4; Popper, 1988). This is the case with recreational subdivisions, which usually have an impact of greater than local significance. This realization has prompted many states to implement statewide land-use management mechanisms (DeGrove and Stroud, 1987, 3–5).

The federal response to recreational land development has been limited to consumer protection legislation administered by either the Office of Interstate Land Sales Registration or the Securities and Exchange Commission. As a result, the federal government has had little influence over the location or the quality of recreational land development. But some federal initiatives, while not impacting recreational subdivisions directly, control land uses that may influence land development; the Coastal Zone Management Act, for example, significantly controls development along the coasts, and the Water Pollution Control Act has jurisdiction over any development that could increase sediment or otherwise pollute water resources. However, the cumulative effects of federal laws on recreational land development have been far more potential than real (American Society of Planning Officials, 1976, 114–15; Henderson, 1991).

Land developers build in remote locations because regulation is weak or nonexistent and most land is unincorporated and under the jurisdiction of county governments, which have not been particularly interested in land management (Platt and Macinko, 1983, 16). Historically, land-use decisions have been made by individuals, corporations, and government agencies ignorant of ecological design and planning techniques. To improve land-use policy, we need to ask, What should be controlled? Who should do the controlling? Who will pay for the controls? and What uses should be encouraged? (Jackson, 1981, 9–11).

One of the best ways to reduce the negative impact of land development is to establish a land-use management system that covers all uses of land and is applied to all regions, nonmetropolitan as well as metropolitan (Porter, 1986, 3–6). This system should preserve adequate land for growing food and fiber; protect land with scenic, historic, or other cultural value; restrict building in hazardous areas, such as floodplains and earthquake (seismic) zones; provide adequate recreational land; provide housing and community services for all citizens; reduce the pollution of land, air, and water through local planning and the proper location of industries and disposal sites; preserve fragile environments and wilderness areas; conserve wildlife habitat; reduce urban sprawl by maintaining and connecting greenbelts, greenways, and open space; and guard against land use that may be detrimental to the health, safety, and welfare of the public and the environment (R. Jackson, 1981, 11–12).

One issue central to land-use management is control. Who will make decisions and what policies and guidelines will control decision-makers? What uses will be restricted? Who will enforce these restrictions? How much control can be imposed on the use of land before the government, in effect, takes away the right of individuals to own land (Yearwood, 1971, 20–23)? These questions illustrate the complexities in establishing equitable land-use management (Arnn, 1991).

Seventy-five years ago, urbanization brought about a revolution in land-use regulation in the United States. In 1916, New York City adopted the nation's first comprehensive zoning ordinance. In 1922, the Standard State Zoning Enabling Act was adopted, giving states the power to delegate zoning power. Eventually, all fifty states adopted some form of control. Yet these regulations are far from adequate because of an absence of state standards, especially regarding ecological design and planning. In far too many cases, local governments have promoted development they considered beneficial to their jurisdiction, without regard for state and regional impacts (Pelham, 1979, 1–9). Too many planners, especially at the local level, are trained only in economics and engineering; if more planners understood landscape architecture they would be more aware of environmental-ecological problems and could alleviate potential difficulties from subdivisions with flawed designs. If we are to move forward to better community developments, environmental-ecological awareness is crucial. Unfortunately, designing and planning with nature is still a foreign concept to most local and state government planners.

11 Examples of Progress and the Status Quo

Throughout the history of the United States, land-use controls, if they existed at all, were implemented at the local level, but this approach to land-use decisionmaking is beginning to change. States and local communities are becoming aware that states are more capable than local governments of devising techniques and structures to solve problems of pollution, the destruction of natural resources, the housing shortage, and other such social and environmental problems (De-Grove and Stroud, 1987). By the mid-1970s, several states—including California, Florida, Hawaii, New York, Oregon, and Vermont—had passed legislation giving state governments a direct role in approving significant changes in land use (Swan, 1977). In some cases, the state's role was limited to critical areas, such as coasts or mountains. Given the rising concern over the environment and a general trend toward the centralization of regulatory authority, it was considered only a matter of time until all states had comprehensive land-use management programs. Even federal legislation to encourage state efforts was given serious consideration (Healy and Rosenberg, 1979, 1).

Colorado and Oregon require that local governments adopt regulations; there is a threat of state intervention if local governments fail to act. More than half the states have adopted land-use plans that assess land and water resources, project future needs for these resources, examine current land-use problems and government responses, and direct future growth. In addition, several states have adopted legislation to deal with developments creating greater than local impacts. Legislation in Florida, Vermont, and Maine govern large land development projects; other states have adopted an environmental impact review process. Unfortunately, many of these reviews apply only to such projects as road construction and public works. Some of the most significant regulations are those designed to protect areas of special scenic, natural, scientific, or historic value. These regulations help protect areas unsuitable for recreational subdivisions and areas that should serve the recreational needs of the public rather than being subdivided for private recreation. Some states have also taken steps to protect their coastlines, beaches, shorelines, and wetlands. These and other methods of land-use control are available for those states willing to take the necessary steps to manage growth and development before, rather than after, the fact.

The following discussion highlights the land-use programs in Florida, Oregon, and Vermont, all of which have made impressive strides in statewide land-use management, and in New Mexico and Arkansas, where state legislators have been reluctant to adopt comprehensive statutes.

Florida

Florida's history as a poor, sparsely populated state is important to an understanding of current growth management policies, processes, and attitudes. From the time Florida was first inhabited by Europeans until the 1940s and 1950s, it experienced little growth and economic development. Local governments were weak, fragmented, and ill-prepared for the rapid growth and development of recent decades (DeGrove, 1984, 99–176). Much of this development and change has been concentrated in the state's most unique and sensitive natural environments.

Actually, Florida's problems began more than a century ago, with the intensive settlement of delicate, low-lying areas. Growth and environmental degradation in these areas continued until an environmental crisis was proclaimed during the early 1970s (L. Carter, 1974, 1–6).

During the 1970s, as many as 25,000 people per month moved to Florida, attracted by its mild winters, hundreds of miles of coastline, and abundant recreational facilities (Healy and Rosenberg, 1979, 126). Land developers eagerly capitalized on these desires (Vesterby and Heimlich, 1991), and now Florida has more large recreational-retirement subdivisions than any other state and leads the nation in the number of subdivision lots. Over 2.1 million lots have been subdivided along Florida's coastal zone and other fragile wetland locations (U.S. Dept. of Housing and Urban Development, 1993). Although many lots remain vacant, the subdividing itself created environmental problems (Schnidman, 1987); in addition, tremendous environmental pressure has been caused by population growth. These threats to the environment have stimulated public interest in growth management and control mechanisms (Stroud, 1984).

In 1973, one of every seven new homes constructed in the United States was in Florida (Healy and Rosenberg, 1979, 127–28). Although growth slowed during the slump in housing starts, it resumed after only a brief decline. Growth has been particularly rapid near Orlando and Disney World, along the coast north of Miami, and from Tampa–St. Petersburg southward along the Gulf Coast. This concentrated growth is attributable to the warm winter climate, the ocean shoreline, and employment opportunities generated by an expanding economy. A substantial portion of Florida's new population is retired or goes to Florida for vacations, so they have no need to live near a center of employment (R. Jackson, 1981, 37). Recreational developments now occupy more than 1 million acres of Florida real estate, which has been subdivided into enough lots to house more than 6 million residents (Stroud, 1984, 14–15). Although relatively few people actually live on these lots, the potential is that they will. The speculative subdivision that has been going on since the turn of the century did not physically change the land ("paper subdivisions"). Today, however, in part because of federal and state regulations, recreational subdivisions build roads and canals, artificial lakes, and other facilities long before a large permanent population moves in. Such urbanization is a major source of environmental alteration and is premature, given present rates of home building and settlement. Such developments must be closely monitored to avoid environmental degradation and the misallocation of land.

The subdivision of wetlands and coastal areas demonstrates the conflict that can arise between private rights and public needs. The carving out of lots in these locations causes irreparable damage. The continued subdivision of fragile ecosystems and the scale of development in other areas of Florida, along with the seeming inability of local ordinances to control large developments, resulted in state action to protect Florida's land and water (R. Jackson, 1981, 35–41). State task forces, commissions, and committees have made recommendations and drafted legislation. These groups have been a major force in formulating a growth management system and in building a consensus to get regulations adopted.

The first growth management task force, appointed by Governor Reuben Askew, prepared and presented to the 1972 session of the legislature four major pieces of legislation: the Environmental Land

and Water Management Act, the Water Resources Act, the State Comprehensive Planning Act, and the Land Conservation Act. These laws and a companion law mandating that local governments adopt plans approved by the 1975 legislature were for the time (the 1970s) far-reaching and progressive (DeGrove, 1991; Outland, 1988). The most significant law was the Environmental Land and Water Management Act of 1972, which allows the state to designate "areas of critical state concern" and directs local governments to protect statewide interests if and when these areas are developed. The act also provides for state overview of large land development projects. These "developments of regional impact" (DRIs), which include gigantic residential developments (recreational subdivisions, in many cases), are regulated by a complex process involving local government, regional planning agencies, and the state (McCahill, 1974).

AREAS OF CRITICAL STATE CONCERN

Areas of critical state concern are defined as geographical areas with special environmental, historical, archaeological, and other significance of regional or state importance. Any person or group can recommend an area for designation, but the final approval, as mandated by the Environmental Land and Water Management Act, is the responsibility of the Florida Administration Commission (DeGrove, 1984, 116–17). The commission consists of the governor of Florida and six popularly elected constitutional state officers. The designation *area of critical state concern* is limited to the following categories:

—an area containing, or having a significant impact upon, environmental, historical, natural, or archaeological resources of regional or statewide importance;
—an area significantly affected by, or having a significant effect upon, an existing or proposed major public facility or other area of major public investment;
—an area of major development potential, which may include a proposed site of a new community designated in a state land development plan.

The regulation of these areas involves both state and local governments. Local governments have six months to adopt development regulations that comply with the principles established by the Florida Administration Commission. The state has the authority to take local governments to court if their enforcement is improper (Healy and Rosenberg, 1979, 135–36; Pelham, 1979, 99–100).

The first critical area to be designated was Big Cypress Swamp, a vast, virtually uninhabited wetland of ponds and grasslands located north and west of Everglades National Park. Big Cypress has been extensively subdivided in some locations. One land development company, for example, has carved out a network of unimproved roads and drainage canals across 113,000 acres of Big Cypress, scarring the land and disrupting ecological patterns. Other developments planned within Big Cypress would further degrade the environment. Big Cypress lies over an aquifer and is a source of groundwater for urban areas. Water from Big Cypress provides irrigation water for agriculture and surface water for Everglades National Park; it is the location of estuarine fisheries and related ecosystems that compose important commercial and sport fishing grounds.

In 1973, faced with the possibility of losing the swamp's vital resources, the Florida legislature partially bypassed the administrative process and conferred critical area status on Big Cypress (Pelham, 1979, 110–12). Legislative approval, rather than governor and cabinet approval, allowed a swifter designation and meant that the area would not count toward the 5 percent acreage limits. (The law states that no more than 5 percent of Florida's total land area can be designated as critical areas.) No more than 10 percent of a critical area can be disturbed, and only 5 percent can be covered by an impermeable surface. Development of mangroves and salt marshes is prohibited; also prohibited are finger canals and drainage works that allow fresh water to escape into the ocean (Healy and Rosenberg, 1979, 136–42).

Big Cypress Swamp, Green Swamp, and the Florida Keys have all been designated areas of critical state concern in order to protect a major wetland (Big Cypress Swamp), a groundwater recharge area and pine woodland (Green Swamp), and an area of historic and environmental value (the Keys). Apalachicola Bay, along the northwest Gulf Coast, was added to the program in 1985 to protect its estuarine environment. The state made the designation because the local government (Franklin County) does not have the financial capability or planning expertise to adequately protect the Bay. Guidelines for land development in these designated areas are clear and enforceable, and enforcement is controlled by the state through performance standards and a permitting system (deHaven-Smith, 1984, 416–17). Additional designations are not likely in the near future, since the state now requires each county to prepare a detailed comprehensive plan. Each plan should identify—and establish a means of protecting—environmentally sensitive locations. Current legislation allows the state to assign areas-of-critical-state-concern status to any county that fails to incorporate adequate environmental protection into its comprehensive plan (Quinn, 1993).

DEVELOPMENTS OF REGIONAL IMPACT

The developments of regional impact process applies to large projects and is one of the most important means of regulating large recreational subdivisions. Specifically, the act defines a DRI as "any development which, because of its character, magnitude, or location, would have a substantial effect upon the health, safety, or welfare of citizens of more than one county." Measures adopted and approved by the Administration Commission and the legislature in 1973 add specific content to this definition. The following projects may be designated developments of regional impact: a shopping center covering more than forty acres or providing parking for more than 2,500 cars; a power plan providing more than 100 megawatts of electricity; a postsecondary educational campus having more than 3,000 students; a racetrack or sports stadium; a housing development, mobile home park, or subdivision larger than 250 units in sparsely populated counties and larger than 3,000 units in the more densely populated counties; an airport; a large port facility; an oil storage tank; a high-voltage electric transmission line crossing county borders; a mine disturbing more than 100 acres annually; a hospital serving more than one county (hospitals of fewer than 100 beds are exempt); and a manufacturing plant or industrial park providing parking for more than 1,500 cars.

A DRI application involves the developer, the local government, a regional planning council, the state planning agency, and Florida's governor and cabinet; together, the governor and cabinet serve as the Land and Water Adjudicatory Commission. Local government plays a crucial role in this process, since there is no state permit at all and the developer's final goal is to obtain a "development order" issued by the local government. The local government, however, must adhere to a state-mandated process, whereby it is clearly stated what can be built and under what conditions (Healy and Rosenberg, 1979, 144–46).

A developer proposing a DRI must submit an application for development approval to the local government, to the appropriate Regional Planning Council, and to the Department of Community Affairs. The Regional Planning Council prepares an advisory report on the project's regional impact for the local government, and a hearing is then held by the local government, which approves the development, or approves it with conditions, or denies it. This decision can be appealed by the developer or the Department of Community Affairs; these appeals go directly to the governor and the Land and Water Adjudicatory

Commission. The appeals process provides for state override of city or county land-use decisions if regional or state interests have been inadequately considered (Thomas and Griffith, 1974; Burr, 1993). State legislation enacted in 1993 removed the appeal authority of the Regional Planning Councils, eliminating important checks and balances. Regional Planning Councils still have the option of requesting that the Department of Community Affairs appeal a particular DRI decision (Burr, 1993).

Unfortunately for the environment, the Florida DRI law contains a vested-rights provision that exempts development authorized prior to the effective date of the act. Furthermore, grandfather clauses are well established in Florida law and help to protect the rights of landowners who have begun development based on previous land-use laws. Vested rights are determined by the Division of State Planning, and its decision is binding on the developer and all state, regional, and local authorities (Pelham, 1979, 38).

Tabulations from the Department of Community Affairs' yearly status report on DRIs reveal some interesting statistics (Florida, 1983). For example, of the more than 390 DRI applications filed between 1973 and 1982, 272 were either approved outright or approved with conditions, while over 60 applications were withdrawn or denied approval. The overwhelming majority of the applications were for residential developments, but there were also applications for shopping centers, electrical installations, and so on. The greatest number of applications, 143, were filed in 1973–74, but applications dropped to only 11 in 1976–77, reflecting the economic recession and the downturn in the building industry.

After that, applications again increased, and in 1981–82, forty-two DRI applications were filed, concentrated in a few locations, with only thirteen counties having ten or more applications (figure 11.1). Dade and Hillsborough counties each had over thirty applications, with Broward, Orange, and Palm Beach having twenty or more. Many of the developments in these counties are being built in conjunction with growth in and around Tampa–St. Petersburg (Hillsborough County), Miami, Fort Lauderdale, and West Palm Beach (Dade, Broward, and Palm Beach counties), and in the Orlando area near Disney World (Orange County). In more recent years, DRI applications have maintained a relatively constant level, totaling between fifty and sixty each year. In 1990, for example, fifty-nine DRI applications were filed (D. Harris, 1991; Quinn, 1993). The large number of DRI applications by developers of massive residential settlements indicates the size of the land development boom in Florida when the DRI process began.

In 1973–74, more than 630,000 residential units were proposed, enough to house nearly 2 million people. The decline in applications by 1976–77 reflects the slump in home building, particularly those requiring DRIs (DeGrove, 1979, 137–38).

The planned residential community of Three Rivers typifies the DRI process. Significantly, Three Rivers was the first DRI case to be decided on appeal by the Land and Water Adjudicatory Commission. This project was to be built on 5,800 acres of land in Lake County some twenty miles north of Orlando. Its projected 18,000 dwelling units was clearly above the DRI cutoff of 750 units for Lake County. The East Central Regional Planning Council objected to the development because of its potential impact on the Wekiva River and on local public services. Despite these concerns, the local government issued a development permit. Convinced that the local government had not adequately considered regional interests, the regional council voted to underwrite an appeal. Lake County officials and the developer argued that the DRI process unfairly penalized large projects, but the Adjudicatory Commission voted unanimously to accept the hearing examiner's report, and the first DRI appeal ended in a victory for the Regional Planning Council. The decision made it clear to developers and local governments that the DRI process can be a powerful instrument in controlling land use (Healy and Rosenberg, 1979, 150–53).

Despite such success, the DRI process has some inherent weaknesses. All too often, the Regional Planning Council, being composed largely of local elected officials, has strong local interests. Since the Regional Council's recommendations are not mandatory, the local government may ignore them if they choose to. Only rarely does the Adjudicatory Commission overturn local decisions, although, as was the case with the Three Rivers project, it has the authority to do so (deHaven-Smith, 1984, 417–18). But although it is far from perfect, the DRI process has established an intergovernment relationship that allows local, regional, and state agencies to become more familiar with each other's needs and desires. Furthermore, it identifies and regulates the most pervasive types of development. Despite the complexity of the system and the many frustrations developers must face in obtaining project approval, some type of regulatory device was essential in Florida, which has experienced unprecedented growth, widespread environmental degradation, and water shortages. There is little doubt that the DRI process could be refined, but its present functions are crucial; developments of regional impact must be identified and regulated, which is important in a state with so many environmentally sensitive locations.

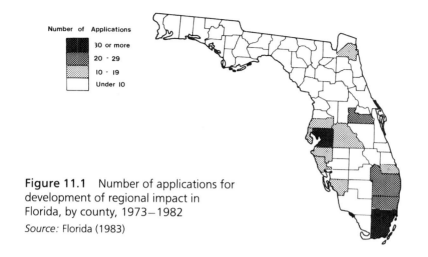

Number of Applications
- 30 or more
- 20 - 29
- 10 - 19
- Under 10

Figure 11.1 Number of applications for development of regional impact in Florida, by county, 1973–1982
Source: Florida (1983)

INITIATIVES OF THE ENVIRONMENTAL LAND MANAGEMENT
STUDY COMMITTEE

Florida's growth management efforts during the 1970s were only partially successful. Overall, the system did not deal adequately with the impacts of new growth. In 1982, in response to these shortcomings, Governor Bob Graham established the second task force to address Florida's growth problems. Referred to as the second Environmental Land Management Study (ELMS II) Committee, the task force comprised a cross section of interests, including all the principle adversaries. The committee's objective was to reach agreement on problems and solutions and, by 1984, be in a position to make recommendations to the legislature that, if adopted, would completely revamp Florida's growth management system. The ELMS II committee made several strong recommendations, and surprisingly, the legislature over the 1984–86 period voted virtually every one into law. The most significant recommendation was the Omnibus Growth Management Act, later renamed the Local Government Comprehensive Planning and Land Development Regulation Act (the law from which the concurrency requirement originated). Believing that many growth issues are too complex to be managed at the local level, the legislature designed the act to be administered from the top down. One of the main features of the act is concurrency, the requirement that infrastructure, such as roads, sewer, and water, must be available before developers can obtain the necessary permit approvals to continue development.

Unfortunately, the act has several significant weaknesses. First, funding is inadequate. Second, the administration of the act is too tightly controlled from above. Third, standards of performance are unclear and arbitrary. Fourth, the system is cumbersome and costly (Claremont Institute, 1991). Consequently, there is polarization regarding concurrency, the heart of the act (Ciccarone, 1991; Daltry, 1991).

Suggestions have been made for improving the act. Some of the most recent suggestions were made at a conference entitled "Fresh Thinking about Florida's Growth" held in Fort Myers in July 1991 and sponsored by the Claremont Institute of Montclair, California. The Institute provided a publication called "Ten Steps to Good Growth Management in Florida" with suggestions ranging from restricting government control of housing density to allowing the government only a limited number of days to rule on an application for development. The institute also stressed that the cost of environmental regulation should be levied equitably and that a development be charged only the costs directly associated with its building and not the costs of the long-term effect of population growth on traffic and infrastructure.

One of the most significant aspects of the act is that it made the Florida legislature aware that the growth crisis is significant, needs immediate attention, and should be addressed by all counties in the state. And, while it is far from perfect, the act does provide a growth management process. Its problems are attributed not to the "Growth Management Act and its ambitious objective of aligning public facilities demand with public facilities capacity, but to the failure of Florida and Floridians to face the obligations that go with growth and prosperity during the last thirty years" (Siemon, 1988, 1). Taxpayer revolts and no-growth initiatives are seen as possible if Floridians continue to ignore the disparity between their facilities' capacity and demand. Failure to face up to this reality will be tantamount to a failure to preserve the natural and human-made resources that make Florida desirable (ibid.). This position notwithstanding, the act in its present form undoubtedly has shortcomings, and changes are needed. Some planners and growth management experts are convinced that refinements and improvements will continue to be made (Daltry, 1991).

Efforts to improve growth management have continued into the 1990s. In 1991, Governor Lawton Chiles named the members of the third Environmental Land Management Study (ELMS III) Committee. This influential committee was charged with several important tasks, including recommending ways to improve the State Comprehensive Planning Act, examining the need for new legislation, reassessing the role of Regional Planning Councils, examining ways to make the system more "user friendly," exploring methods to improve the integration of the coastal zone management system into the overall growth management system, and recommending ways to strengthen the economic component of the system. The ELMS III committee made 174 specific recommendations to the governor in a report that is a blueprint for the changes needed to make the growth management system more efficient and effective as Florida continues its twenty-year effort to manage its growth (DeGrove and Miness, 1992). Since the 1993 legislature adopted many of the ELMS III recommendations into law, it is only a matter of time until the ELMS report has a substantial impact on the growth management process. Once again, Florida has successfully used a task force to build consensus and shape the future of growth management (Quinn, 1993).

Oregon

Oregon's land-use planning program is one of the most innovative and comprehensive in the United States. Its aims and objectives are expressed in nineteen statewide planning goals. Goal 1 ("Citizen Involvement") is to develop programs that will ensure citizen involvement in planning. Goal 2 ("Land-Use Planning") outlines the basic procedure of the program. Goal 3 ("Agricultural Lands") defines agricultural land and requires the inventory and preservation of agrarian resources. Goal 4 ("Forestlands") defines forestlands and requires the inventory and conservation of this valuable resource. Goal 5 ("Open-Space, Scenic, and Historic Areas, and Natural Resources") establishes the process for inventorying and evaluating resources. Goal 6 ("Air, Water, and Land Resources Quality") requires that local comprehensive plans be consistent with state and federal regulations. Goal 7 ("Areas Subject to Natural Disasters and Hazards") requires appropriate safeguards when planning development in hazardous locations. Goal 8 ("Recreational Needs") requires that each community evaluate its recreational facilities and develop plans to deal with projected demand.

Goal 9 ("Economy of the State") calls for the diversification and improvement of the economy. Goal 10 ("Housing") requires that each community plan for and accommodate a variety of housing. Goal 11 ("Public Facilities and Services") calls for the efficient planning of services such as sewers, water, law enforcement, and fire protection. Goal 12 ("Transportation") provides for a safe, convenient, and economic transportation system. Goal 13 ("Energy") requires that land use plans maximize the conservation of energy. Goal 14 ("Urbanization") mandates that all cities estimate their future growth and their need for land and to plan and zone accordingly. Goal 15 ("Willamette Greenway") sets procedures for administering the 300 miles of greenway that protects the Willamette River. Goal 16 ("Estuarine Resources") describes the types of land use and activity permissible in Oregon's twenty-two major estuaries. Goal 17 ("Coastal Shorelands") specifies how certain types of land and resources in the area bounded by the ocean on the west and the coastal highway (State Route 101) on the east are to be managed. Goal 18 ("Beaches and Dunes") sets planning standards for development on various types of dunes; residential development is prohibited, for example, on beaches and active foredunes. Goal 19 ("Ocean Resources") aims to conserve the long-term values, benefits, and natural resources of the nearshore, ocean, and continental shelf.

Unlike those of any other state, these goals bind all levels of government (DeGrove, 1984, 235–36) and are designed to ensure citizen involvement in all phases of the planning process. The program establishes that comprehensive plans will be the basis of land-use decisions and that suitable implementation ordinances (such as zoning) needed to put the plan's policies into effect must be adopted (Oregon, 1985a).

Why has Oregon taken such a potentially far-reaching action? One very important factor is the widespread feeling among Oregonians that their state has special natural features and that these should be protected. A beautiful, rugged coast, pastoral valleys, picturesque mountains, valuable timberlands, and the sparsely populated arid and semiarid eastern region are a valuable heritage and make the state distinctive. Second, Oregonians are determined to avoid the problems California has had with uncontrolled growth and development and its concomitant environmental degradation. Finally, the rapid loss of farmland in the Willamette Valley by urban encroachment helped provide the motivation needed for adopting a comprehensive land and growth management law (DeGrove, 1984, 235–37).

Oregon's program originated with Senate Bill 100 in 1973, which sets forth nineteen planning goals. Rather than vague statements and vague objectives, these goals are specific, detailed, mandatory, and enforced by law. Numerous adjustments and refinements have been made to the original law through subsequent legislation, which has reduced the power and force of the original bill (Oregon, 1985). For instance, the 1983 Legislative Assembly relaxed the standards for approving exceptions, opened the door for local governments and landowners to negotiate solutions to planning problems unforeseen by statewide legislation, and moderated the requirements for securing Land Conservation and Development Commission approval of plans (Nelson, 1985, 3–4).

Prior to 1970, the state's role in land-use planning was minimal, with local governments planning and zoning largely at their discretion.

Some counties had very effective plans and land-use ordinances; others had none at all. However, this inconsistency changed with Senate Bill 100, which specifies the planning concerns to be addressed, sets standards that local plans and ordinances have to meet, and establishes a review process to ensure that those standards are met. Compliance and review processes are managed through three organizations: the Land Conservation and Development Commission, the Department of Land Conservation and Development, and the Land Use Board of Appeals. Each city and county is required to submit its comprehensive plan and associated land-use regulations to the state Department of Land Conservation and Development for review. A hearing is then held before the Land Conservation and Development Commission. State approval of city and county plans is required by law, and those cities and counties that do not present their plans for approval are subjected to a much more rigorous review. After state approval is given, local governments need only consider their own local standards; compliance with statewide goals is theoretically ensured by the approval process (Oregon, 1985).

Oregon is, of course, experiencing development pressure from a number of sources: the suburbanization of the Willamette Valley, the subdivision of rangeland in the semiarid east, and urban sprawl and recreational development along the Pacific Coast (R. Jackson, 1981, 69–70). Problems associated with the subdivision and development of some of Oregon's most aesthetically pleasing landscapes for recreational purposes has been particularly significant. Recreational subdivisions, occupying over 95,000 acres, are concentrated along the Pacific Coast and the eastern side of the Cascades in Deschutes and Klamath counties. These land developments have been subdivided into more than 84,000 lots and range in size from less than 100 acres to more than 5,000 acres (U.S. Dept. of Housing and Urban Development, 1993). While Oregon's comprehensive planning is intended to combat some of the development mistakes of the past, the program has done little to remedy the problems caused by existing subdivisions.

Salishan Resort, which began in 1961, was built long before land-use planning and subdivision regulations had been established. The 600-acre resort with its two and one-half miles of ocean frontage extends south from the Siletz River along an active foredune and to the east up the slopes of the coastal mountain range. The active foredune, referred to locally as the Salishan spit, contains over 150 lots (G. W. Carter, 1985). Severe beach erosion has been an ongoing problem along the spit. Most foredune lots have been temporarily stabilized by riprap, a pile of large boulders, to reduce erosion and provide a buffer during tidal surges. But it is only a matter of time until expensive beachfront homes are destroyed at Salishan (Granger, 1985). Development of such an unstable site would not be allowed today under the comprehensive planning program; yet lots continue to be resold and homes built on them. Salishan illustrates the importance of environmental management and growth planning whereby sites suitable for development can be identified and places such as active spits, fragile estuaries, and other environmentally sensitive zones can be designated as open space or as unsuitable for development.

The implementation of Oregon's planning program has been slow, and it has taken over a decade for city and county plans to be written and approved by the state. Further, some Land Conservation and Development officials feel that too much power remains in the hands of local officials who "manage to find a way around the law when it meets their needs to do so" (Hale, 1985). Other problems occur because Land Conservation and Development does not have the staff to monitor land development and must rely on individuals—adjacent property owners for example—to lodge complaints when a violation occurs. According to an Oregon attorney specializing in land use, "county recording officials uniformly refuse to reject a deed that is in proper form, even if it conveys an interest that clearly conflicts with zoning" (Epstein, 1985). This practice permits the sale of substandard lots in recreational subdivisions even though they fail to meet land-use regulations. In addition, enforcement is expensive; or it is too late to effectively manage growth. Attention is now being focused on problems caused by the premature subdivision of land and the need for sound land-use practices for subdivisions outside urban areas (ibid.).

The implementation of Oregon's planning program has been a slow process; it has taken more than a decade for city and county plans to be written and approved by the state. But the passage of the comprehensive land-use plan was made possible when it became evident to a majority of the state's residents that land-use planning on a statewide basis is the most logical way to ensure that development will be guided in a direction that will provide maximum satisfaction of the needs of everyone. Oregon's governor was committed to environmentally sound land-use practices. Further support was provided by a strong environmentalist movement and by residents interested in the wise use of the state's natural resources. Such widespread support led to a comprehensive statewide planning program that can do much to effectively manage growth and development in the state.

Vermont

During the 1960s and early 1970s, Vermont experienced a boom in large recreational subdivisions and in population (Natural Resources Defense Council, 1977, 276; Bevins, 1989, 113). Growth in major Northeast cities like New York, Boston, and Hartford, and the completion of the national interstate highway system in New England, made Vermont attractive to recreational subdivision developers (Zwick, 1989, 117). Public officials became increasingly concerned about the impact of this recreational explosion on the state, particularly the commercial and industrial development that could occur in association with growth (King and Harris, 1989, 183–89). In 1968, the International Paper Company's proposal to develop 20,000 acres in southern Vermont prompted a large public outcry and extensive news coverage. Concerns centered on dramatic increases in seasonal populations; soaring land prices; the inability of small towns to provide utilities and such public services as road maintenance, police and fire protection, and schools; the loss of Vermont's rural landscape and picturesque villages; and the shift in political power when new residents outnumber local inhabitants (Blucher et al., 1971; Bosselman and Callies, 1971, 54–56; DeGrove, 1984, 65–94).

Ironically, during the late 1950s and early 1960s, Vermont actively sought industry and tourism. But the rapid rate at which growth occurred made residents become concerned about the quality of life in the future (Healy and Rosenberg, 1979, 40–43), concerns that led to the passage of the Vermont Environmental Control Act (Act 250) in 1970. In essence, the act provided district and state control of certain types of development and listed environmental and other criteria that these developments must meet. It also established a land capability plan, explicit land-use controls, and an innovative tax on capital gains from land speculation; it specifically addressed problems associated with recreational subdivisions by stating that "no person shall sell or offer for sale any interest in any subdivision located in this State, or commence construction on a subdivision . . . without a permit" (Bosselman and Callies, 1971, 59).

The act defined a "subdivision" as all tracts of land owned or controlled by a common entity and divided for the purpose of resale into ten or more lots of less than ten acres each, within a radius of five miles of any point on any lot. The act also provided protection against unauthorized subdivision, since it stipulated that the property transfer tax form, required with every property transfer, include a certificate of compliance with, or exemption from, both the Environmental Control

Law and Board of Health, requirements. Permits were generally required for residential construction of ten or more units and for subdivisions of ten or more lots (Byers and Wilson, 1983, 17–19). The law also provided stiff penalties, including fines up to $500 per day or two years' imprisonment—or both—for violations. Except for the transfer tax report for subdivisions, it was essentially self-policing, relying on private individuals to report developments that did not come to the attention of the state through applications to other agencies (Bosselman and Callies, 1971, 59; DeGrove, 1984, 71–74).

One of the act's greatest virtues was that it was designed to be more than a stopgap measure. As we know, legislation is often simply a reaction to events rather than a preventive measure. The focus of reactive legislation is often narrow and treats symptoms rather than the problem. Although Vermont's Environmental Control Act originated primarily in reaction to existing problems, it was visionary (Marshall, 1971, 10). For more than twenty years, the act, broadened now by several amendments, was a publicly accepted and effective project review process (Wilson, 1987, 1–13).

The review process involved several agencies, committees, and boards. Persons who sought to subdivide or undertake some other kind of development had to obtain a permit from district commissions, assisted administratively by regional coordinators who served as administrative officers. As long as they gave specific reasons for denial, local district commissions could deny permits if they found that the proposed development would be detrimental to public health, safety, or the general welfare. Before a district commission could issue a permit, it had to declare that the proposed development would not result in undue water or air pollution; would have sufficient water available to meet future needs; would not cause an unreasonable burden on the existing water supply; would not cause unreasonable soil erosion or reduce the capacity of the land to hold water so that a dangerous or unhealthy condition might result; would not cause unreasonable highway congestion or unsafe conditions with respect to highways existing or proposed; would not unreasonably burden educational or government services; would not adversely affect the scenic and natural beauty of the area; was in compliance with a duly adopted development plan, land-use plan, or land capability plan; and was in compliance with a duly adopted local or regional plan. Although few permits were denied outright, most were approved only conditionally. Substantial improvements could be required in a development's design by imposing conditions regarding sewage disposal, population density, setback requirements, erosion control, and architectural and landscape design (Bosselman and Callies, 1971, 66–68).

The district commission, instrumental in the regulatory process, was only one element controlling development. For example, a proposal for a 198-unit apartment complex was approved by the district commission but was successfully opposed by the local planning commission and selectmen (the New England equivalent of a mayor). The local planning commission extensively reviewed a proposal for a 9.9-acre shopping center, theoretically exempt from district review. However, the planning commission's approval with conditions was only an advisory opinion to local selectmen, while a district commission decision would have been binding (ibid., 68–70).

One of the primary reasons for implementing this act was to limit the proliferation of large recreational land developments, but its impact is difficult to measure. Whereas some developments were prevented and others were forced to redesign or alter their projects, the act was less successful in controlling small subdivisions and in restraining commercial strip development. These limitations were primarily the result of the "over ten acre" rule. The act applied only to subdivisions that exceeded ten acres or that platted ten or more lots (DeGrove, 1984, 95–98).

During the 1980s, Vermont evaluated its growth management program. Unlike several states that made administrative corrections to simplify the law and to coordinate bureaucratic procedures in hopes of defusing conservative critics, Vermont tightened its law. Two studies were made of Vermont's program, which resulted in a 1987 law that extended state regulation to developments with fewer than ten lots, thus closing a loophole developers had used to avoid regulation and control (Popper, 1988, 297).

Although the process seemed to work reasonably well, it was understaffed, underfunded, and addressed only about one-third of the development taking place in Vermont. As growth pressures mounted during the 1980s, it became obvious that the act could not deal with the cumulative impact of population growth and land development. Increasing concern over protecting Vermont's unique quality of life resulted in the passage of a number of laws between 1985 and 1987, including statutes dealing with groundwater classification, toxic materials, pesticides, water quality, and wetlands. But even the addition of these resource protection statutes to the existing act was not enough to solve many growth management problems. Continuing frustration with the act and the fear among local residents that Vermont was going to be exploited by developers from other states prompted the governor (Madeleine Kunin) to undertake a second attempt at state growth management (DeGrove and Miness, 1992).

On September 22, 1987, Governor Kunin, by executive order, created a Commission on Vermont's Future with the following charge: to plan for desirable and orderly growth, to create a statement of goals and principles for the preservation of Vermont's character, to provide for the preservation of agriculture, and to help create affordable housing and jobs for all of Vermont's citizens. The governor appointed a twelve-member commission, which held a series of public hearings to determine what Vermonters were concerned about and what they wanted to preserve. Based on the findings from these hearings, the commission organized its recommendations under the following headings: the planning process, economic development, natural resources, agriculture, and affordable housing. After much debate and some compromise, the law passed. The Growth Management Act of 1988 addresses such policy areas as the planning process, quality of resources, public and private investment, planning for growth, economic development, agriculture and forestry, planning for housing, transportation systems, and public utilities. It establishes a basic framework within which growth management is to function. The act requires from each municipality a statement of objectives and policies, a land-use plan and a map of present and future land uses, and a provision of community facilities and services linked to regional needs, identified by regional planning commissions.

Opposition to the act surfaced from a group organized as Citizens for Property Rights, which charged that private property rights would be taken away if the act were implemented and that the process was top-down planning and would ultimately shift most control of growth to state and regional levels. After much debate and some compromise, the act survived this challenge and was implemented. Compromises include a reduction in the number of goals and the inclusion of an option allowing municipal planning members to be elected as well as appointed. Although the compromises weakened the law, the alternative was to risk repeal. Proponents emphasized the importance of keeping the planning process moving even if the Growth Management Act of 1988 was not as strong as originally intended (ibid.).

In spite of the opposition raised by Citizens for Property Rights and others, Vermont's regulation of land is one of the most comprehensive and visionary in the nation. The permit procedure, performance standards, property tax relief, and a capital gains tax on land sales have produced substantial changes in the way development has occurred. The nine district commissions, each made up of three unpaid citizens appointed by the governor, is an important part of the system. The performance standards that these commissions enforce, being part of the law, have improved many projects. The act has been more effective in regulating recreational development and suburbanization than in retarding commercial strip development, but the emphasis is shifting. The act is now being applied to projects associated with the state's efforts to diversify and stimulate its economy.

New Mexico

Subdividing land into smaller parcels dates back to early Rome and Egypt. These techniques were adopted by Europeans and brought to the New Mexico Territory by the Spanish, French, and English. A federal land survey was done in 1858; all subsequent legal land descriptions have relied upon this survey (Anderson, 1968).

New Mexico, unlike Florida, Oregon, and Vermont, is not noted for its progressive land-use planning or growth management legislation. By 1600, the Spaniards had settled the part of northern New Mexico known today as the Rio Arriba, and so the power structure within these sections has been slow to change, because Hispanic people generally oppose state involvement in property rights (Carlson, 1991). And in the eastern and southern sections of the state, where ranching is predominant, resentment runs deep concerning county or state government interference in ranchers' rights to dispose of their land. These attitudes account for the lack of even modest land-use and subdivision regulations and permitted vast acreages to be subdivided without concern for water availability, liquid waste disposal, terrain, flooding, road construction and maintenance, and habitability (Miller, 1984, 4–5).

In 1960, New Mexico's population was 951,023; by 1980 it had grown to 1,266,600 (Wombold, 1979), resulting in increased demand for housing and land development. By 1990, the population reached 1,515,069, representing a 16.5 percent increase since 1980 (U.S. Bureau of the Census, 1991). Pressure for land development is compounded by in-state residents seeking new homes and by out-of-state investors (notably from California) seeking recreational facilities. These demands have made it highly profitable for developers to subdivide and sell their land in small parcels.

The federal government owns more than 43 percent of New Mexico's nearly 78 million acres of land. Despite these vast government holdings, more than 1 million of the 34 million acres of land in private ownership has been subdivided, resulting in the shifting of a large amount of acreage from agricultural and grazing use to urban or residential use ("Land Use Planning—New Mexico's Green Belt Law," 1968). This extensive land development has not been without problems. New residents and new communities have placed a tremendous burden on local governments and taxpayers. Because poorly financed land development projects fail to provide roads, water, or other basic services promised to lot owners, counties have been burdened with providing these services, paying for them through local taxes. Furthermore, many subdivisions have been abandoned after being partially sold out, creating a checkerboard of parcels and removing large tracts of land from beneficial use, like grazing. In view of these and other problems, the belief that growth and development pays for itself is no longer widely accepted in New Mexico; many residents believe that planning and growth management are essential if local governments are to guide local patterns of growth and land use in a responsible manner (New Mexico, 1984, 12–13).

Because of its vast tracts of relatively inexpensive land and comparatively weak controls on land use, New Mexico now ranks fifth among states in number of subdivision lots (more than 518,000). Thirty-eight subdivisions are larger than 1,000 acres, with some projects exceeding 200,000 acres (U.S. Dept. of Housing and Urban Development, 1993). Horizon's Rio Communities near Albuquerque, with its 240,000 acres, was possibly the largest recreational subdivision in the United States before some of its holdings were sold or passed on to property owners' associations. This massive subdivision was built largely without planning, environmental regulation, or controls.

New Mexico's first comprehensive attempt to manage and control land subdivision and sales in unincorporated areas was the 1963 Land Subdivision Act. The statute contained new advertising and disclosure standards and criminal sanctions against misrepresentations made in the sale of subdivided land; it also required that disclosure be made concerning water availability and the depth of water when only subsurface water was available. No performance standards or specific regulatory authority was provided, however, and exemption was allowed for subdivisions with fewer than twenty-five lots. As a result, counties approved subdivisions even if the developer did little more than prepare a survey plat map and stake boundaries (New Mexico, 15).

The 1973 New Mexico Subdivision Act provides for the involvement of various state agencies in the approval process. The attorney general, the Environmental Improvement Division, the state engineer, and Regional Conservation Districts provide advisory opinions to counties concerning disclosure statements, water availability, and other aspects of subdivision. Increasingly, county officials withhold approval of subdivision until all the concerns of reviewing state agencies are satisfactorily addressed (ibid.). This procedure allows city and county governments to guide growth in an affirmative manner in advance of development. Land-use planners are optimistic that this system of regulation will produce subdivisions that are assets to the area rather than burdens on the taxpayers.

Furthermore, the 1973 act defines a subdivider as any person creating a subdivision and defines a subdivision as an area of land the surface of which had been divided by a subdivider into five or more parcels within a three-year period for the purpose of sale or lease. But "a subdivider could divide land into five lots, sell four of them to a family member or a related entity, each one of such lots could be further divided into five lots, four of which could be sold over three years" (Miller, 1984, 6). If continued over a long period and practiced by numerous subdividers, this process could carve up a large number of lots, none of them regulated under existing statutes. Nor does the 1973 law govern subdivisions located wholly within the boundaries of a city or that were annexed by a city at the time of approval. The act also does not apply to the sale of apartments, offices, condominiums, or time-share units so long as no fee interest or division in land is sold or leased (New Mexico, 1984, 27–32).

A county can add subdivision regulations if the board of county commissioners feels they are needed. Unfortunately, very few counties have adopted regulations adequate to cope with environmental conditions. If a county fails to adopt regulations, statewide standards may be applied, but in many instances, these standards do not take local conditions into account. While most counties will not approve a subdivision unless the developer meets state concerns, some counties, eager to take advantage of perceived economic benefits, ignore problems and approve land development despite reservations by state agencies (Miller, 1984, 7).

There is currently no state agency with statewide supervisory authority over subdivision development. However, some monitoring and control is provided by the state engineer, the environmental health division, soil and water conservation districts, and the highway department. The state engineer ensures that water supplies are adequate for the proposed subdivision; the environmental health division tests water quality; soil and water conservation districts are concerned with watershed protection; and the highway department determines if the road network is adequate to meet the subdivision's needs (Martinez, 1993). The 1963 and 1973 acts both grant specific enforcement power to New Mexico's attorney general to require compliance by subdividers and the county officials who administer these laws. In addition, subdividers are required to file all disclosure statements as well as advertising and promotional materials with the attorney general's office (Miller, 1984).

Large-scale developers have a great deal of political clout and occasionally have been strong enough to stymie legislation that would hamper their operations. In 1972, a dispute arose over legislation that provides permits for domestic wells on individual lots and allows promoters to avoid the time-consuming and expensive business of acquiring water rights for the entire subdivision. A bill before the New Mexico legislature to limit water abuse at two stages in the subdivision process would require the developer to prove that water was available for the projected population prior to approval of subdivision plans. Furthermore, water quality and sewage disposal plans were to be approved by the director of the state Environmental Protection Agency. The developer could not sell any lots until all these stipulations were met. The bill would also have prohibited recourse through existing legislation. Since the current law granted permits for domestic wells without assurance that sufficient water was available, denial of this section would have protected consumers. Refusing the use of domestic wells would also have protected the water supply of established farmers and homesteaders. The legislation was simply an attempt to ensure that land developers could sell lots only if there was enough water so that lot owners would not impinge on water rights already established by prior appropriation (Wolff, 1973, 100–103).

Having the support of a number of groups, the governor recommended the new law to the House and Senate, but the bill was attacked by prodevelopment supporters, who added several amendments to the bill. Additional difficulty arose in the Senate, where an influential senator introduced a substitute bill that supposedly would accomplish the same objective. The substitute bill restored domestic well permits and omitted the authority given the state engineer to regulate water rights for subdivisions. After a third attempted compromise was voted down, the proponents of effective subdivision legislation let the bill die.

The governor ordered the Environmental Improvement Board to form a special task force to write a subdivision bill for consideration by the next legislature. The task force bill was enacted by the legislature in 1973, but the bill disappointed supporters of subdivision control; it grants the authority to control subdivisions to the state's thirty-two county commissions, each of which is to set up its own regulations. Critics argued that many county commissions supported careless subdivision activities in the past and are likely to do so in the future. The law also allows developers to shop around until they find a supportive commission, and more important, it does not apply at all to existing subdivisions, currently occupying hundreds of thousands of acres (Wolff, 1973, 100–109). This situation shows how difficult it is to pass restrictive legislation in a prodevelopment environment.

In spite of the many setbacks encountered by those interested in effective land-use management in New Mexico, there are a few positive signs on the horizon. Although there is no county planning or zoning except in urban areas such as Albuquerque, Santa Fe, Los Alamos, and Los Cruces, all counties have the authority to consider density in their subdivision regulations. Santa Fe County passed its Land Use Plan in 1980, establishing two-acre-minimum lots. Deviation from this density can occur only if the subdivider can prove there are sufficient water rights to provide water for lots of smaller size. And Torrance County encouraged a developer who purchased a dormant subdivision to replat the subdivision and implement clustering and open-space preservation to preserve water. The developer, who expressed interest in replatting at the time (mid-1980s), failed to take advantage of the opportunity to redesign the subdivision (Miller, 1984, 8; Miller, 1994).

In general, New Mexico has lagged behind many states in managing land use and subdivisions. Furthermore, it has neither comprehensive statewide planning nor state and regional environmental regulation. There is a need for dramatic improvements in growth management in New Mexico before other areas suffer environmental degradation. Clair Reiniger's (forthcoming) bioregionalism approach for the Rio Grande watershed is a promising beginning.

Arkansas

Arkansas, also, has not made substantial progress in developing a statewide land-use planning program and in regulating large subdivisions, although many residents and public officials have long recognized the need for them (Stroud, 1985a). The state legislature granted planning and zoning authority to municipalities in the 1920s and to counties in the 1930s and 1950s. Act 9 of 1935 provided for the establishment of state land-use and capital improvement plans, and other land-use planning statutes were adopted in subsequent years, including Act 246 in 1937, Act 353 in 1953, and Act 202 in 1957. Acts 353 and 202 were replaced by Act 422 in 1977 and its subsequent amendments (V. Jackson et al., 1979, 6).

Act 422 mandates that the county quorum court participate in the planning process, in creating a county planning board, in providing for the enactment of county ordinances related to planning, and in repealing all subsequent land-use planning acts. The county judge may create, with the approval of the majority of the members of the quorum court, a county planning board that would prepare a county plan and receive and make recommendations on public and private proposals for development. If a county plan is developed, it would direct economic development and reflect the county's development policies. The plan may also recommend the conservation of natural resources, the protection of areas of environmental concern, and the provision of adequate recreation, education, and community facilities. In addition, the county planning board has the option of regulating the location and size of buildings, open spaces, the density and distribution of population, and other land uses (West Central Arkansas Planning, 1977; Stroud, 1985a).

The act seems comprehensive enough to deal with growth management and to control all types of development. It authorizes local officials to establish plans and to enforce such plans through zoning and other devices. The latter are optional, since the act is only an enabling act, but county judges may, at their discretion, establish a planning board or take steps to see that countywide land-use plans are implemented. As would be expected, most counties have opted not to implement county land-use plans, let alone to zone unincorporated areas, which illustrates why statutes need to be followed by a means of enforcement—without follow-up and implementation, legislation is ineffective. An amendment to Act 422 resulted in additional limitations: Act 532 of 1981 prohibits the county planning board or the county quorum court from restricting or limiting the right of any person to file a deed or other instrument for the transfer of property (Bonner, 1984), thus reducing a county's authority to prohibit unplatted subdivisions and negating much of the regulatory authority provided by Act 422 (Stroud, 1985a).

Despite substantial growth and development in recent years, most counties have not implemented effective land-use guidelines. Counties and states tend to wait until a crisis before they implement growth management techniques. Although Arkansas's growth and development pressures are not as great as those in Florida and other high-growth states, it does have more than 310 active subdivisions, ranging in size from Hot Springs Village, which covers 60,000 acres, to extremely small developments like Whitewater, with only 230 acres. Arkansas ranks tenth among the fifty states in total number of subdivision lots.

Benton and a few other counties have established county planning commissions, but these commissions, with their limited authority and inadequate staff and funding, cannot effectively manage large land developments (Deen, 1984). Thus no government agency or regulatory body is authorized to scrutinize these subdivisions other than the state health department (Kirsch, 1984). Baxter County, for example, is experiencing phenomenal rates of population growth and tremendous subdivision pressure; Mountain Home, the county seat, grew from a mere 2,105 in 1960 to more than 9,000 in 1990 (U.S. Bureau of the Census, 1991). Subdivisions, particularly small ones, accounted for much of this growth. Twenty-eight projects of less than 1,000 acres each (5,200 acres in all) account for more than 10,500 lots.

Many local inhabitants believe that the growth associated with recreational subdividing will stimulate the county economy. But in fact, economic benefits may be offset by the cost of providing services to these subdivisions, especially if they are allowed to be developed without meeting certain standards. Subdivision roads are usually dedicated to the county, but if these roads are poorly designed and below county standards, the county must pay for improving them. Such problems prompted the planning commission in Baxter County to establish minimum subdivision road standards, which any developer must meet before the roads can be dedicated to the county (Hall, 1984).

In 1984, a forum on land use was held as part of a series of projects sponsored by Winthrop Rockefeller on critical public policy issues in Arkansas. Experts and leaders from across the state discussed problems associated with agriculture, forestry, water, mining, and tourism, problems ranging from soil loss and water resource depletion to the degradation of prime recreational areas. A recreational planner with the Arkansas Department of Parks and Tourism noted that "the areas of greatest scenic attraction ironically come under the most intense development pressure" (Rice, 1985). Haphazardly built commercial strips and housing units may spoil the very features of the physical landscape that draw people to the area in the first place. One participant suggested establishing an Arkansas Department of Natural Resources; another suggested a State Agency Coordinating Committee. Other participants proposed specific legislation to deal with land resources and ways to raise public awareness and support for legislation before it is introduced (K. J. Coyle, 1984).

Counties with a high concentration of recreational subdivision lots have experienced tremendous rates of population growth since 1970. Despite this, many county officials fail to implement a growth management system that could help preserve those qualities that make these counties appealing as recreational areas. Few of the state's land-use and planning acts have been successfully implemented. Apparently, a different approach is needed. First, guidelines should provide for the health and safety of Arkansas and for the public good. Second, land-use plans should infringe on individual rights as little as possible.

More than 1,600 Arkansans were asked in a survey to select the form of land-use planning they would support from among choices that included safety and sanitation controls, controls to keep the same land uses in the same areas (use zoning), and exclusionary zoning controls (regulation of uses that lower property values, for example). Safety and sanitation controls were overwhelmingly supported by Arkansans, and support for the other two types of control was higher than expected (V. Jackson et al., 1979), which indicates that Arkansans are not totally opposed to land-use controls. The key is to present a plan that both provides for the public good and allows individual owners flexibility in using their land (Stroud, 1985a).

Progress in land-use management will undoubtedly be slow. Some residents support certain kinds of land-use management, but there is widespread opposition to comprehensive land-use planning. Despite the many problems that result from planning after the fact, Arkansas will probably do as Florida and a number of other states have done—enact growth management policies only after a crisis has occurred. Arkansas is not a high-growth state, but it does have the second highest percentage of elderly of any state in the United States, and several of Arkansas's Ozark Mountain counties are among the fastest growing in the nation (K. J. Coyle, 1984; Schneider, 1987). Unmanaged and uncontrolled growth and development cannot continue if these places are to retain the characteristics that make them special.

There were no significant changes in Arkansas's land-use regulatory mechanism during the latter half of the 1980s. Apparently, government officials are content with Arkansas having no state-level planning legislation or planning department and inconsistent local planning. Nor are there indications that the state's land-use regulations will change any time soon. This is unfortunate, because land-use planning and growth management today could prevent a land-use crisis in the future.

The current controversy over wetlands and wetland delineation in the United States is particularly troublesome in Arkansas and indicative of the problems that occur when state and local officials fail to inventory land use, establish state and county land-use plans, and develop a land-use regulatory mechanism. When the Arkansas Soil and Water Conservation Commission asked a staff engineer to determine how many acres in Arkansas were added to the wetlands category as defined by the federal government's definition adopted in 1989, the engineer answered that "the information does not exist." The commission was also interested in how many acres would be lost from the wetlands category under the new definition proposed by the Bush administration. But the engineer indicated that numbers varied widely depending on the source.

The absence of a reliable figure about wetland acreage is only one problem Arkansans may face in the future. On the horizon are such issues as solid waste disposal, industrial pollution, water degradation and depletion, loss of wetlands, and developments that aesthetically degrade beautiful landscapes, especially in the Ozarks. While land-use planning departments and regulatory guidelines will not automatically resolve all these problems, a competent staff of environmental planners and landscape architects, as well as a rational planning and land-use process that accounts for ecological planning and design, would address many of these environmental, social, and economic problems.

12 Trends in Land-Use Planning and Regulation

Building Citizen Support

State and local governments often spend a great deal of time and money developing land-use plans and growth management techniques that are then ignored. Why have planning efforts in many states failed to meet expectations? A partial explanation is associated with the failure to establish adequate citizen support for the proposed programs. While many problems plague planning efforts, few are as serious (even fatal) as those that result when planners fail to obtain citizen support for their proposed land-use management mechanisms. Communities have wasted thousands of dollars on proposed courses of action only to have them rejected by voters. Such problems are not necessarily unique, but they are serious enough to cause significant setbacks when citizen support has not been cultivated.

STRATEGIES

Wilford Winholtz (1968, 546–76) suggests that the majority of people in a typical American community are not interested in what their local planning department is doing until they are affected personally. Effective communication is important if the planning department expects to build a coalition of citizen support. A variety of media can be used to reach the public, including the press, radio, television, public hearing, informal meetings, reports, maps, charts, photographs, models, and exhibits.

Unfortunately, planners often have little influence over the way plans are implemented. How can planners increase their power base so they can fulfill their legal mandate? The answer is related to the planners' approach; they need to be attentive to the special problems at hand rather than planning for planning's sake. Because they know where the data are, what questions to ask, and how to analyze the data, planners can influence the decision-making process. In addition, planners know who to ask for information, how to get a project approved with minimum delay, and what sorts of design problems to avoid. Knowing the ropes can be an important source of power. Planners can anticipate and counter efforts by those interests that threaten the planning process by misrepresenting cases, improperly involving authority, or distracting attention from key issues. The strategy used depends on the issue or the type of planning being done. In environmental planning, for example, this means making environmental impact reports intelligible to the public to improve public understanding and support (Forester, 1981, 67–69).

Frederick Steiner (1991) suggests several techniques for encouraging public participation in the planning process, including establishing task forces to deal with well-defined problems usually relating to a single subject; establishing citizens' advisory committees made up of groups representing local ideas and attitudes; holding workshops; polling the public to identify issues and set goals; and holding town meetings and public hearings. Barry Checkoway prescribes the following for enhancing the public participation in the planning process: establishing goals, setting priorities, identifying issues, educating the public, establishing relationships with influential people in the community, developing constituencies, and building coalitions (1986, 136–44).

Setting goals and priorities is essential to providing direction to the planning staff and to demonstrate to the community that the planning agency has a reason for existence and has specific objectives it is trying to accomplish. The Oregon experience underscores the importance of specific and comprehensive goals. The planning goals implemented by each county not only give the planning staff direction but also signify to the public that Oregon's planning staff will follow certain guidelines (DeGrove, 1984, 235–90). In Eugene, for example, no haphazard development has encroached upon the rich Willamette Valley farmland. Comprehensive planning goals—approved by the public—have achieved this. It is a welcome sight indeed to still see the separation of town and country.

Planners must address issues important to local residents and must attempt to resolve problems people face in their daily lives; obviously, planners dealing with issues important to large constituencies have a greater likelihood of successfully implementing their plans. Planners can also enhance their image by avoiding esoteric issues or highly technical theoretical rationales that few local residents even want to understand. Planners would be well advised to pay close attention to those people affected by issues and who can support planning efforts. Such support does not happen automatically but results from planners' efforts to identify these people and develop their support. One of the best ways for planners to obtain a group's support is to invite its members to select representatives to work with the planners. These representatives will help develop community support (Checkoway, 1986, 138–39).

Planners can, through a priority-setting process, make sure that planning is not misunderstood and mistrusted and that goals can be met through constituent participation. One of the most logical ways to involve the public is to ask interested constituents (consumer organizations, for example) to advise the agency about its programs. Experience shows that responses are often positive, if cautious. A workable system of information exchange can be beneficial to all parties (Barkdoll, 1983).

Samuel Stokes and his colleagues (1989) discuss ways private citizens can impact the planning process. As they point out, one individual can accomplish a great deal, but each person's efforts can be far more effective when the individual becomes part of an organized group, since a group can spread responsibilities among—and use the talents of—the whole membership. In addition, a group grows and changes over time as new members are added. With the proper timing and appropriate leadership, a group can dramatically alter the outcome of decisions affecting the welfare of a community.

Planning efforts can be greatly enhanced by an education program that provides a better understanding of the planning agency and its overall objective. Citizens cannot be expected to support planning efforts if they understand neither the nature of the agency nor the problems they are trying to resolve. Planners should help people learn about their problems (environmental, transportation, social, and economic) and the ways these problems can be resolved. Possibilities for education include public hearings, public service announcements, radio and television appearances, mass mailings, leaflets, town meetings, and personal outreach by staff and board members. Other possibilities include creating a speakers' bureau to facilitate board and staff presentations, conducting training programs, and publishing educational guides to develop leaders and activate citizens (Checkoway, 1986, 140–41).

Planners should not overlook the important role that community leaders play; these people are indispensable in helping a planning agency meet its objectives. They are interested in community affairs and are a source of influence when planning proposals need local support. Although there is no pat way of identifying leaders, planners should be aware of the importance of community leaders and cultivate their participation. Equally, perhaps even more, important are groups who exercise power and influence decisions. Planners should cultivate these groups and make special efforts to involve their leaders in decisions. Planners should respond quickly to requests from public officials, labor unions, chambers of commerce, and other groups with large constituencies. Further, they should help elect officials likely to support planning. Some planning agencies have specific strategies for building support among community leaders and public officials who can affect planning. One is to analyze power structures to identify influentials and then include them on governing boards, councils, and committees (ibid., 141–42).

Donald Craig (1991), planning director of the Department of Community Development in Lee County, Florida, stresses the importance of determining what is on the minds of the local population. His suggestions for making such a determination include workshops, mail and phone surveys, public forums, and video presentations that ask for letters and phone calls. The information gathered from these sources can be used to acquire a sense of the community. The planning staff would develop a list of pertinent issues, and community leaders would make sure environmental issues are on this list. Possible solutions are also listed, as are the planning department's goals. The people can then rank order these issues, solutions, and goals. By participating in this ordering process, the general population is more likely to support planning efforts. This citizen process is an extremely important part of rational planning.

THE CASE OF CAPE CORAL

Cape Coral has had a planning department for a number of years; its planners spend much of their time trying to find solutions to the problems created by the original developers. Since problems are so widespread, planners have a prescribed procedure for dealing with issues and for resolving the problems created by poor planning and development. These planners have developed techniques to gain citizen support for their work. The following committees participate in the planning process: the Citizen's Advisory Committee, the Architectural Review Committee, the Planning and Zoning Committee, the Historic Preservation Advisory Committee, the Building and Fire Code Resolution Committee, the Parks and Recreation Advisory Committee, and the Senior Citizen's Advisory Committee. In addition, the City Council is heavily involved in the process. While the original comprehensive plan was being prepared, for example, outreach to citizens was required. Fifty hearings were held during the preparation of the comprehensive plan. Each amendment to the comprehensive plan must be considered and approved in sequence by the Citizen's Advisory Committee, the Planning and Zoning Committee, the City Council, and state officials before going to the City Council for final approval (Generous, 1991).

Furthermore, the city advertises the need for participation and awareness. Planning meetings are held to maximize this possibility. Planners also talk about various issues to such citizen's groups as the Board of Realtors, the Chamber of Commerce, and the Kiwanis. There are notice requirements for zoning amendments. Planners also use the media (weekly radio talk shows, for example) and mailing campaigns. As a result, citizens are generally well informed and citizen participation is active. A large retiree population with ample time for involvement has engaged in heated debates concerning two of the more controversial issues, the dual water system and pretreated effluent pumping. Unfortunately, some of the hearings have become unruly. Threats were even made on the mayor's life after a meeting to discuss the merits of water independence for Cape Coral (Leger, 1990).

Cape Coral has had several unusual experiences with citizen support, some of them successful and others overwhelming failures. A major success was the passage of a general obligation bond in 1989 to raise funds to improve roads, water systems, and sewer systems. Planners set the stage for this bond vote through a mailing of a pamphlet to each resident explaining the proposed bond. The response was positive, and Cape Coral residents voted overwhelmingly to support the general obligation bond (Generous, 1991).

Other proposals were not as successful. One of the most significant issues is obtaining enough potable water to meet current and future needs. Although Cape Coral is situated over several aquifers, their yields are limited. The surficial aquifer was severely damaged by canal construction and pollution from septic systems. And the Mid-Hawthorne formation has been severely drawn down by excessive pumping. The Lower Hawthorne is now being tapped. Although water in deeper formations is expensive to reach and is more saline than water in shallower aquifers, the city has been forced to drill deeper wells into these aquifers where drawdown is not a current problem.

One possible option for dealing with this water resources dilemma is water independence for Cape Coral (WICC), an option proposed by the city's utilities director and others. WICC is based on the concept of a two-pipe (dual) water system that prevents people from using potable water to irrigate lawns. Although the dual water system failed to receive support from a majority of Cape Coral residents in previous years, the outcome of the 1989 city election indicates public support for the system. Four of the eight council seats were being decided, and the dual water system was the primary issue of the campaign, with candidates for each seat either supporting or denouncing the program. Only those candidates supporting dual water were elected. The 1989 ballot also included the following referendum: "Do you favor the use of reclaimed waste water for residential irrigation?" Sixty-six percent of the voters voted yes (Boyle Engineering, 1990).

Cape Coral has over 300 miles of freshwater canals throughout the city, discharging an estimated 58–274 million gallons of water into the Gulf of Mexico daily. Water resource studies have concluded that, although the "freshwater" in the canals is not a viable source of potable water, it could be used for irrigation. Most important, canal water could be used without extensive treatment and without the usual water storage system (ibid.). With a dual water system, estimated future water demand (when all lots are built on) will be reduced from 80 million gallons per day to 36 million gallons a day. The first phase of the dual water system, covering eight square miles of the city, was completed in 1993. Its use in this portion of the urban service area has reduced the demand for potable water from 14 million gallons a day to only 8 million gallons a day, permitting the city to delay expansion of water treatment facilities.

Local officials had to work diligently to build citizen support for the system, particularly since it requires an initial assessment charge of $1,500 per lot in addition to regular monthly fees. As one would expect, many residents considered the assessment exorbitant. The assessment is particularly problematic because a high percentage of residents are elderly and tend to be more concerned with short-term solutions than with long-term investments (Kiss, 1991). In addition, the organized opposition group, the OWLS (Owners Watchdog League), portrayed the system negatively. To build citizen support for the dual water system, utility officials, planners, and community groups made presentations to public groups, homeowner's associations, and church groups, prepared television shows, conducted radio talk shows, and sent press releases to local newspapers. Families for the Future, made up of builders, developers, and younger citizens, strongly supported the dual water system and mailed out a brochure explaining the benefits of WICC to every resident of Cape Coral. These efforts paid dividends, and residents approved the dual water system in the spring of 1989.

By contrast, the city failed to obtain the support it needed to implement a relatively inexpensive sewer system. The system, pretreated effluent pumping (PEP), proposed by the utilities director, was designed to provide relatively inexpensive sewage treatment. Engineers conducted feasibility studies and concluded that PEP was the best system for Cape Coral since the water table is high and much of the surface material is resistant coral-type rock that is very difficult for backhoes to dig. The high water table is a problem for gravity sewer systems, since pipes must be deeper and must be dug at grade (perfect slope). The deeper ditches (trenches) must then be dewatered before pipes can be installed. Consequently, a gravity sewer system is much more expensive than PEP and much more harmful to the environment (ibid.).

Planners, utility officials, and others worked hard to promote PEP, holding public hearings and making presentations to explain its advantages. The city assumed it had the support it needed from citizen's groups and the general public and issued a contract for preliminary work. The contractor even ordered some of the necessary pipe. After the city had invested well over $1 million on the initial phases, opposition began to surface. A citizen's opposition group was formed to fight PEP. Citizens for Gravity Sewers held meetings and press conferences, during which they labeled PEP a "Mickey Mouse" system and pointed out that the PEP system is largely untried. Worst-case scenarios were publicized, including the likelihood that raw sewage could back up into people's homes. Unfortunately for those supporting PEP, Citizens for Gravity Sewers did not have to substantiate their charges to influence public opinion (ibid.). Residents of Cape Coral rejected PEP in favor of a gravity system, which is now being implemented. The initial assessment on each lot exceeds $5,300, instead of the $1,800 that PEP would have cost (Generous, 1991).

Despite the lessons they learned from the WICC experience, Cape Coral officials failed to obtain the needed support for the implementation of PEP and proceeded with the project, assuming that local residents would support it. Unfortunately, this was not the case. It is not clear whether a better job of building citizen support would have made a difference. On certain issues, it may be virtually impossible to convince the general population that a proposed project is in their best interest. Such seems to be the case with PEP. Whenever the city offered supportive documents, the Citizens for Gravity Sewers countered with negative information—and even misinformation. As a result, the PEP proposal stood little chance of being approved. Sadly enough, city officials proceeded with a plan to implement PEP only to have it rejected. Such miscommunication between city officials and local residents proved to be an expensive lesson indeed. Not only did the city lose $1 million, it now must implement the more costly gravity system.

The lesson is clear: the successful completion of a project is unlikely without the support of the local population.

Beyond State Planning

Some states have adopted statewide land-use plans to protect environmentally critical areas and other resources (such as farmland), while other states have made little progress in such growth management and land-use planning. Most regulatory tools were not designed to manage large subdivisions and consequently ignored many important considerations; local governments often find their regulations based on legislation more than fifty years old. Many planners and local officials eagerly waited for the completion and release of the American Law Institute's model land development code, which was to provide invaluable aid in the modernization of state enabling acts. Completed in 1974, the code has not been adopted as national policy, and few states or local governments have implemented the code as part of their land-use planning programs.

Equally exciting to the land-use planning community in the early 1970s was the ultimate in land-use regulation, the National Land Use Policy Act, designed to provide federal grants (approximately $100 million annually in the 1975 bill) for states to draw up land-use plans, establish procedures for protecting environmentally sensitive areas, and regulate large developments. The legislation was introduced by Democrats every year from 1968 to 1975. In 1974 the Senate passed it by a wide margin, but the House rejected it when President Nixon withdrew his support (Popper, 1988). The bill has faded from the political scene and is unlikely to be reintroduced any time soon.

Despite these failures, there are positive signs, including federal acts passed during the 1970s: the 1972 Coastal Zone Management Act, through which the U.S. Department of Commerce gave thirty Atlantic, Pacific, Gulf, and Great Lakes states grants totaling about $16 million a year to plan for and regulate coastal development; the 1977 Surface Mine Control and Reclamation Act, which gives states $110 million annually in Department of Interior grants to regulate strip mining; the 1970 Clean Air Act, the 1972 Clean Water Act, and the 1974 Safe Drinking Water Act, which give states almost $3 billion annually in Environmental Protection Agency grants to carry out regulatory and construction programs with land-use implications; and the 1973 Flood Disaster Protection, which requires states and localities to regulate development in floodplains before they or their residents can buy federal flood insurance or receive federal flood disaster aid (ibid., 283; National Resources Defense Council, 1977, 18–132). These and other acts indicate that land-use regulation shifted away from the local control of the 1960s to centralized control (Popper, 1988).

During the 1980s, regulation reverted to state and local control, yet centralized land-use regulation did not disappear. The fortunes of centralized land-use regulation "ebb and flow depending mainly on the politics of the individual states, federal agencies, or land-use fields that apply it; but on the whole it is quietly thriving" (ibid., 296). There is more centralized regulation now than ever before, but this regulation is likely to be specialized, oriented to particular purposes, rather than comprehensive (ibid.; Brower and Carol, 1987, 1–6). This is not to imply that the specialized approach is less effective than the comprehensive approach. Although Florida adopted its comprehensive Growth Management Act in 1985, the state is having numerous problems with implementation (Arnn, 1991), due to inadequate funding, unequal enforcement, and polarization between proponents and opponents (Ciccarone, 1991). New Jersey, on the other hand, has managed land use effectively with its single-purpose laws (Popper, 1988). There are state-required and state-reviewed local regulations; regional control of the pinelands, urban areas, and high-growth regions; and state laws regarding protection from hazardous waste and protection of coastal zones, wetlands, and farmlands (Duerksen, 1983, 218–19; Popper, 1988, 297). Single-purpose legislation is likely to be more palatable to the general population and may receive less opposition than all-encompassing legislation.

Dealing with Special Problems

Much environmental legislation has been passed since the publication of Rachel Carson's *Silent Spring* in 1962, and many methods are available to improve land-use management. But few regulations have been specific enough to deal with the vexing problems associated with growth management. During the 1970s, several seminal articles outlined innovative possibilities for controlling growth. A good example is Robert Freilich's "Development Timing, Moratoria, and Controlling Growth," (1974), in which he suggests dividing growth controls into short-term controls, long-term controls, permanent controls, and federal and state controls (147–51). Short-term controls can halt development until the planning process is completed. Many stop-growth or freeze-growth ordinances are, however, nothing more than interim controls that protect the planning process during the implementation stage, prevent new nonconforming use, and promote public debate. Short-term control can be initiated by a temporary ordinance preventing additional development until the planning process is finished and permanent controls established (ibid., 151–54).

Long-term controls include timing and sequential controls; subdivision regulations; public acquisition of land (land banking); urban and rural service areas; bonus, incentive, and conditional zoning; and development rights transfers. These and other options may be necessary to deal with the problems of urbanization, urban sprawl, and uncontrolled land subdivision in rural locations (ibid., 150). The concept of timing and sequential controls, one of the most important long-term options, requires that development proceed only in conjunction with the provision of municipal services. This control mechanism requires an ordinance stating that development must be coordinated with provision of adequate municipal facilities and that developers must obtain a permit before proceeding with development (ibid., 162–63).

Permanent controls include regulations covering wetlands, floodplains, and coastlines; large-lot zoning; mobile home restrictions; minimum floor-area regulations; and population density regulations. Some cities, concerned about explosive population growth and diminishing resources, have even placed absolute limits on population. Boulder, Colorado, Boca Raton, Florida, and Petaluma, California, have adopted ordinances establishing an upper limit on their populations. Such limits have been hotly contested, and most have failed when contested in court (ibid., 191–211; Porter, 1986, 25–31). Many techniques are available for controlling growth; the problem is not lack of options but apathy and reluctance on the part of government officials to address issues likely to trigger political opposition (Freilich, 1974, 191–217). Officials are often perplexed over ways to implement growth management mechanisms, but criteria exist for establishing better land-use policies and a framework within which these criteria can be implemented (Steiner, 1991).

In their *Land Use and the States*, Robert Healy and John Rosenberg (1979, 248–58) provide five criteria for land-use policies. First, they suggest that "power over land be lodged with the level of government appropriate to the problem." This suggestion addresses the need to break away from the tradition of local land-use planning and control; many land-use decisions need to be made at regional, state, or even national levels. While local governments should continue to make most land-use decisions, the state needs to make decisions in cases where nonlocal interests are at stake. These include decisions about developments of state or regional impact, development in unregulated areas, and developments affecting or affected by major state investments. For example, to help clean up the Chesapeake Bay, Virginia farmers in the upper reaches of the Shenandoah River watershed, well over 100 miles away, may soon be regulated to ensure proper soil conservation and water pollution abatement measures.

Second, "the state decision process should be open and 'political'" to include all land users in the process. Although the political process is far from perfect, it is the institution best suited for making these decisions. Land-use policy will succeed only if it is open to public participation and scrutiny. Third, "effective controls require a clear definition of goals and knowledge about how the land resource relates to those goals." For example, Oregon's nineteen major goals represents an important part of the state's highly acclaimed planning program. The setting of goals should be followed by establishing the land uses that will help achieve them. Fourth, "land-use controls need not await the adoption of comprehensive plans." Fifth, "land policies should promote desirable forms of development as alternatives to those which do environmental or social damage." This can be accomplished without retarding economic growth: development can be encouraged in areas that are not environmentally sensitive, where they will not overtax services or destroy the character of the community.

For states with a high concentration of recreational development, the regulatory process is more complicated. Few controls introduced during the 1960s and 1970s were designed to resolve problems created by recreational subdivision (Reilly, 1973, 24–31). The development of recreational communities should not be prevented as long as they create livable and ecologically sound amenity settlements. Problems arise from large-scale lot sales operations where the creation of actual new communities is unlikely. Sporadic attempts to control such development have generally been unsuccessful. William Reilly's suggestions for managing their growth include requiring developers to meet the same environmental and land-use standards applied to first-home developments. In other words, local governments should establish subdivision requirements that ensure that all projects, permanent and seasonal, meet development standards. Steps should then be taken to prohibit lot sales in unsuitable places.

State and federal laws regarding full disclosure should be amended to provide lot buyers a nonwaivable cooling-off period of thirty days (rather than the present two to seven days), and it should apply whether the buyer has made an on-site visit or not. In addition, federal securities legislation should be amended so that the sale of lots in any project with more than fifty lots be considered a securities transaction. Such legislation would also require a prospectus and other specifications of the Securities and Exchange Commission. Since full disclosure regulations are inadequate for the inexperienced buyer, federal and state legislation should obligate the developer to guarantee to each property owner that lots will be made suitable for building on a specific date—and no later than the date the lot owner receives title to the lot. Furthermore, a portion of a lot buyer's payments should be deposited in escrow to ensure that the seller fulfills his obligations. These funds would be available for construction of promised improvements if they are not provided by the developer (ibid., 30–31). If implemented as part of a statewide or nationwide regulatory plan, these suggestions should promote viable new communities and retard development of raw land for speculation.

Some of the most difficult land-use problems are associated with subdivisions platted years before any land-use control and environmental and consumer protection guidelines were established. Many of these older subdivisions were inadequately planned and poorly designed, development was scattered, and land-use practices were unsound. Once roads, canals, and dredging and filling have destroyed thousands of wetland acres, it is ridiculous and ineffective to require a master plan and sound development practices. Older subdivisions must be reviewed on a case-by-case basis by county officials, in conjunction with establishing county development tolerance zones. Thus the degree to which particular developments are in compliance with these zones could determine whether corrective measures are needed. For example, if a developer has destroyed vital wetlands, the county should consider rezoning the property and restoring the drainage system to its predevelopment condition (Melinsky and Maier, 1980).

Antiquated subdivisions were approved under regulations that are inadequate by today's standards (Bergeson and Glickfield, 1987). These platted lands are a major concern because of their size and number and because a majority were approved prior to environmental impact considerations and review and permitting procedures. Platting is the formal process by which subdivision maps are recorded with appropriate local officials. Since the platted lands in subdivisions are so gigantic, it will be extremely difficult for local governments to make services available as homes are built on these lands. And if existing roads and canals are not maintained, they will deteriorate and need restoration. These roads and canals were often poorly designed in the first place, so the cost of bringing them up to current standards would be substantial.

Water can be polluted by septic systems installed in unsuitable soil or on lots too small for the drainage system. Unless sewers are provided, building permits may have to be denied. Another concern is meeting rising demands for potable water from a limited supply. These are only a few of the problems that may result when vast tracts of land are prematurely committed to single-family detached homesites in what are supposed to be recreational-retirement communities. Because this land is preempted from alternative use, other developers use other tracts of land to meet the demand, leaving much of the older subdivided lands vacant (Schnidman, 1984, 21–22).

In their monograph, Frank Schnidman and R. Lisle Baker (1985, 508–97) provide several options for dealing with some of the problems created by older subdivisions, including restricting the use of existing platted lands, controlling the timing and location of development within platted lands, requiring impact fees, reassembling platted lands, restoring some areas in whole or part to a natural condition, and promoting government-developer negotiations (1983, 508–97). The following discussion examines some of the difficulties in implementing these suggestions.

Some older subdivisions may have areas that should be developed only if specific conditions are met, and thus it may be useful to delay development until these improvements are made. In fact, it would be better to declare a moratorium on development than to allow irreparable damage. Some areas should not be developed at all, either because services are unavailable or because the land is ecologically fragile. In this case, it would be better to cluster development in a small area and leave other areas undeveloped (Schnidman, 1984, 24). Restricting the development of platted lands might also be accomplished by rezoning them to a lower density.

Individual lot owners, of course, may protest if their homesites are rendered unbuildable and claim they have vested rights that protect them from a change in the zoning. But when rezoning power has been contested in the courts, local governments have won (*Euclid v. Ambler Realty Company*, 272 U.S. 365, 1926). In certain situations, however, landowners may have the right to develop their land even though zoning changes have been made. Grandfathering is technically referred to as *vested rights,* or *estoppel.* Actually, the question is whether platted lots are protected from a change in minimum size. In Florida, municipalities cannot rezone if it is inequitable to property owners (Schnidman and Baker, 1985, 532–34).

Another means of restricting use is through the issuance of special permits, which allow local governments to control a particular kind of development in a specific location (in residential zones for example). Or a ban may be placed on a particular type of development or building for a limited time. If restriction of land use is not permissible, a feasible option may be acquiring the land through purchase or through the power of eminent domain (ibid., 549–50).

Rather than restricting use, it may be better to require that development be phased to coincide with provision of services. Building would be banned in areas where services are not provided, and a timetable would be established for the provision of facilities and services as they are needed. Impact fees force developers to pay a portion of the costs of development and allow local governments to cover the cost of the capital improvements caused by new development (impact fees are currently being levied in many Florida counties). The use of some form of taxation may also provide income, although this method is often more appropriate for undeveloped areas (ibid., 553–62). Finally, statutory authority could be given to state and local governments so they can pay for such basic services as hospitals, fire protection, and water supply (see, for example, O'Keefe, 1972, 837–39; Juergensmeyer and Blake, 1981; McMahan, 1978, 1211–15).

Recombining platted lands may be desirable if much of the subdivision has remained unbuilt for a number of years and if existing lot lines block more reasonable uses of the land. Reassembling platted land may be accomplished through deplatting and eminent domain. Deplatting can be initiated by the local government if the plats have been recorded for five years and if not more than 10 percent of the total area has been sold. A vacating order must conform to the comprehensive plan and must be done only to promote the public welfare. Deplatting can be done through cluster zoning and transferable development rights. Land may be reassembled through eminent domain but only if the property to be taken is for "public use" and only upon payment of "just compensation" (Schnidman and Baker, 1985, 566–90).

In wetlands where environmental degradation has occurred, partial or complete restoration of the land could have many positive effects. The damming of selected canals would allow the land to recover, even if slowly and only partially, from the destruction caused by development. Full restoration of a wetland would increase groundwater recharge and wildlife habitat and reduce salinization and contamination of water (ibid., 590–93). Negotiations between government officials and developers are possible because a number of developers continue to have a vested interest in their projects. Developers' involvement may be the ownership of lots that have been platted but not sold or of property that has not been subdivided; or they may be committed to the provision of services and other facilities. When developers have something at stake, they may be willing to negotiate with governments and to take action voluntarily to delay more restrictive action. This could be one of the easiest ways to obtain significant changes in subdivision design (ibid., 593–94). The selection of the specific regulatory device should be based on the specific problem, because there can be legal ramifications. Wise decisions can be made only after an understanding of the problem, of the needs of the local community, and of the ramifications of the regulation.

By following a specific sequence of action, state and local officials can establish an efficient land-use management mechanism. It would be beneficial if all levels of government were involved in the regulatory process, with much of the actual guidance and control being handled at the local level. State governments should provide local governments with sufficient funds and enact statutes that give local governments the financial means and the authority to address the problems. After counties are provided with the necessary authority and funding, they should establish a department of land-use management and environmental planning, or some comparable agency (assuming one does not already exist) to manage land development. This department would prepare and implement guidelines for comprehensive land management designed to prevent the land-use legacies of the past.

First, the department should require developers to file an intent-to-develop application. This application would indicate what steps are necessary for the development to receive approval of its proposed project. Second, the developer should complete a master plan and environmental impact statement so the department can decide on the feasibility of the project. Developers should then be required to adhere to sound land-use practices and ecological design, such as developing in phases, that will protect both the environment and the inhabitants of these subdivisions. Developers should protect sources and limit water use to an environmentally safe yield. Last, developers should provide services prior to lot sales (as Florida now requires with its concurrency regulation) and restrict the sale of lots to developed segments. Developers' advertisement claims, sales practices, and other consumer issues should be closely monitored. Local agencies would submit information received from developers to the new department of land-use management for review. This department would assist counties when necessary and obtain federal assistance from appropriate agencies when warranted.

These suggestions, if followed, could greatly reduce the negative impact of recreational subdivision and assist in attaining sound land-use practices and ecological design. Without such a framework for monitoring land use and design, abuse and mismanagement will undoubtedly continue. Since the potential for environmental devastation is so great, much thought and consideration should be given by local, state, and federal officials before they allow vast acreages of land to be irretrievably subdivided years or decades prior to its expected use.

Coping with Red Tape

There is a growing concern among developers and some local officials over extended delays and substantial cost increases attributable to the regulatory process (Brower and Carol, 1987, 3–4). Some developers view planning mechanisms as formidable. This is the basic conservative perspective adhered to by many Americans. They argue that land-use initiatives create centralized regulatory mechanisms and that since the 1970s the nation has had too much federal regulation of land use (Popper, 1988, 291).

The concerns of planners, town managers, and developers were expressed in journals and monographs during the late 1970s. The following titles indicate the concerns associated with too much regulation: "Developing in a Hostile Environment," "Tips on Cutting the Delays of Regulation," *The Permit Explosion,* and "Development Regulations Must be Reasonable." These publications suggest how developers can deal with the regulatory process and point out that regulations often cause long delays, cost increases, and greater risks (Nahas and Eskind, 1978; So, 1978; Bosselman, Feurer, and Siemon, 1975; Geiler, 1976). A land development company in California could obtain all the permits for a project in only ninety days during the mid-1960s (Geiler, 1976). By 1975 the same company took more than two years to receive permission to build a similar project. The company's director of legal services found thirty-two types of regulation—each of which contain other areas of regulation—applicable to the use and development of privately owned land in southern California. The controls involve the environment, energy, planning, zoning, subdividing, economic impact, taxation, politics, and disclosure (ibid., 3). These controls were partially the result of reactions to problems caused by uncontrolled growth in previous years.

If developers designed and planned well and served their customers fairly and honestly, there would be no need for regulation. But after years of developer abuse, many states have developed an elaborate regulatory framework. Have these regulatory devices gone too far? Are the negative aspects—delays, cost increases, and greater economic risks—too high a price to pay for land-use management (see, for example, Patrick, 1991)? Are middle-income and lower-income families being priced out of the housing market because of regulatory delays? These are arguments against complex permitting procedures. The solution probably lies in a compromise between developers and regulatory agencies (Plotkin, 1987). A successful regulatory system utilizes the highest possible standards, implements appropriate regulations, encourages developer flexibility, and streamlines the process. But developers must accept some delay and cooperate with regulatory authorities throughout the process in order to achieve a good environmental design. Success is no longer based on location, location, location but rather on location, product, and management (Geiler, 1976, 4): today's more sophisticated clientele demand much more than a good location. Their demands are partly responsible for real estate ventures that sell a complete package of services, amenities, and housing in communities managed by the developer or a property owners' association. Some of these recreational-retirement communities are now incorporated cities.

The complexity of the regulatory process and the need for simplification prompted several scholars to explore how planning and regulatory agencies can streamline the process. Suggestions include coordinating state permitting programs, establishing development impact committees to review development proposals, reducing the number of government levels involved, and expanding local permitting authority. Although reducing the number of government agencies involved can be beneficial in some situations, the centralization of development decisions at either the state or local level has significant disadvantages; furthermore, delegation of all authority over land-use issues to a single agency is unrealistic because of the complexity of the issues and the variations in political institutions. The aim is to simplify the process and at the same time improve the quality of development—that is, to make the system both fair and efficient (Bosselman, Feurer, and Siemon, 1975; Connerly, 1986; DeGrove, 1991; Lynch, 1990; Scott, 1975).

Frank So (1978), a deputy director of the American Society of Planning Officials, discusses several possibilities for reducing the delays: first, make local ordinances easy to read and understand; second, consolidate all local ordinances that deal with development into one ordinance; third, develop a form that includes all relevant information on local regulations; fourth, have all permits filed at one location; and fifth, assign one person to be an ombudsman, or permit expediter. *Streamlining Land Use Regulation: A Guidebook for Local Governments,* by John Vranicar, Welford Sanders, and David Mosena (1980) also addresses the red tape in land development regulation. The relationship between delays and the cost of housing is a major reason for simplifying the regulatory process by streamlining the preapplication and staff review stages; clarifying the ground rules, plans, ordinances, and review procedures; and putting reforms into action (1–74). Suggestions range from fast-tracking applications and reducing public hearing backlogs to establishing an approval system for routine cases.

Windsor, a small town in Connecticut, provides a good example of how to reduce regulatory red tape. In this town, a staff development team meeting is held for each developer proposing a project. The team consists of the town engineer, the environmental health officer, the public works director, the building inspector, and the fire marshal. This meeting eliminates the necessity for the developer to meet individually with each department, provides the developer with all the information he or she needs, and familiarizes town officials with all aspects of the proposed development. This approach moves away from the uncoordinated individual staff review process, which often emphasizes negative restrictions, and allows the developer to become a member of the problem-solving group. The result has been fewer enforcement problems, fewer lawsuits, and greater cooperation between developers and local officials (Ilg, 1974).

13 Fulfilling the Promise

Land development for recreational-retirement communities has created numerous economic and environmental problems. Although the era of the unwieldy, uncontrolled land development corporation that subdivided vast tracts of land has largely passed, many unresolved issues remain. As U. S. Congressman Morris K. Udall said, "the installment land-sales business bears little resemblance to the traditional and honorable real estate transaction, where a well-informed buyer deals on an even footing with a locally based firm for a clearly identified parcel of land. Increasingly, the business has degenerated into an updated version of the old snake-oil racket, sold by the acre instead of the bottle. Companies aim for volume sales, not development, and this goal has created a built-in incentive to over-promise; once the contract is signed and the paper is peddled to a finance company, the promoter's only incentive to carry through on promises is tough, persistent, even nagging regulatory efforts" (Allan, Kuder, and Oakes, 1976, vii–viii).

The recreational subdivision industry has been plagued by many negative features: selecting the wrong locations for development, using deceptive or fraudulent promotional practices, ignoring environmental constraints, and failing to provide even the most basic services to lots. Many sites were developed not because of their suitability but because they were available at a cheap price and because there were few regulations in place to control development. Not surprisingly, few people wanted to buy vacation homesites in these locations, so demand had to be created through elaborate promotional schemes.

Moreover, many locations selected for development were ecologically fragile and possessed extraordinary scenic beauty. Much environmental and aesthetic destruction occurred before states adopted environmental controls. In addition, enactment of protective legislation has been slow, so ecological destruction is likely to continue, especially where older subdivisions are exempt from compliance because they were in operation before regulations were adopted. These grandfather clauses make correcting mistakes of the past difficult. The extent of environmental destruction is largely dependent upon decisions developers made before subdivision began. Cape Coral, Lake Havasu City, and many other subdivisions show how extensive the environmental damage can be when developers blatantly disregard the environment.

Some locations are unsuitable for subdivision even if sound land-use practices are used. Naturally, developers are attracted to prime recreational locations with aesthetically pleasing environments, but many of these beautiful locations cannot withstand the pressure associated with extensive subdivision. If their recreational and aesthetic qualities are to be maintained, extreme care must be taken; a high concentration of any kind of land development—in particular, subdivision—can rapidly degrade environmental quality. The six states in which over 60 percent of subdivision is occurring—Arizona, California, Colorado, Florida, New Mexico, and Texas—possess extensive ecologically fragile areas: mountains, deserts, wetlands. These fragile areas are being subdivided, which is why there is an urgent need for growth management guidelines and regulations to control the rate at which these lands are converted to uses that may not suit the needs of the public at large. Also, more attention must be paid to the concept of ecological design and planning on a local and regional scale.

The economic impact of recreational subdivision is likely to be both positive and negative. Whether a project contributes to county and state revenues depends largely upon whether the subdivision ever becomes a new community. County governments can be forced to provide services to the residents of the new community and maintain the community's roads. Increased revenues from real estate taxes and local expenditures by subdivision residents may, but often do not, offset county expenditures; thus, local governments should not welcome new land development blindly.

Consumer problems alone have warranted restraining orders against many subdivision operations; some of the largest and most reputable firms have had multi-million dollar lawsuits filed against them and been forced to refund money to thousands of lot owners. Such occurrences (along with the OPEC-generated energy crisis of the 1970s) severely eroded the industry's credibility and contributed greatly to the slump in lot sales during the mid-1970s. Some of the deception and fraud has been eliminated by the industry, but high-pressure tactics are still widely used. Consumer protection has been provided through full-disclosure legislation; unfortunately, such legislation does not cover all problems. For example, although the Federal Trade Commission has taken action from time to time, there is no protection agency that specifically deals with the giant subdividers other than the Office of Interstate Land Sales Registration. And its authority is based on full disclosure laws, under which subdividers can sell land that is underwater or on a vertical slope as long as they make full disclosure to prospective buyers. Full disclosure is totally inadequate to protect an ignorant, land hungry client. It has been suggested that protection should be provided under the auspices of the Securities and Exchange Commission or a similar agency, with the authority to require much more than full disclosure from the subdivider; it could impose regulations like those applied to companies selling stocks and bonds.

One of the most vexing questions is, What can be done with existing but incomplete land developments? Many planners and land-use experts argue that nothing can be done. These projects, they contend, were platted years ago prior to the adoption of growth management guidelines, and lot owners have vested rights. Some of the most advanced work in the field of platted lands (existing or old subdivisions) was done by Frank Schnidman, a land-use attorney. He suggests, among other things, subdivision redesign. His most successful redesign project is Ocala Springs, a subdivision in Florida that was platted years ago. Lots were never marketed and sold, so the entire property was under a single ownership (the developers); thus redesign was feasible (Getman, 1988). Over the course of several months, starting in 1984, the subdivision redesign was worked out. The end result was a state-of-the-art master plan based on sound land-use planning. Many lots platted prior to requirements that subdivisions meet certain standards were eliminated, and a new design was superimposed. More troublesome are platted subdivisions whose lots have been sold to thousands of property owners across the country. To make changes in these subdivisions requires the overwhelming task of dealing with individual lot owners. Before redesign could be accomplished, subdivision reassembly would first be required. The task is great, but it is possible and has been accomplished for small projects (Schnidman, 1988).

Other options available to local officials in dealing with older subdivisions include calling a moratorium on development until the local infrastructure is prepared to absorb demands for services; charging impact fees for development; deplatting lots in subdivisions that are vacant and unused; reassembling lots into unified ownership; rezoning to require a lower density by aggregating development; transferring development rights; calling for voluntary land pooling; and establishing time limits on development. These options are controversial, and their feasibility has not been proved, but they are excellent topics for future research. Transfer of development rights (TDR), for example, can preserve fragile locations that were inappropriately subdivided before land-use regulations were implemented. The shifting (transfer) of development to more suitable locations is obviously desirable, but the TDR procedure is fraught with difficulties. One of the most significant shortcomings is marketability (finding someone interested in purchasing a TDR). Another problem is finding a zone where densities can be increased without disrupting existing land-use patterns, upsetting adjacent property owners, or creating an undue burden on services. Despite these and other problems, TDR can work under the proper circumstances. Its applicability to existing but incomplete subdivisions located in fragile environments merits further research (Stokes et al., 1989).

Whether government officials implement a comprehensive approach or a more selective approach, the key is to provide the proper mix of land-use regulations that will provide a balance between economic growth and environmental protection. Some states have numerous regulations and elaborate permit procedures; other states have few if any regulatory devices. Florida, for example, has enacted several land-use management mechanisms and has a complicated framework within which developers must work before subdivision can occur.

But while scrutiny and regulation are necessary and can alleviate many problems, care must be taken that the regulatory process does not result in inappropriate delays, which can increase costs to the point where housing is priced beyond the reach of many middle-income families (Lerman, 1987; Pollakowski and Wachter, 1990). It is unfortunate that developers and government officials are caught in such a "Catch 22" situation. Management and control over development is essential, but they inevitably create delays, which push the price of vacation real estate beyond the reach of some citizens. And too often, properly designed, environmentally sound projects can be afforded only by large, well-financed corporations. These costs are then passed on to a wealthy clientele. Ecologically sound design should not mean higher costs or higher real estate prices. Regulation is a necessity, but it must be reasonable and administered so that decisions can be made quickly.

The development of such a precious resource as land and the fulfill-ment of such vital needs as recreation and retirement housing should be undertaken only by developers committed to meeting the needs of the public and the environment. Social responsibility is the issue here.

The first and most important step in creating a "good" recreational-retirement subdivision is site selection. Since so many aesthetically pleasing locations are unsuitable for subdivisions, many problems can be averted if government officials establish tolerance zones for devel-opment and limit subdivision projects to those areas. The laissez-faire attitudes of many local governments have allowed subdividers to pro-vide an oversupply of "vacation lots" and created an environmental nightmare in the process. A good example is Lee County, Florida, where 242,000 of more than 350,000 lots remain vacant and environ-mental damage is widespread. There are many locations where recrea-tional developments can be built without creating environmental dev-astation or exacerbating the oversupply of lots.

In the past, far too many sites were selected for the wrong reasons. Developers chose counties where development constraints were lax or areas where land was cheap and available. Or they chose areas where another developer had built a successful subdivision, ignoring the fact that just one developer may have produced enough vacant lots to meet local housing needs for hundreds, even thousands of years. Some counties should not allow additional land to be subdivided until their current supply of lots is built on or until these lots are redesigned into some other land use. The lots available in Lee County, Florida, could house 900,000 people if all were built on and occupied, but despite this incredible number of vacant lots, new subdivision projects are under way—with the county's blessing. Granted, the new projects must conform to the more stringent development standards now in place. But why produce more lots when the supply already exceeds the demand by an extremely wide margin?

Many locations suited to subdivision have not been overrun by mas-sive land development ventures. These are the places where land de-velopment might occur in the future—at a scale appropriate to the region. And land development should be allowed only after careful consideration has been given to the local situation. In some counties, subdivisions may already have created an oversupply of lots or are overtaxing water supplies. For example, on the Cumberland Plateau, or in east Texas, or in any "tolerant" location, subdivisions should be permitted only if market studies by land-use planners show that there is a demand and only if the developer is committed to a master plan, to developing within the environmental constraints of the site, to phasing in the project, and to providing consumers needed services and facilities for home construction.

Too many projects have been created because the developer owns a tract of land and decides to do something with it. Market research can be invaluable to developers in designing the right product: the right product will be accepted; the wrong product will require high-pressure sales tactics and an expensive sales program. In the long run, competent and unbiased market research prevents worthless planning and wasted effort and leads to a development accepted by all concerned (Poeschl, 1973, 32–33). Included in market research would be an inventory of natural resources; an evaluation of population statistics, demographics, and leisure living trends; and statistics on other subdivisions—the supply that already exists. The developer needs to know who the buyers are, how many there are, and what their personal and psychological characteristics are—do they want social interaction? seclusion? sports? Physical planning needs to consider compatibility: snowmobiling (noisy and fast) and cross-country skiing (quiet and slow) do not mix, nor do hiking and hunting (ibid.).

The days are numbered for land development that is insensitive to the needs of buyers. Gone, too, are those mammoth subdivisions selling lots through extensive advertising and high-pressure sales techniques. However, for those developers who implement environmentally sound land-use practices, who market a sensible product, and who promote it honestly and innovatively, the future is bright. The customers for recreational land development are increasing, as people become weary of living in urban environments and have higher per capita income, more leisure time, and greater mobility (ibid., 35; Hawks, 1991).

Although it is changing, the recreational-retirement land development industry still faces significant challenges. Many inactive large subdivisions have left behind land-use problems that will require land-use management techniques beyond the capabilities of many of the local governments left holding the bag. These problems, plus the problems of managing the growth of current and future projects, show the need for a thorough understanding of the land development industry, an understanding that will allow government officials to anticipate and possibly avoid future problems.

The key for governments is to establish ecological and other land-use regulations before development occurs. It is already too late for many projects to undo the damage from unwise land-use decisions, but immediate government action would ensure that the remaining prime locations for recreational-retirement communities would be developed wisely and equitably. The objective is not to stop growth but to allow growth within the context of sound economic and ecological management. Growth and development are needed, but only in the proper locations, at a scale suited to the needs of the population, and with architectural and landscape design in harmony with nature and the regional environment. It is time for land developers to understand their economic, social, and environmental responsibilities, so that future recreational-retirement communities will fulfill their promise.

References

Adams, Victoria, and Bill Mundy. 1991. "The Valuation of High-Amenity Natural Land." *Appraisal Journal,* 59; 48–55.

Aghemo, Lorenzo. 1992. Planning director, Monroe County Dept. of Community Development, Key West, Florida. Personal interview, July.

Albertson, Robert. 1988. Regional vice president, Fairfield Communities, Inc., Little Rock, Ark. Personal interview, October.

Allan, Leslie, Beryl Kuder, and Sarah L. Oakes. 1976. *Promised Lands.* Vol. 1, *Subdivisions in Deserts and Mountains.* New York: Inform.

——. 1977. *Promised Lands.* Vol. 2, *Subdivisions in Florida's Wetlands.* New York: Inform.

American Society of Planning Officials, Conservation Foundation, Urban Land Institute, and Ragatz Assoc., Inc. 1976. *Subdividing Rural America: Impacts of Recreational Lot and Second Home Development.* Washington, D.C.: Council of Environmental Quality.

"AMREP Accused of a $200-Million Swindle of 45,000 Land Buyers." 1975. *House and Home* (December).

AMREP Southwest, Inc. 1988, 1990, 1993. Corporate files. Rio Rancho, N.M.: Public Affairs Dept. October 1988, July 1990, April 1993.

Anderson, Richard. 1991. Director of operations, Westinghouse Gateway, Inc., Lee County, Fla. Personal interview, July.

Anderson, Robert M. 1968. *American Law of Zoning.* Vol. 2., *Subdivision Controls.* Rochester, N.Y.

Arizona, State of. *Arizona Community Profile.* 1984, 1985, 1991, 1993. Phoenix: Arizona Office of Economic Planning and Development.

Arkansas, State of. 1980. Aerial photograph REF-71-11, roll 80-5. Little Rock, Ark.: Arkansas Highway Dept.

Arnn, Larry. 1991. Remarks made during conference, "Fresh Thinking about Florida's Growth." Fort Myers, Fla., Claremont Institute, July.

Arnon, Lee. 1993. Senior planner, Dept. of Community Development, Lake Havasu City, Ariz. Personal interview, November.

Barkdoll, Gerald L. 1983. "Involving Constituents in Agency Priority Setting: A Case Study." *Evaluation and Program Planning,* 6:31–37.

Barker, Joe. 1989. Environment Health, Lee County Health Dept., Fort Myers, Fla. Personal interview, July.

Barker, Kim. 1991. Investor relations coordinator, Fairfield Communities, Inc., Little Rock, Arkansas. Personal interview, September.

Barlowe, Raleigh. 1979. "Soils, Plants, and Land Use in the United States." In *Planning the Uses and Management of Land,* ed. M. T. Beatty, G. W. Petersen, and L. D. Swindale. Madison, Wis.: American Society of Agronomy.

Barnwell, Ralph. 1993. Tax assessor, Cumberland County, Crossville, Tenn. Personal interview, June.

Barraclough, J. T., and O. T. Marsh. 1962. *Aquifers and Quality of Ground Water along the Gulf Coast of Western Florida.* Report Inventory 29. Washington, D.C.: U.S. Geological Survey.

Baumkirchner, Gary. 1993. President, McCulloch Realty Co. Lake Havasu City, Ariz. Personal interview, November.

Beattey, Timothy. 1994. *Ethical Land Use: Principles of Policy and Planning.* Baltimore: Johns Hopkins University Press.

Beaumont, Peter. 1989. *Environmental Management and Development in Drylands.* London: Routledge.

Bender, Gordon L., ed. 1982. *Reference Handbook on the Deserts of North America.* Westport, Conn.: Greenwood.

Bendix, Selina, and Herbert R. Graham. 1978. *Environmental Assessment: Approaching Maturity.* Ann Arbor, Mich.: Ann Arbor Science Publishers.

Bergeson, Marian, and Madelyn Glickfield. 1987. "The Evolution of Land Readjustment Law in California: Solving a Hidden Land Use Problem." *Land Assembly and Development* 1:45–64.

Bevins, Malcolm. 1989. "Impact of Ski Areas on Vermont Rural Communities." General Technical Report NE-132, Northeastern Forest Experiment Station. In *Proceedings of the 1989 Northeastern Recreational Research Symposium.* Broomall, Pa.: U.S. Dept. of Agriculture.

Blanchard, Robert E. 1991. Growth planning director, Collier County, Naples, Fla. Personal interview, July.

Bloom, George F., Arthur M. Weimer, and Jeffery D. Fisher. 1982. *Real Estate.* New York: John Wiley and Sons.

Blucher, Walter, et al. 1971. *An Analysis of Social and Economic Characteristics of Vermont.* Montpelier: Vermont State Planning Office.

Boggess, D. H. 1968. *Water-Supply Problems in Southwest Florida.* Open-file report FL-68003. Washington, D.C.: U.S. Geological Survey.

"Boise Cascade Agrees to $58.5 Million Settlement of Land Sales Lawsuits." 1973. *House and Home* (February).

Bonner, William. 1984. Professor, Dept. of Sociology, University of Arkansas, Fayetteville, Ark. Personal interview, July.

Borchers, Ron. 1988. Planning director, Polk County, Bartow, Fla. Personal interview, July.

Borchert, John. 1967. "American Metropolitan Evolution." *Geographical Review* 57:301–32.

————. 1993. Regent's professor emeritus, Dept. of Geography, University of Minnesota. Personal interview, November.

Bosselman, Fred P., and David Callies. 1971. *The Quiet Revolution in Land Use Control.* Washington, D.C.: Council on Environmental Quality.

Bosselman, Fred P., Duane A. Feurer, and Charles L. Siemon. 1975. *The Permit Explosion: Coordination of the Proliferation in Management and Control of Growth.* Washington, D.C.: Urban Land Institute.

Boyle Engineering. 1990. "City of Cape Coral, Florida, Utility Expansion Plan, Dual Water System—Phase I." Fort Myers, Fla.: Boyle Engineering.

Brower, David J., and Daniel S. Carol, eds. 1987. *Managing Land Use Conflicts: Case Studies in Special Area Management.* Durham: Duke University Press.

Brown, Richard N., Jr. 1970. *Economic Impact of Second Home Communities—A Case Study of Lake Latonka, Pennsylvania.* ERS 452. Washington, D.C.: U.S. Dept. of Agriculture, Economic Resource Service.

Budenkov, Yuri P., and Lawrence S. Hamilton. 1991. "Transformation of Mountain Environments Conference." *Environment* 33.

Burr, David. 1991, 1992, 1993. Planning director, Southwest Florida Regional Planning Council, North Fort Myers, Fla. Personal interviews, July 1991, July 1992, and November 1993.

Byers, N. G., and Leonard U. Wilson. 1983. *Managing Rural Growth: The Vermont Development Review Process.* Montpelier: Vermont Environmental Board.

Cahn, Robert. 1973. "What You, the Reader, Say Should Be Done about Land Sales." *Christian Science Monitor* (April 6).

California, State of. 1971. *Environmental Impact of Urbanization on the Foothill and Mountainous Lands of California.* Sacramento: Dept. of Conservation.

Canter, Larry W. 1977. *Environmental Impact Assessment.* New York: McGraw-Hill.

Cape Coral, City of. 1988. *Population and Demographics.* Cape Coral, Fla.: Planning Division.

Carlson, Alvar. 1991. *The Spanish-American Homeland: Four Centuries in New Mexico's Rio Arriba.* Baltimore: Johns Hopkins University Press.

Carson, Rachel. 1962. *Silent Spring.* Boston: Houghton Mifflin.

Carter, G. W. 1985. Designated broker, Salishan Realty, Gleneden Beach, Oregon. Personal interview, July.

Carter, Luther J. 1974. *The Florida Experience: Land and Water Policy in a Growth State.* Baltimore: Johns Hopkins University Press.

Cavanaugh, James C. 1988. "Vacation Homes: Before and After the Tax Reform Act of 1986." *Real Estate Law Journal* 17:3–28.

Chant, Davis R. 1986. "Buying Time—and—Financing It." *ABA Banking Journal* 78:161–64.

Checkoway, Barry. 1986. "Building Citizen Support for Planning at the Community Level." In *Interdisciplinary Planning: A Perspective for the Future,* ed. M. J. Dluhy and K. Chen. New Brunswick, N.J.: Rutgers University Press.

Chinity, Benjamin. 1990. "Growth Management: Good for the Town, Bad for the Nation?" *Journal of the American Planning Association* 56:3–8.

Ciccarone, Michael. 1991. Remarks made during conference, "Fresh Thinking about Florida's Growth." Fort Myers, Fla., Claremont Institute, July.

Cinelli, Arlene. 1975. "County Commentary: Let Us Not Forget the Flood." *Sandoval County Times Independent* (November 28).

Claremont Institute. 1991. *Ten Steps to Good Growth Management in Florida.* Mandate for Prosperity Series. Montclair, Calif.: Claremont Institute.

Clark, Brian D., Ronald Bisset, and Peter Wathern. 1980. *Environmental Impact Assessment: A Bibliography with Abstracts.* London: Mansell.

Cloud, Jack. 1993. Development Review Board chairman, Albuquerque, N.M. Personal interview, June.

Cobb, Bryan. 1993. Planner, Dept. of Community Development, Cape Coral, Fla. Personal interview, July.

Colegrove, Jim. 1986. Director of public affairs, AMREP Corp. Rio Rancho, N.M. Personal interview, April.

Conboy, Vince. 1972. *Florida's Billion Dollar Land Fraud.* Naples, Fla.: V. Conboy.

Connerly, Charles E. 1986. "Growth Management Concern: The Impact of Its Definitions on Support for Local Growth Control." *Environment and Behavior* 18:707–32.

Cornick, Philip. 1938. *Premature Subdivision.* New York: Columbia University Press.

Costello, David F. 1975. *The Mountain World.* New York: Thomas Crowell.

Cottington, Jim. 1993. Port LaBelle project manager, Atlantic Gulf Communities, Port LaBelle, Fla. Personal interview, November.

Coyle, Kevin J. 1984. "Arkansas Land: The Wealth of a State, a Forum Report." *American Land Forum* (Bethesda, Md.).

Coyle, Richard. 1993. Property manager, Fairfield Bay, Inc., Fairfield Bay, Ark. Personal interview, June.

Craig, Donald L. 1991. Planning director, Dept. of Community Development, Division of Planning, Lee County, Fort Myers, Fla. Personal interview, July.

Crawford, Anne, ed. 1983. "Resort Condominiums International and Vacation Horizons International." *Perspectives* 1:1–3.

Dady, Mike. 1993. Director, planning and development, Atlantic Gulf Communities, Miami, Fla. Personal interview, October.

Daltry, Wayne. 1988. Executive director, Southwest Florida Regional Planning Council, North Fort Myers, Fla. Personal interview, July.

———. 1991. Remarks made during conference, "Fresh Thinking about Florida's Growth." Fort Myers, Fla., Claremont Institute, July.

Davidson, Donald A. 1980. *Topics in Applied Geography: Soils and Land Use Planning.* New York: Longman.

Davis, Tony. 1993. "Water Battle Brewing: Intel, Corrales Bickering about Plant's Well Plan." *Albuquerque Tribune* (August 11).

Deen, J. D. 1984. Division of Real Estate, Tax Assessor's Office, Benton County, Ark. Personal interview, June.

DeGrove, John M. 1979. "The Political Dynamics of the Land and Growth Management Movement." *Law and Contemporary Problems* 43:11–143.

———. 1984. *Land Growth and Politics.* Chicago: American Planning Assoc.

———, ed. 1991. *Balanced Growth: A Planning Guide for Local Government.* Washington, D.C.: International City Management Assoc.

DeGrove, John, and Nancy Stroud. 1987. "State Land Planning and Regulation: Innovative Roles in the 1980s and Beyond." *Land Use Law and Zoning Digest* 39:3–8.

DeGrove, John M., with Deborah A. Miness. 1992. *The New Frontier for Land Policy: Planning and Growth Management in the States.* Cambridge, Mass.: Lincoln Institute of Land Policy.

deHaven-Smith, Lance. 1984. "Regulatory Theory and State Land-Use Regulation: Implications from Florida's Experience with Growth Management." *Public Administration Review* (September/October): 416–17.

Didion, Larry. 1986. Planner, Dept. of Community Development, Lake Havasu City, Ariz. Personal interview, April.

Downie, Leonard, Jr. 1974. *Mortgage on America.* New York: Praeger.

Drake, Ronald, et al. 1968. *Selected Economic Consequences of Recreation Development: Tuolumne County, Case Study.* Berkeley: University of California, Agricultural Extension Service.

Duerksen, Christopher J. 1983. *Environmental Regulation of Industrial Plant Siting: How to Make It Work Better.* Washington, D.C.: Conservation Foundation.

Economic Development Council of Northeastern Pennsylvania. 1976. *Impact of Second Home Development on Northeastern Pennsylvania: Trends and Projections.* Avoca, Pa.: EDC.

Englander, Todd. 1988. "Making a Dull Job Fun." *Incentive* 162:59–61.

Epstein, Larry. 1985. "Legislative Approach to Antiquated Subdivisions in Oregon." *Platted Lands Press* 2:4–6.

Evans, David D., and John L. Thames, eds. 1981. *Water in Desert Ecosystems.* Stroudsburg, Pa.: Dowden, Hutchingson, and Ross.

Fairfield Communities, Inc. 1984, 1990, 1993. Corporate files. Little Rock, Ark., July 1984, November 1990, October 1993.

Federal Interagency Committee for Wetland Delineation. 1989. *Federal Manual for Identifying and Delineating Jurisdictional Wetlands.* Washington, D.C.: U.S. Army Corps of Engineers, U.S. Environmental Protection Agency, U.S. Fish and Wildlife Service, and USDA Soil Conservation Service.

Ferguson, Sharon. 1991. Administrative assistant, Fairfield Communities, Inc., Little Rock, Ark. Personal interview, October.

Fields, Barry. 1993. Public works director, Fairfield Glade Community Club, Fairfield Glade, Tenn. Personal interview, June.

Fins, Antonio N. 1990. "I Thought Florida Land Scams Were Over." *Business Week* (April 23).

Fischel, William A. 1990. "Introduction: Four Maxims for Research on Land-Use Controls." *Land Economics* 66:229–236.

Florida, State of, 1983. *Developments of Regional Impact Status Report.* Tallahassee: Bureau of Land and Water Management, Dept. of Community Affairs.

Forester, John. 1981. "Planning in the Face of Power." *Journal of the American Planning Association,* 48:67–80.

Freilich, Robert. 1974. "Development Timing, Moratoria, and Controlling Growth." *Planning, Zoning, and Eminent Domain* 147:147–219.

Gardner, Judy. 1973. "Consumer Report/Land-Sales Industry Braces for Tighter Federal, State Regulation." *National Journal,* 90–98.

Gates, Thomas U. 1983. Sales manager, Port LaBelle, Fla. Personal interview, July.

Gautier, Charles. 1990. Senior planner, Planning and Zoning Division, Dept. of Community Development, Lee County, Fort Myers, Fla. Personal interview, July.

Geiler, Richard M. 1976. "Development Regulations Must Be Reasonable." *Urban Land* (October): 3–4.

General Development Corp. 1982. *General Development Profile.* Miami: GDC.

Generous, Robert E. 1991. Planner, Dept. of Community Development, Cape Coral, Fla. Personal interview, July.

Getman, Dennis. 1988, 1993. Vice president and general counsel, Avatar Holdings, Inc., Coral Gables, Fla. Personal interviews, December 1988, June 1993.

Granger, Oscar. 1985. Director of planning, Lincoln County, Newport, Ore. Personal interview, July.

Gravely, Richard. 1993. District engineer, Tennessee Dept. of Transportation, Cookeville, Tenn. Personal interview, June.

Griffee, Carol. 1991. "No Wetlands Statistics Exist for Arkansas." *Jonesboro Sun* (October 17).

Grogen, Ken. 1993. Hall County Sheriff's Dept., Gainesville, Ga. Personal interview, June.

Hale, Glenn. 1985. Field representative, Dept. of Land Conservation and Development, Newport, Ore. Personal interview, July.

Hall, Gwin. 1984. Tax assessor, Baxter County, Mountain Home, Ark. Personal interview, July.

Hammer, Siler, and George Assoc. 1984. *Economic Impact Analysis, Fairfield Bay, Arkansas.* Silver Spring, Md.: SH and G.

Hammond, William. 1991. Director of Curriculum Services, Lee County Schools, Fort Myers, Fla. Personal communication, July.

Hansen, David E., and Thomas E. Dickinson. 1975. "Undivided Interests: Implications of a New Approach to Recreational Land Development." *Land Economics* 2:124–32.

Harris, Donna. 1991. Dept. of Community Affairs, Tallahassee, Fla. Personal interview, October.

Hawks, John. 1991. "The Next Boom in Real Estate." *American Demographics* 13:46–48.

Healy, Robert G., and John S. Rosenberg. 1979. *Land Use and the States.* Baltimore: Johns Hopkins University Press.

Healy, Robert G., and James L. Short. 1983. "Changing Markets for Rural Lands: Patterns and Issues." *Beyond the Urban Fringe: Land Use Issues of Nonmetropolitan America,* ed. Rutherford H. Platt and George Macinko. Minneapolis: University of Minnesota Press.

Helweg, Otto J. 1985. *Water Resources: Planning and Management.* New York: John Wiley and Sons.

Henderson, Roger. 1982, 1986, 1991, 1993. Director, Program Development and Control Division, Office of Interstate Land Sales Registration, U.S. Dept. of Housing and Urban Development, Washington, D.C. Personal interviews, January 1982, March and November 1986, October 1991, and May 1993.

Herbert, Lynn. 1993. Chief, Land Sales Enforcement Branch, Office of Interstate Land Sales Registration, U.S. Dept. of Housing and Urban Development, Washington, D.C. Personal interviews, May and June.

Heritage, John. 1973. "Exploitation Run Wild," *Progressive* (July): 25–27.

Herrera, Joe. 1993. Engineer, Public Services Company of New Mexico, Rio Rancho, N.M. Personal interview, November.

"Horizon Corporation Warned to Curb Sand." 1973. *Albuquerque Journal* (June 14).

Howe, Charles W., et al. 1972. *Residential Development in the Mountains of Colorado: A Handbook of Problems and Guidelines.* Denver: United Banks of Colorado.

Howeth, Becky. 1990. *Fairfield to Reorganize to Deal with Liquidity Problems: Business Operations to Continue.* Press release, October 3. Little Rock, Ark.: Fairfield Communities, Inc.

Humphrey, R. R. 1958. *The Desert Grassland.* Tucson: University of Arizona Press.

Ilg, Albert G. 1974. "Dealing with Real Estate Developers." *Public Management* (December): 8–9.

Intel Corporation. 1993. "Background Memorandum on Intel's Expansion." Rio Rancho, N.M.: Intel.

Ives, Jack D. 1979. "Applied High Altitude Geoecology: Can the Scientist Assist in the Preservation of the Mountains?" In *High Altitude Geoecology,* ed. Patrick J. Webber. AAAS Selected Symposia Series. Boulder, Colo.: Westview.

Jackson, Richard H. 1981. *Land Use in America.* New York: John Wiley and Sons.

Jackson, Virginia, Diana M. Danforth, Gerald T. Hudson, and Donald E. Voth. 1979. *Attitudes toward Planning and Management of Land Resources in Arkansas.* Bulletin 838. Fayetteville: University of Arkansas, Division of Agriculture, Agricultural Experiment Station.

Jaffe, Austin J., and C. F. Sirmans. 1982. *Real Estate Investment Decision Making.* Englewood Cliffs, N.J.: Prentice-Hall.

Jezeski, James J., et al. 1973. *Impact of Large Recreational Developments upon Semi-Primitive Environments: An Overview of the MSU-NSF Galla-tin Canyon Study.* Bozeman: Montana State University, Center for Interdisciplinary Studies.

Johnson, Arthur H., Jonathan Berger, and Ian L. McHarg. 1979. "A Case Study in Ecological Planning: The Woodlands, Texas." In *Planning the Uses and Management of Land,* ed. Marvin T. Beatty, Gary W. Petersen, and Lester D. Swindale. Agronomy series 21. Madison, Wisc: American Society of Agronomy, Crop Science Society of America, and Soil Science Society of America, Inc.

Johnson, Jack D. 1982. "Desertification in the United States." In *Proceedings of an International Conference on Alternative Strategies for Desert Development and Management.* New York: Pergamon.

Joyce, Rick K. 1991. Principal environmental planner, Dept. of Community Development, Division of Environmental Services, Lee County, Fort Myers, Fla. Personal interview, July.

Juergensmeyer, Julian C., and Robert M. Blake. 1981. "Impact Fees: An Answer to Local Governments' Capital Funding Dilemma." *Florida State University Law Review* 9:415–521.

Jundt, Dwight. 1980. *Buying and Selling Farmland: A Guide to Profitable Investment.* St. Louis, Mo.: Doane Agricultural Services.

Keller, Brian. 1993. Vice president of sales administration, Fairfield Communities, Inc., Little Rock, Ark. Personal interview, November.

Kenzel, Barry. 1993. Arkansas Dept. of Education, Little Rock, Ark. Personal interview, June.

King, Leslie, and Glenn Harris. 1989. "Local Responses to Rapid Growth: New York and Vermont Cases." *Journal of the American Planning Association* 55:181–91.

Kirsch, Bruno. 1984. Director, Division of Engineering, Arkansas Dept. of Health, Little Rock, Ark. Personal interview, July.

Kiss, Stephen K. 1991. Assistant director, Utilities Dept., City of Cape Coral, Fla. Personal interview, July.

Knight, Howard. 1990. Environmental planner, Dept. of Community Development, Cape Coral, Fla. Personal interview, July.

Lachman, Leanne. 1990. "Demographics: The Key to Successful Real Estate Projects in the 1990s." *Real Estate Finance Journal* 6:16–21.

Laitin, Jon. 1988. "Down East Drama." *Planning* (August): 21–24.

Lake Havasu City. 1991. Base map. Lake Havasu City, Ariz.: Dept. of Community Development.

"Land Boom Swells in Southwest Utah." 1973. *Salt Lake Tribune* (July 8).

"Land Sales Boom: Let the Buyer Beware." 1972. *Consumer Reports* (September): 606–8.

"Land Use Planning—New Mexico's Green Belt Law." 1968. *Natural Resources Journal* 8:190.

Lawson, James C. 1988. "Casting for Sales Superstars." *Insurance Review* 49:54–57.

Lee, Al. 1986. Realtor, McCulloch Realty, Lake Havasu City, Ariz. Personal interview, July.

Leger, Ken. 1990. Student intern, Dept. of Community Development, Cape Coral, Fla. Personal interview, July.

LeJune, Harold. 1972. *Economic Impact of Artificial Lake Development: Lakes Sherwood and Camelot, a Case History.* Madison, Wis.: Upper Great Lakes Regional Commission.

Leonard, Tracy. 1993. Commercial and industrial marketing specialist, AMREP Southwest, Inc., Rio Rancho, N.M. Personal interview, April.

Lerman, Donald. 1987. "The Affordability of Adequate Housing." *American Real Estate and Urban Economics Association Journal* 15:389–404.

Levin, M. R., J. G. Rose, and J. S. Slavet. 1974. *New Approaches to State Land-Use Policies.* Lexington, Mass.: D. C. Heath.

Lewis, Gordon D. 1975. "The Benefits of Vacation Home Developments to County Governments." In *Proceedings, Man, Leisure, and Wildlife: A Complex Interaction.* Vail, Colo.: Eisenhower Consortium for Western Environmental Forestry Research.

Limb, Max. 1993. Tax assessor, Beaver County, Beaver, Utah. Personal interview, June.

Littell, Ronald. 1993. Fairfield Bay Community Club utilities field supervisor, Fairfield Bay, Ark. Personal interview, November.

Loyd, Lynn. 1988. Planner, Warren County Planning Dept., Front Royal, Va. Personal interview, May.

Lynch, Rodney C. 1990. "Bethel's Plan for Managing Growth." *Public Management* 72:11–14.

McCahill, Edward. 1974. "Florida's Not-So-Quiet-Revolution." *Planning* (March): 10.

McConnell, John. 1991. *Fairfield Communities Files Plan of Reorganization.* Press releases, May 8 and June 28. Little Rock, Ark.: Fairfield Communities, Inc.

McCoy, Jack. 1993. Division of Natural Resources Management, Lee County Dept. of Community Development, Fort Myers, Fla. Personal interview, November.

McHarg, Ian L. 1969. *Design with Nature.* New York: Natural History Press.

Machida, Dennis. 1988. Director, California Tahoe Conservancy, South Lake Tahoe, Calif. Personal interview, December.

McIntosh, John. 1973. Director of market research, Fairfield Communities Land Co., Little Rock, Ark. Personal interview, October.

———. 1983. Executive vice president and general manager, Fairfield Bay, Ark. Personal interview, July.

Mackert, Ken. 1988. County planning administrator, Clarke County, Va. Personal interview, May.

McMahan, Sandra L. 1978. "One Tier beyond Ramapo: Open Space Zoning and the Urban Reserve." *San Diego Law Review* 15:1211–40.

Mandelker, D. R., and R. A. Cunningham. 1979. *Planning and Control of Land Development.* New York: Bobbs-Merrill.

Manning, John. 1991. Lee County commissioner, Fort Myers, Fla. Remarks made during conference, "Fresh Thinking about Florida's Growth." Fort Myers, Fla., Claremont Institute, July.

Marshall, John, Jr. 1971. *The Efficacy of Act 250: The Evolution of an Environmental Law.* Montpelier, Vt.: Environmental Planning Information Center.

Martin, Ann. 1993. Vice president, Fairfield Bay Community Club Board of Directors, Fairfield Bay, Ark. Personal interview, April.

Martin, David G., Jr. 1980. "New Rules for Subdivision Lot Sales." *Real Estate Review* 10:90–96.

Martin, Wendell H. 1971. "Remote Land: Development or Exploitation." *Urban Land* 30:3–10.

Martinez, Eluid. 1993. New Mexico state engineer, Santa Fe, N.M. Personal interview, November.

Massara, Dennis. 1993. Financial services director, Lake Havasu City, Ariz. Personal interview, November.

Mather, Cotton. 1993. President, New Mexico Geographical Society, Mesilla, N.M. Personal interview, October.

Melinsky, D., and E. Maier. 1980. "Florida Wetlands Subdivisions: Protecting the Consumer? the Environment? or the Developer?" *Florida Environmental and Urban Issues* (July): 4–29.

Miller, Anita. 1984. New Mexico's Subdivision Ills." *Platted Lands Press* 1:4–8.

———. 1987, 1994. Attorney at Potter and Kelly, Albuquerque, N.M. Personal interviews, July 1987 and March 1994.

"Million Recovered by State for People Bilked Buying Land." 1969. *New York Times* (December 8).

Mitsch, William J., and James G. Gosselink. 1986. *Wetlands.* New York: Van Nostrand Reinhold.

Montana, State of. 1986. *A Manual for the Administration of Montana Subdivision and Platting Act 15.* Helena: Dept. of Commerce.

Morgan, Richard B. 1988. Assistant regulatory administrator, Northwest Florida Water Management District, Tallahassee, Fla. Personal interview, July.

Morgenson, Gretchen. 1988. "Suckering the City Bumpkins." *Forbes* 142: 39–40.

Mosena, David. 1972. "A Report on Recreational Land Development." *Planning* (December): 297–300.

Nahas, Ronald C., and Neil Eskind. 1978. "Developing in a Hostile Environment." *Urban Land* (November): 7–10.

National Time-sharing Council. 1981. *Resort Timesharing: A Consumers' Guide.* Washington, D.C.: American Land Development Assoc.

Natural Resources Defense Council, Inc. 1977. *Land Use Controls in the United States: A Handbook on the Legal Rights of Citizens,* ed. Elaine Moss. New York: Dial Press/James Wade.

Nelson, Arthur C. 1985. "Negotiated Replatting in Oregon." *Platted Lands Press* 2:1–7.

New Mexico, State of. 1984. *Subdividing Land in New Mexico.* 2d ed. Santa Fe: Office of the Attorney General.

Odum, Eugene P. 1959. *Fundamentals of Ecology,* 2d ed. Philadelphia: W. B. Saunders.

Office of Technology Assessment. 1984. *Wetlands: Use and Regulation.* Washington, D.C.: Government Printing Office.

O'Keefe, Thomas C. 1972. "Time Controls on Land Use: Prophylactic Law for Planners." *Cornell Law Review* 57:827–49.

Oregon, State of. 1985. *Oregon's Statewide Planning Program.* Salem: Dept. of Land Conservation and Development.

Outland, John. 1988. Dept. of Environmental Regulation, Tallahassee, Fla. Personal interview, July.

Page, Barbara Kerr. 1977. "The Land of Enchantment Is also the Land of Ripoff." *Planning* (April/May): 48–51.

Parsons, James J. 1972. "Slicing up the Open Space: Subdivisions without Homes in Northern California." *Erdkunde* (March): 1–8.

Patrick, Beaton W. 1991. "The Impact of Regional Land-Use Controls on Property Values: The Case of the New Jersey Pinelands." *Land Economics* 67:172–94.

Patrick, Ruth, Emily Ford, and John Quarles. 1987. *Groundwater Contamination in the United States,* 2d ed. Philadelphia: University of Pennsylvania Press.

Paulson, Morton C. 1972a. *The Great Land Hustle.* Chicago: Henry Regnery.

———. 1972b. "*Caveat Emptor:* Beware, Buyers, of Dusty Lots." *National Observer* (June 10).

———. 1974. "Reselling Land: Profits Rare for Second Home Sites." *National Observer* (April 20).

Pelham, Thomas G. 1979. *State Land-Use Planning and Regulation.* Lincoln Institute of Land Policy. Lexington, Mass.: D. C. Heath.

Peterson, Edward. 1988. Gordon county administrator, Calhoun, Ga. Personal interview, May.

Platt, Laurence E. 1987. "Caveat Emptor, Caveat Faenerator." *Mortgage Banking* (October).

Platt, Rutherford A., and George Macinko, eds. 1983. *Beyond the Urban Fringe: Land Use Issues of Nonmetropolitan America.* Minneapolis: University of Minnesota Press.

Plotkin, Sidney. 1987. *Keep Out: The Struggle for Land Use Control.* Berkeley: University of California Press.

Poeschl, William H. 1973. "The Right Way to Market Vacation Homes." *Real Estate Review* 3:31–35.

Pollakowski, Henry O., and Susan M. Wachter. 1990. "The Effects of Land-Use Constraints on Housing Prices." *Land Economics* 66:315–24.

Popper, Frank J. 1988. "Understanding American Land Use Regulation since 1970: A Revisionist Interpretation." *Journal of the American Planning Association* (Summer): 291–301.

Porter, Douglas R., ed. 1986. *Growth Management: Keeping on Target.* Washington, D.C.: Urban Land Institute.

Quinn, Jim. 1993. Administrator, Areas of Critical State Concern Program,

Dept. of Community Affairs, Tallahassee, Fla. Personal interview, November.

Ragatz, Richard L. 1976. "Analysis and Overview." In *The Real Estate Development Industry.* Washington, D.C.: American Land Development Assoc.

Rawn, Douglas. 1973. Research analyst, Fairfield Communities Land Co., Fairfield Glade, Tenn. Personal interview, November.

Reed, Don. 1993. Deschutes County Tax Assessor's Office, Bend, Ore. Personal interview, June.

Reed, Jim. 1984, 1993. Vice president of finance and administration, Fairfield Communities, Inc. Fairfield Glade, Tenn. Personal interviews, July 1984 and May 1993.

Reilly, William K., ed. 1973. *The Use of Land: A Citizen's Policy Guide to Urban Growth.* New York: Thomas Y. Cromwell.

Reiniger, Clair. Forthcoming. "Bioregional Planning: Merging Ecology and Economics." In *Ecological Design and Planning,* ed. George F. Thompson and Frederick R. Steiner. Baltimore: Johns Hopkins University Press.

Rice, Joe D. 1985. Planner, Arkansas Dept. of Parks and Tourism, Little Rock, Ark. Personal interview, September.

Richey, Clyde W. 1972. "Value and Property Taxes of a Second-Home Subdivision: Case Study." *Land Economics* 48:387–92.

Roane, Alton. 1990. Planning director, Dept. of Community Development, Division of Planning, Lee County, Fort Myers, Fla. Personal interview, July.

Rodgers, William H., Jr. 1972. "Boise Cascade: The One That Didn't Get Away." *Washington Monthly* (November): 50.

Rodin, Neal I. 1991. "Approaches for Real Estate Development and Investment for the 1990s." *Real Estate Finance Journal* 7:83–86.

Sampson, Robert E. 1988. Senior planner, Polk County Planning Division, Bartow, Fla. Personal interview, July.

Sanchez, Isabel. 1993. "Intel's Smell Could Go up in Smoke: Incinerator May Burn Off Chip-Making Fumes." *Albuquerque Tribune* (September 2).

Schaenman, Philip S., and Thomas Muller. 1974. *Measuring Impacts of Land Development: An Initial Approach.* Washington, D.C.: Urban Institute.

Schneider, Mary Jo. 1987. "Arkansas' Growth Industry: Retirement." *Arkansas Business and Economic Review* 20:1–8.

Schnidman, Frank. 1984. "Resolving Antiquated Subdivision Problems." *Florida Environmental and Urban Issues* 12:20–24.

———. 1987. "Resolving Platted Lands Problems: The Florida Experience." *Land Assembly and Development: A Journal of Land Readjustment Studies* 1:27–44.

———. 1988. Senior research fellow and visiting professor, FAU/FIU Joint Center for Environmental and Urban Problems, Florida Atlantic University, Fort Lauderdale, Fla. Personal interview, December.

Schnidman, Frank, and R. Lisle Baker. 1985. *Planning for Platted Lands: Land Use Remedies for Lot Sale Subdivisions.* Monograph 85-2. Cambridge, Mass.: Lincoln Institute of Land Policy.

Schnidman, Frank, June A. Silverman, and Rufus C. Young, eds. 1978. *Management and Control of Growth: Techniques in Application*, vol. 4. Washington, D.C.: Urban Institute.

Schofield, J. A. 1987. *Cost-Benefit Analysis in Urban and Regional Planning*. London: Allen and Unwin.

Scott, Randall W., ed. 1975. *Management and Control of Growth: Issues, Techniques, Problems, Trends*. Washington, D.C.: Urban Institute.

Sears, Paul. 1972. "How to Ignore a Flood." *New Mexico Review* (September): 3–5.

Shands, William E., and Patricia Woodson. 1974. *The Subdivision of Virginia's Mountains: The Environmental Impact of Recreational Subdivisions in the Massanutten Mountain–Blue Ridge Area, Virginia, a Survey and Report*. Washington, D.C.: Central Atlantic Environment Center.

Shultz, Michael M., and Jeffery B. Groy. 1986. *The Premature Subdivision of Land in Colorado: A Survey with Commentary*. Monograph 86-10. Cambridge, Mass.: Lincoln Institute of Land Policy.

———. 1988. "The Failure of Subdivision Control in the Western United States: A Blueprint for Local Government Action." *Utah Law Review* 1988:569–674.

Siemon, Charles L. 1988. "The Growth Management Act of 1985: A Bitter Pill, but Better than 'Growth Management Anarchy.'" *Environmental and Urban Issues* 16:1–5.

Smiley, Emma. 1993. Property appraiser, Van Buren County, Clinton, Ark. Personal interview, June.

Smith, Herbert H. 1979. *The Citizen's Guide to Planning*. Chicago: American Planning Assoc.

Smith, Martin R. 1987. "From Subdivision Improvement Requirements to Community Benefit Assessments and Linkage Payments: A Brief History of Land Development Exactions." *Law and Contemporary Problems* 50: 5–30.

So, Frank S. 1978. "Tips on Cutting the Delays of Regulation." *Planning* (October): 26–30.

Soucie, Gary. 1973. "Subdividing and Conquering the Desert." *Audubon* (July): 29–35.

Squires, Kitty. 1993. Tax collector, Van Buren County, Clinton, Ark. Personal interview, June.

Srader, Dave. 1981. Project manager, Horizon City, El Paso, Tex. Personal interview, July.

Standon, Don. 1993. Tax assessor, Winsor County, Hartford, Vt. Personal interview, June.

Steiner, Frederick. 1991. *The Living Landscape: An Ecological Approach to Landscape Planning*. New York: McGraw-Hill.

Stephenson, Larry K. 1987. Strategic Planning, City of Glendale, Glendale, Ariz. Personal interview, July.

Stokes, Samuel N., et al. 1989. *Saving America's Countryside: A Guide to Rural Conservation*. Baltimore: Johns Hopkins University Press.

Stroud, Hubert B. 1974. "Amenity Land Development as an Element of Geographic Change: A Case Study, Cumberland County, Tennessee." Ph.D. diss. University of Tennessee.

———. 1977. "Recreational Land Development in Arkansas," *Arkansas Business and Economic Review* 10:9–13.

———. 1978. "The Land Development Corporation: A System for Selling Rural Real Estate." *Journal of the American Real Estate and Urban Economics Association* 6:271–86.

———. 1983a. "Raw Land to Time-sharing in Arkansas." *Arkansas Business and Economic Review* 16:11–16.

———. 1983b. "Environmental Problems Associated with Large Recreational Subdivisions." *Professional Geographer* 35:303–13.

———. 1984. "Florida's Challenge: Balance between Subdivision and the Environment." *Florida Environmental and Urban Issues* 11:14–22.

———. 1985a. "Problems Associated with the Regulation of Recreational Land Development in Arkansas." *Arkansas Journal of Geography* 1:12–25.

———. 1985b. "New Community Developments: An Element of Change for Selected Locations." *Ekistics* (May/June): 253–57.

———. 1985c. "Port LaBelle." *Landscape Planning* 12:193–96.

———. 1991. "Water Resources at Cape Coral, Florida: Problems Created by Poor Planning and Development." *Land Use Policy* 6:143–57.

"Subdivision 'Benefits' Mixed Bag." 1972. *The Bulletin* (February 8; Bend, Ore.): 3.

Sussna, Stephen, and Jack Kirchhoff. 1971. "The Problem of Premature Subdivision." *Appraisal Journal* (October): 592–601.

Swafford, Tom. 1984, 1988. Vice president of Engineering, Fairfield Glade, Tenn. Personal interviews, December 1984 and October 1988.

Swan, Raymond H., ed. 1977. *Report 6: A Summary of State Land Use Controls*. Silver Spring, Md.: Business Publishers.

Syme, Geoffrey J., Clive Seligman, and Duncan K. Macpherson. 1989. "Environmental Planning and Management: An Introduction." *Journal of Social Issues* 45:1–15.

Tahoe Regional Planning Agency and U.S. Forest Service. 1971a. *Geology and Geomorphology of the Lake Tahoe Region*. South Lake Tahoe, Calif.: Tahoe RPA.

———. 1971b. *Limnology and Water Quality of the Lake Tahoe Region*. South Lake Tahoe, Calif.: Tahoe RPA.

Tampa, City of. 1972. "Environmental Assessment of Development Atlas." Tampa, Fla.: Tampa Bay Regional Planning Council.

Thomas, Joseph M., and George Griffith. 1974. "DRI." *Florida Environmental and Urban Issues* 1 (April/May).

Thompson, Lamar. 1973. Project sales manager, Fairfield Communities, Inc., Fairfield Glade, Tenn. Personal interview, March.

Thurow, Charles, William Toner, and Duncan Erley. 1975. *Performance Controls for Sensitive Lands*. Washington, D.C.: American Society of Planning Officials.

Tillson, Gregory D., et al. 1972. *Local Tax Impact of Recreational Sub-Divisions: A Case Study.* Special Report 365. Corvallis: Oregon State University Extension Service.

"Time-Share Industry Is Trying to Shed Its Once Sleazy Reputation." 1993. *Jonesboro Sun* (June 18).

Topper, Erwin. 1993. Resource manager, U.S. Army Corps of Engineers, Lake Lanier, Buford, Ga. Personal interview, June.

Tossier, Robert. 1983. Senior planner, Cape Coral, Fla. Personal interview, July.

Trescott, Daniel. 1993. Principal planner and DRI coordinator, Southwest Florida Regional Planning Council, North Fort Myers, Fla. Personal interview, July.

Trudnak, Stephen J. 1989. Director of planning and design, Bonita Bay Properties, Bonita Springs, Fla. Personal interview, July.

Tuan, Yi-Fu. 1989. *Morality and Imagination: Paradoxes of Progress.* Madison: University of Wisconsin Press.

Tucker, Sunni. 1993. Director, Rio Rancho Economic Development, Rio Rancho, N.M. Personal interview, October.

Turner, Phillip. 1993. Tax assessor, Windham County, Brattleboro, Vt. Personal interview, June.

Twiss, Robert H. 1973. "Planning for Areas of Significant Environment and Amenity Value." In *Environment: A New Focus for Land-Use Planning,* ed. Donald M. McAllister. Washington, D.C.: National Science Foundation.

Tymon, Dorothy. 1973. *America Is for Sale.* Rockville Centre, N.Y.: Farnsworth.

U.S. Bureau of the Census. 1991. *Census and You.* Washington, D.C.: Government Printing Office.

U.S. Dept. of Agriculture. 1964. Aerial photograph BSU-3FF-62. Washington, D.C.: Agricultural Stabilization Conservation Service.

———. 1982. Aerial Photograph HAP-81-F. Washington, D.C.: Agricultural Conservation Service.

———. 1984a. Aerial photograph HAP-84-F. Washington, D.C.: Agricultural Conservation Service.

———. 1984b. *Soil Survey of Lee County, Florida.* Fort Myers, Fla.: Soil Conservation Service.

U.S. Dept. of Housing and Urban Development. 1984a. Interstate Land Sales Full Disclosure Act, sec. 1419, 15 U.S.C. 1718. Washington, D.C.: Office of Interstate Land Sales Registration.

———. 1984b. *Catalog Report,* August. Washington, D.C.: Office of Interstate Land Sales Registration.

———. 1986. *Catalog Report,* July. Washington, D.C.: Office of Interstate Land Sales Registration.

———. 1989a. *Before Buying Land—Get the Facts.* Washington, D.C.: Government Printing Office.

———. 1989b. *Buying Lots from Developers.* Washington, D.C.: Government Printing Office.

―――. 1990. *Land Registration, Purchaser's Revocation Rights . . .* Washington, D.C.: Office of Interstate Land Sales Registration.

―――. 1993. *Catalog Report,* May. Washington, D.C.: Office of Interstate Land Sales Registration.

U.S. Department of the Interior. Various years. Geological Survey Water supply papers. Washington, D.C.: U.S. Government Printing Office; and U.S. Geological Survey maps. Washington, D.C.: Map Information Office.

Vanderblue, Homer B. 1927. "The Florida Land Boom." *Journal of Land and Public Utility Economics* (May): 113–31.

Van Hoy, Chris. 1993. Administrative assistant for sales, Fairfield Glade, Tenn. Personal interview, May.

Vaux, H. J. 1974. *Desert Land Use and Residential Subdivision.* Riverside: University of California, Dry-Land Research Institute.

―――. 1977. "Rural Land Subdividing: A Lesson from the Southern California Desert." *AIP Journal* (July): 271–78.

Vesterby, Marlow, and Ralph E. Heimlich. 1991. "Land Use and Demographic Change: Results from Fast-Growing Counties." *Land Economics* 67:279–91.

Vranicar, John, Welford Sanders, and David Mosena. 1980. *Streamlining Land Use Regulation: A Guidebook for Local Government.* Chicago: American Planning Assoc.

"Warning: Land Frauds Are Flourishing." 1967. *Changing Times: The Kiplinger Magazine* (May): 7.

Weber, Bruce, Russell Youmans, and Rick Harrington. 1977. *Rural "Recreational" Subdivisions and Local Taxes: The Fiscal Impact of Rural Subdivisions in Klamath County, Oregon.* Corvallis: Oregon State University Extension Service.

Weiss, Joseph E. 1981. *Rio Rancho: A Study.* Ph.D. diss. University of New Mexico.

Weiss, Ted. 1986. Vice president, Avatar Holdings, Inc. Coral Gables, Fla. Personal interview, December.

Welch, Pam. 1993. Administrative assistant, property management, Fairfield Glade, Tenn. Personal interview, May.

Werner, William. 1993. Director, Habitat Protection Division, Arizona Game and Fish, Yuma, Ariz. Personal interview, November.

West Central Arkansas Planning and Development District, Inc. 1977. *Land Resource Management: 1977–1979.* Hot Springs, Ark.: West Central Ark. PD.

Westman, Walter E. 1985. *Ecology, Impact Assessment, and Environmental Planning.* New York: John Wiley and Sons.

Whiting, Bill. 1973. "The Land May Turn Barren, Naturalist Warns Florida." *Miami Herald* (May 27).

Williams, Robert. 1988. Director of planning, Hendry County, LaBelle, Fla. Personal interview, May.

Wilson, Leonard. 1987. "Origins of Vermont Development Regulation." In *Report of the Governor's Commission on Vermont's Future: Guidelines for Growth.* Montpelier: Governor's Commission on Vermont's Future.

Winholtz, Wilford G. 1968. "Planning and the Public." In *Principles and Practice of Urban Planning*. Washington, D.C.: International City Managers' Assoc.

Wolff, Anthony. 1972. "'Invest in the West'—New Yorkers Fall for the Land Con." *New York Magazine* 5:52–57.

———. 1973. *Unreal Estate*. San Francisco: Sierra Club.

Wombold, Lynn. 1979. *Estimates and Projections of the Population of New Mexico, by County, 1975–1990*. Albuquerque: University of New Mexico, Bureau of Business and Economic Research.

Workman, J. P., et al. 1973. *A Taxpayer's Problem—Recreational Subdivision in Utah*. Logan: Utah State University Press.

Wulhorst, Peter. 1988. Planner, Pike County Planning Dept., Milford, Pa. Personal interview, April.

Yearwood, Richard M. 1971. *Land Subdivision Regulation*. New York: Praeger.

Ziner, Charles I. 1974. "The Impact of Leisure Homes on the Economy of the Area within the "Blue Line" of the Adirondack Park." Ph.D. diss., University of Illinois.

Zwick, Rodney. 1989. "Images of Vermont Communities and the New England Region: Constructed Typologies." General Technical Report NE-132, Northeastern Forest Experiment Station. In *Proceedings of the 1989 Northeastern Recreation Research Symposium*. Broomall, Pa.: U.S. Dept. of Agriculture.

Index

Page numbers in italics denote figures; those in boldface denote tables.

Cape Coral, Florida (*continued*) 105; Matlacha Pass, 105; pattern of roads and canals in, 105; planning problems at, 110–11; population growth rates at, 109; potential population at, 36, 109; retirement age population at, 109; reverse osmosis (R/O) use at, 107; size of (acres), 104; use of unscrupulous sales practices at, 107; water pollution problems at, 105

Carnegie, Andrew, 3

Carson, Rachel, 178

"Catch-22." *See* management and control

caveat emptor, 70. *See also* consumer protection

centralized land-use regulation. *See* regulation

Chesapeake Bay, Virginia, 180

Claremont Institute, growth management guidelines, 152

class-action suits, against GAC, 107

Clean Air Act, 177

Clean Water Act, 177

Coastal Zone Management Act, 141

comprehensive approach. *See* regulation, proper mix of

comprehensive zoning ordinance. *See* regulation, revolution in

concurrency requirement, 35

consumer abuses, 62–66, 72–74. *See also* consumer victimization; deceptive advertising; fraudulent sales practices; sales tactics

consumer complaints, 69–70

consumer problems, 64–65, 189–90. *See also* consumer abuses

consumer protection, 65–76; improvements in, 74–75

consumer victimization, 62

contract defaults, 66

cooling-off period, 30-day. *See* regulation, suggestions for

Corrales, New Mexico, 113, 117. *See also* Rio Rancho, Intel Corporation expansion

Costilla County, Colorado. *See also* recreational subdivisions, location of

cultural features, consideration of, 38

Cumberland County, Tennessee, 80. *See also* Fairfield Glade

Cumberland Plateau, scenic beauty of, 89–90. *See also* Fairfield Glade

customer expectations, 97–100

customer naivete, 65

deception and fraud, 1, 109. *See also* consumer abuses

deceptive advertising, 62

Deltona, 31. *See also* wetlands, subdivision of

Department of Land-Use Management, objectives of, 184

deplatting, 131, 183, 191

Deschutes County, Oregon. *See* tax rates

deserts: environmental damage to, 28–30; limiting factors of, 28; subdivision of, 28; water supply in, 29

developmental framework, phases of, 13

developmental tolerance zones, 30, 38–39, 181, 192

Developments of Regional Impact (DRI), 32, 148–50; definition of, 148; positive features of, 150; weakness of, 150

Disney Vacation Development, Inc., 93

Disney's flextime, 95

dredge and fill: elimination of, 31; negative impact of, 24, 31; use of, 105

ecological design and planning, importance of, 140–41

economic consequences, options for evaluating, 58–61

economic impact: factors determining, 44–45; management of, 60; negative, 51–58; positive, 46–50

El Paso, Texas, 28

eminent domain, 182–83

employment, 49

endangered species, 24

environmental damage, 105, 112–13; extensive nature of, 19, 24–25; from developer negligence, 189

environmental-ecological awareness, importance of, 142

environmental impact. *See also* Cape Coral; dredge and fill; Lake Havasu City; land-use practices; phasing schedule; Rio Rancho; septic systems

Environmental Improvement Agency, in New Mexico, 113

environmental laws, 42

Environmental Protection Agency, grants, 177

erosion, 19, 21–23, 25–26, 28, 30; beach, 24

estoppel. *See* vested rights

estuarine environments, 24

Euclid v. Ambler Realty Company, 182

Everglades, as precious ecosystem, 32. *See also* Florida; wetlands

expenditures, by developer, 47

Fairfield Bay, 125–30; bankruptcy and reorganization at, 130; basic services at, 126–27; consumer issues at, 128–29; economic benefits of, 129; environmental limitations at, 125; environmental problems at, 125–127; Greers Ferry Lake at, 125; highly acclaimed resort at, 130; high-pressure sales tactics at, 129; location of, 125; population growth potential at, 36, 128, 130; population growth rate at, 129; septic systems at, 126–27; size of (acres), 125; steep terrain at, 125; unpaved roads at, 125; warranty deed at, 129; water resource problems at, 127

Fairfield Communities, Inc., 79–80, 90, 101–2, 125; Chapter 11 bankruptcy, 90, 101–2; corporate organization, 80; decline in operations at, 102; reorganization of, 102. *See also* Fairfield Glade

Fairfield Glade, Tennessee, 78, 79–102; adequate financing at, 87, 101; cash flow at, 86; cost of family visits to, 85; deficit spending at, 83; direct mail advertisement at, 89; high-amenity resort at, 80–81, 101; infrastructure provided at, 80–82; land acquisition, development, and maintenance costs at, 83; location of, 79; lot sales at, 89; major expenses at, 87; promotional costs at, 85; promotional techniques used at, 89, 101; revenue for profit at, 87; sequence of spending at, 83; size of (acres), 80; sources of income at, 85, 87; success of, 80; time-sharing revenue at, 92. *See also* Fairfield Communities, Inc.

federal regulatory initiatives, 177–78

Federal Trade Commission, 190

financial ruin, of many land developments, 79

fire protection, minimal facilities for, 56

First National Bank of Boston. *See also* Fairfield Communities, Inc., Chapter 11 bankruptcy

flash flooding, 22, 120

Flood Disaster Protection, 177

Florida, 30–32, 144–53; acres in recreational subdivision in, 145; Administration Commission, 146; amenity attractions in, 144–45; Apalachicola Bay, 147; Asken, Reuben (governor), 145; Chiles, Lawton (governor), 152; concurrency in, 35; conflict between private rights and public needs in, 145; definition of Areas of Critical State Concern, 146; definition of concurrency in, 35; Department of Community Affairs, 148–49; East Central Regional Planning Council, 150; employment opportunities in, 145; environmental crisis in, 144; Environmental Land and Water Management Act, 32, 136, 145–46; Environmental Land Management Study (ELMS II) Committee, 151; Environmental Land Management Study (ELMS III) Committee, 152–53; environmental threat as stimulus for growth controls, 145; Everglades National Park in, 147; Florida Keys, 147; Fort Myers, 152; Franklin County, 147; Graham, Bob (governor), 151; Green Swamp, 147; Growth Management Act of 1985, 32, 35, 151–52, 178; growth management and control mechanisms, 145; growth management task force in, 145; importance of Big Cypress Swamp in, 146–47; investment potential in, 103; irreparable damage to wetlands in, 145; Lake County, 150; Land Conservation Act, 146; land development opportunities in, 103; land-use control in, 144–53; Land and Water Adjudicatory Commission, 148; Local Government Comprehensive Planning and Land Development Regulation Act,

Florida (*continued*)
151; panther in (*see* endangered species); popularity of Florida real estate, 103; population growth nodes in, 145; population growth trends in, 144; preservation of environmental integrity in, 103; rapid land development activity in, 144; Regional Planning Councils in, 148–49, 152; State Comprehensive Planning Act, 146, 152; subdivision activity in, 103; subdivision of fragile ecosystems (wetlands) in, 103, 145; "Ten Steps to Good Growth Management in Florida" (*see* Claremont Institute); Three Rivers DRI decision, 150; vested-rights provision in, 149; Water Resources Act, 146; Wekiva River, 150. *See also* Developments of Regional Impact

Forbes Inc., 28
Fort Myers, Florida, 105, 107
fraudulent appraisals, 65
fraudulent sales practices, 63–64, 73

General Acceptance Corporation (GAC), 28–30, 103; bankruptcy of, 103; land acquisition by, 103 (*see also* Cape Coral)
General Development Corporation (GDC), 31, 131. *See also* Port LaBelle; wetlands, subdivision of
geographic information systems (GIS), 39
Glades County, Florida. *See* Port LaBelle, location of
grandfather clauses, 149. *See also* Florida, vested-rights provision in
growth controls: long-term, 179; permanent, 179; short-term, 178–79
Gulf American Corporation, 103; Gulf Coast of Florida. *See* wetlands, subdivision of
Gulf Guaranty Land and Title Company. *See* Cape Coral; Gulf American Corporation
Gulf of Mexico, 105

Hendry County, Florida. *See* Port LaBelle, location of
hidden costs, 51
Horizon Corp., 28

impact fees, 191
installment land sales; boom and bust cycles, 2; multi-billion-dollar industry, 1; success factors, 3
Interstate Land Sales Full Disclosure Act of 1968, 62, 67–69; suggested amendments to, 180
ITT, 31. *See also* wetlands, subdivision of

"just compensation." *See* eminent domain

Lake Havasu City, 78, 119–24; alluvial fans at, 119; consumer issues at, 122; environmental limitations at, 119; environmental problems at, 119–20; flash floods at, 120; improvement districts at, 122; Irrigation and Drainage District at, 123–24; location of, 119–20; London Bridge at, 119; lot resale at, 122; population forecast for, 123; population growth potential at, 123; population growth rate of, 123; school enrollment at, 123; septic systems at, 120; shortcomings of, 124; site selection decisions, 120; size of (acres), 119; taxing districts at, 122–24; water shortages at, 120; wildlife habitat destruction at, 120
Lake Havasu dam reclamation project, 119
Lake Latonka, Pennsylvania, 47. *See also* economic impact, positive
land development, future, requirements for, 192–93
land development schemes, 2
land hustling, 3
land sales industry slump, 189
land sales subdivisions: definition of, 4; future of, 193. *See also* recreational subdivisions
land speculation, 2, 51
land-use management system, 20; establishment of, 141, 184; importance of, 141; improving efficiency of, 184; to reduce negative impact, 141
land-use policies, criteria for, 179–80
land-use practices, 20; improvements in, 34–35, 78
land swindles, 63
land switching, 64

land value, 46–48
landscape design, in harmony with nature, 194
leapfrog development, 140
Lee County, Florida, 31, 192; beautiful coastline of, 104; concentration of recreational subdivisions in, 7; number of vacant lots in, 105; prodevelopment attitude in, 104; rapid growth in, 104
Lehigh Acres, Florida, 105
local government: administrative costs of, 57; demands on, 41; key for, 193–94; state-level requirements for, 143
lot owner dissatisfaction, 64–65
lot prices, 47
lot supply, 192

mailing list, 90
mammoth subdivisions, 193; ending of an era, 188
management and control, of development, 191
mapping, of existing land use, 38
Massanutten and Blue Ridge Mountains, Virginia, 26
master plan, government scrutiny of, 33
McCulloch Properties, Inc. (MPI), 29, 119. See also Lake Havasu City
McCulloch, Robert, 119
medical facilities, overtaxing of, 57
Mohave Mountains, Arizona, 119
Monroe County, Florida. See platted lands, in Florida Keys
Montana: Department of Commerce manual, 27; Subdivision and Platting Act, 27
mountain ecology, 25
mountains: environmental limitations of, 25–27; inhabitation of, 25; problems with subdivision of, 25–27
multi-million-dollar lawsuits, 189
multiplier effect, 49
mystique, of buying land. See "American dream"

Nantucket Islanders, concern over loss of "charm," 25
National Land Use Policy Act, demise of, 177

Nevada County, California, 23. See also pollution, water
new communities, problems associated with, 77
New Deal era, 77
New Jersey's single-purpose laws. See single-purpose legislation
New Mexico, 161–65; attorney general, 162; Environmental Improvement Board, 164; Environmental Improvement Division, 162; federal ownership of land in, 161; Hispanic attitudes concerning land-use control, 161; Horizon's Rio Communities, 162; land developer clout in, 164; Land Subdivision Act of 1963, 162; land-use regulation lagging behind in, 165; New Mexico Territory, 161; population totals in, 161; prodevelopment environment in, 165; ranchers' opposition to land-use control in, 161; Regional Conservation District, 162; Rio Arriba, 161; role of state engineer in, 162–63; stymieing subdivision legislation in, 164; Subdivision Act of 1973: —requirements of, 162–63; —subdivider definition, 163; subdivision activity in, 161–63; weak land-use controls in, 161
new towns. See new communities
New York City. See regulation, revolution in

Ocala Springs, Florida. See subdivision redesign
Office of Interstate Land Sales Registration (OILSR), 4, 68–71, 141, 190: exemptions, 71; provisions of fines and jail sentences, 69, 71; suspension orders, 69. See also consumer protection; Interstate Land Sales Full Disclosure Act of 1968
older subdivisions. See platted lands
operational techniques, changes in, 4
Oregon, 153–56; Cascades subdivision, 155; compliance and review process, 155; comprehensive plans, 154; Department of Land Conservation and Development, 155; Deschutes County, subdivision in, 155; development along Pacific coast in, 155; development of

revenue gains, short-term, 26
rezoning power. See *Euclid v. Ambler Realty Company*
Rio Grande River, 112
Rio Rancho 112–18; bladed roads at, 113, *115;* callous disregard of natural terrain at, 112; cost and availability of basic services at, 113–14; customer complaints at, 118; environmental limitations at, 112; environmental problems at, 112–13; federal legal actions against, 118; flooding problems at, 113; fraud and misrepresentation at, 118; Intel Corporation expansion, 116–17; land sales tactics used at, 113; location of, 112; lot prices at, 112; poor layout and design of, 112–13; positive features of, 114–18; road pattern at, 112, *115;* rapid population growth at, 114, **118;** residents' perception of, 118; sales contract defaults, 118; septic systems at, 113; sewage treatment at, 113; size of (acres), 112; slope of terrain at, 113; stormy history of, 118; unexpected costs at, 113
roads: bladed, 24, 113; cost of, 53–55; dedication of, 51

Safe Drinking Water Act, 177
sales contract, provisions of, 71
sales tactics: high-pressure, 62, 65–66, 190; unscrupulous, 1, 65–66, 72–73. *See also* consumer abuses
Sandoval County, New Mexico. *See* Rio Rancho
Santa Cruz River, 30
schools, cost of, 55
Securities and Exchange Commission, 141, 180. *See also* regulation, suggestions for
selective approach. *See* regulation, proper mix of
selling "the American dream," 97–98
septic systems, 181; assessment of, 34–43; factors accounting for, 20; options for reducing, 42–43; potential dangers of, 22; state-initiated review process of, 143
Shenandoah River, 180
Silent Spring. See Carson, Rachel
single-purpose legislation, 178

site analysis data, forms of, 39
site selection, 9–11, 192
special places. *See* new communities
speculative investments, 72
speculative ventures for profit, 77
Standard State Zoning Enabling Act, 142
Subcommittee on Frauds and Misrepresentations Affecting the Elderly, 62
subdivision of land: history of, 2; premature, 2
subdivision redesign, 190
subdivision regulations. *See* zoning
subdivisions, existing, possible solutions for, 190–91. *See also* platted lands
Surface Mine Control and Reclamation Act, 177
system of operation, 12, 13

Tahoe Regional Planning Agency, 23
tax assessment, 47–48; methods of, 51
tax defaults, in Taos County, New Mexico, 57
tax rates, 46–48
Tax Reform Act of 1986, limits on tax deductions for second-homes, 4
tax revenue, 46–49; loss of, 52
time-sharing, 4, 92–97; advantages of, 94–97; disadvantages of, 94–97; exchange program, 95; improving reputation of, 93; investment potential of, 94–95; legal problems, 97; maintenance fee, 95; popularity of, 92; potential cost savings of, 94; price range of (time-share week), 95; resale program for, 97; sales volume of, 92; types of, 94; upsurge in growth of, 93
transfer of development rights (TDR), 191
Truth in Lending Act, 69, 73
Tucson, Arizona, 28; groundwater use in, 29

Udall, Morris K., characterization of the installment land-sales industry by, 188
unbridled growth, changing attitudes toward, 140
undivided interest plans, 4
uninhabited subdivisions, 1
urban sprawl, 24
U.S. Army Corps of Engineers, 32

U.S. Department of Agriculture, Soil Conservation Service, 39
U.S. Department of the Interior, 39
U.S. Geological Survey, 39
U.S. Postal Service, 66
Utah State Tax Commission (USTC). *See* tax assessment, methods of
Utah Tax Code, 52
utilities, cost of, 52–53

"vacation homesites," 13; oversupply of, 192. *See also* Lee County, Florida, number of vacant lots in
Van Buren County, Arkansas, 49, 125. *See also* tax revenue
Vermont, 157–61; Board of Health, 158; completion of interstate highway system, 157; concerns of Vermonters, 157; development review process, 158; district commissions, 158; Environmental Control Act (Act 250), 157–58; evaluation of growth management program, 159; goals of Commission on Vermont's Future, 160; Growth Management Act of 1988, 160; Kunin, Madeleine (governor), 159; land-use regulation in, 157–61; "over ten-acre" rule in, 157, 159; permit requirements in, 158; population growth in, 157; public outcry against International Pa-

per Company land development proposal, 157; recreational subdivision boom in, 157; subdivision definition in, 157; vested rights, 182
vulnerable locations, development of, 25–34. *See also* deserts; mountains; plateaus; wetlands

Washington state, "twenty-acre rule," 139
Water Independence for Cape Coral (WICC), 174–75
Water Pollution Control Act, 32, 141. *See also* dredge and fill
water resources. *See* pollution, water
water supply, for Cape Coral region, 107
West Mesa, of Rio Grande River, 112
Westinghouse Gateway Communities, Inc., 32
wetlands: canal construction in, 31–33; drainage of, 30; intolerance of, 31; subdivision of, 30–31, 145; value of, 30
Windsor, Connecticut. *See* regulation, consequences of
wise and equitable development, importance of, 193

zoning, 140; absence of, 139

About the Author

Hubert B. (Bill) Stroud is a professor of geography at Arkansas State University, where he has spent much of his professional career teaching, conducting research, and writing. His research interests include platted land problems, the impact of recreational-retirement communities on rural landscapes, and growth management in environmentally sensitive locations. Professor Stroud's numerous publications on these and other topics have appeared in several national and international journals, including the *Professional Geographer, Land Use Policy,* and *Ekistics.* He has also co-authored a book on the geography of Arkansas with Gerald T. Hanson. Dr. Stroud is a member of several professional organizations and has served as president and vice president of the Arkansas Geographical Society. He completed a Ph.D. in geography at the University of Tennessee.

Library of Congress Cataloging-in-Publication Data
Stroud, Hubert B.
    The promise of paradise : recreational and retirement communities
in the United States since 1950 / Hubert B. Stroud.
        p.   cm. — (Creating the North American landscape)
    "Published in cooperation with the Center for American Places,
Harrisonburg, Virginia"—T.p. verso.
    Includes bibliographical references (p.   ) and index.
    ISBN 0-8018-4926-8 (alk. paper)
    1. Retirement communities—Economic aspects—United States.
2. Retirement communities—United States—Planning. 3. Retirement
communities—United States—Marketing. 4. Retirement communities—
Environmental aspects—United States. I. Title. II. Series.
HV1454.2.U6S77   1995
307.76'8—dc20   94-13228